Glamorella's daughter

Copyright © 2022 Jerry Bennett and Charles J. Martin

Published by Literati Press Comics & Novels
3010 Paseo, Oklahoma City, OK 73103
Find us online at literatipressok.com & @literatipress

ISBN: 978-1-943988-34-1

Edited by Chloe Harrison, Steve Gooch, and Brandy Williams
Book design by Charles J. Martin, Jerry Bennett, and Joseph Martin

First Edition, 2022
Printed in the United States of America

This is a work of fiction. Any similarity to actual persons living or dead, businesses, organizations, events, or places is entirely coincidental.

Glamorella's daughter

VOLUME 1

JERRY BENNETT
Concept, Art, and Color Finishes

CHARLES J. MARTIN
Script & Lettering

BRANDY WILLIAMS
Sensitivity Editor & Color Flats

"Not Particularly"

LARON CHAPMAN
Script

JERRY BENNETT
Art, Colors & Lettering

JESSICA BENNETT
Color Assist

Issue Two Variant Cover by Jerry Bennett
Issue Three Variant Cover by Jerry Bennett
Issue Two Variant Cover by Marcus Eakers
Issue Three Variant Cover by Tintin Pantoja
Issue One Planet Comicon Variant by Corinne Smith

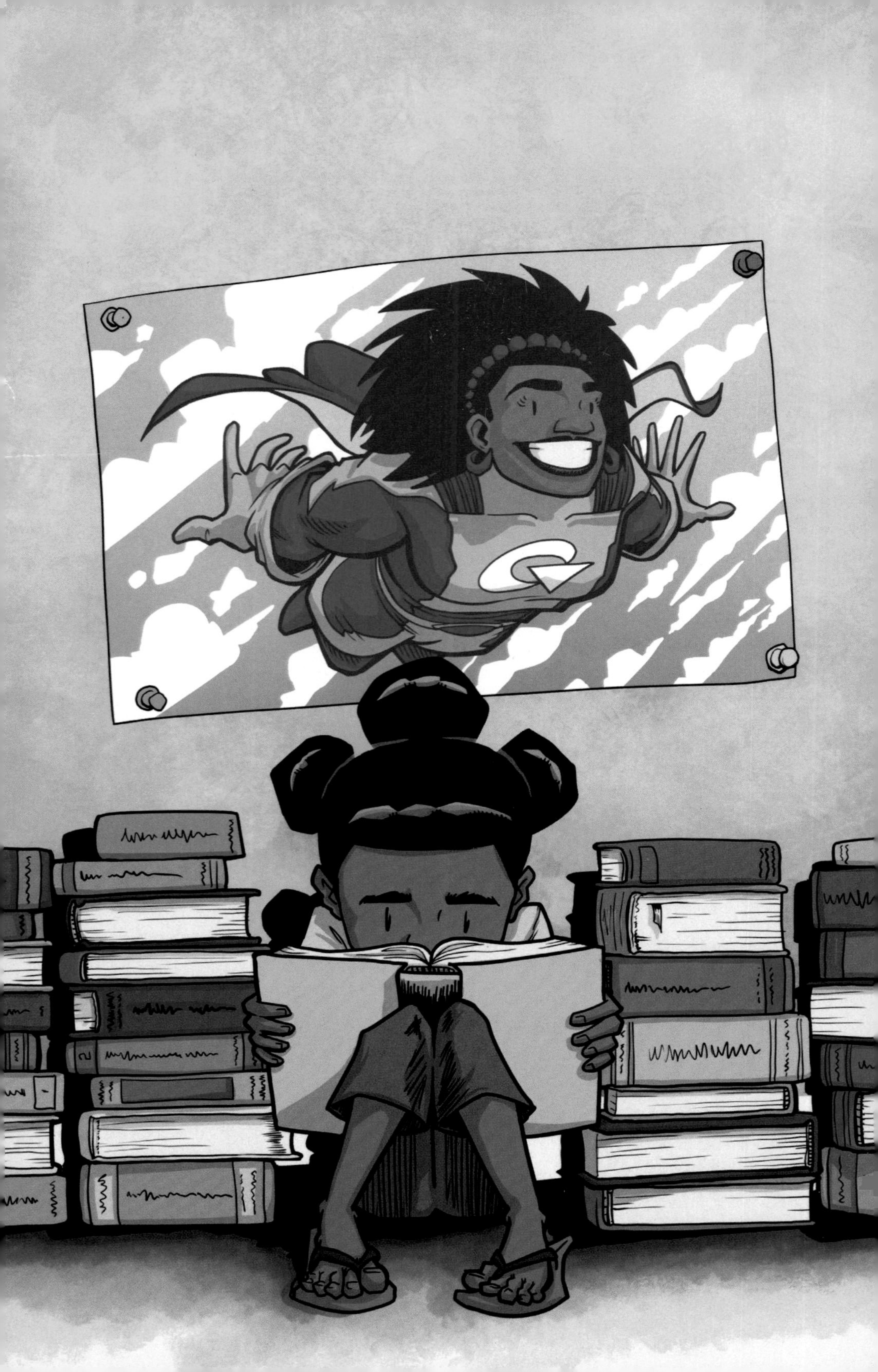

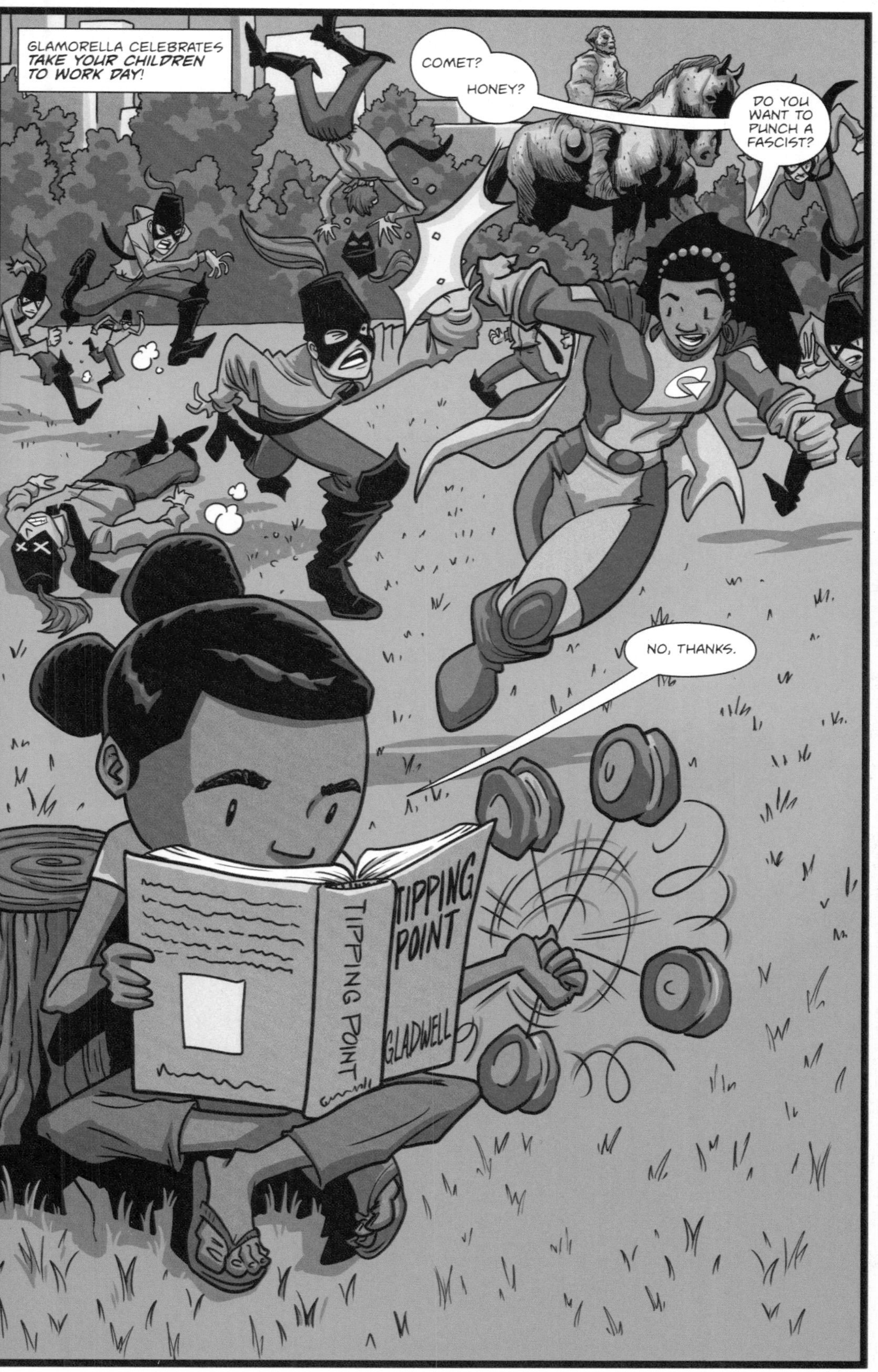
GLAMORELLA CELEBRATES *TAKE YOUR CHILDREN TO WORK DAY*!
COMET?
HONEY?
DO YOU WANT TO PUNCH A FASCIST?
NO, THANKS.
TIPPING POINT
GLADWELL
TIPPING POINT

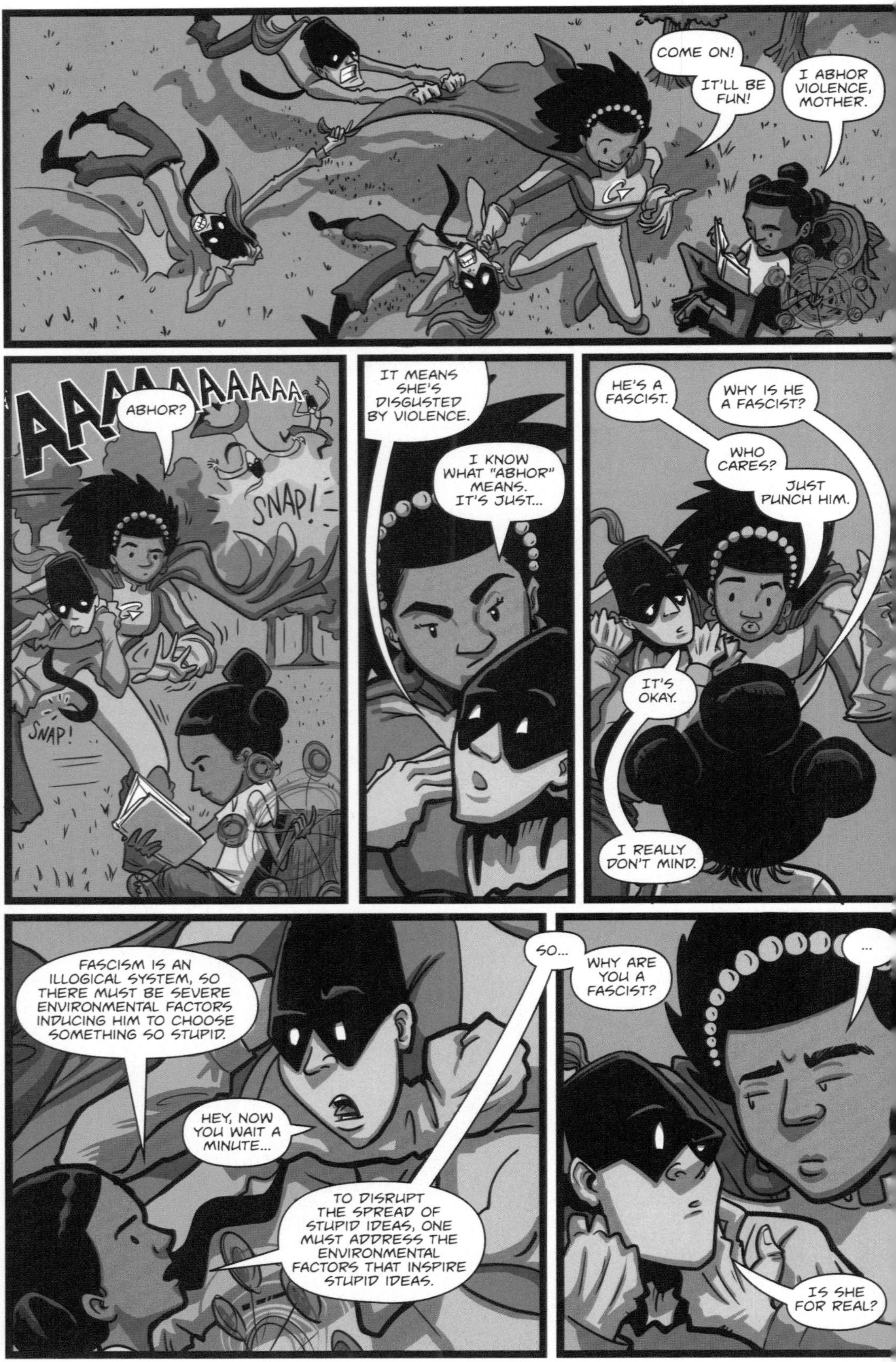
COME ON!
IT'LL BE FUN!
I ABHOR VIOLENCE, MOTHER.
AAAAAAAAAA
ABHOR?
SNAP!
SNAP!
IT MEANS SHE'S DISGUSTED BY VIOLENCE.
I KNOW WHAT "ABHOR" MEANS. IT'S JUST...
HE'S A FASCIST.
WHY IS HE A FASCIST?
WHO CARES?
JUST PUNCH HIM.
IT'S OKAY.
I REALLY DON'T MIND.
FASCISM IS AN ILLOGICAL SYSTEM, SO THERE MUST BE SEVERE ENVIRONMENTAL FACTORS INDUCING HIM TO CHOOSE SOMETHING SO STUPID.
HEY, NOW YOU WAIT A MINUTE...
TO DISRUPT THE SPREAD OF STUPID IDEAS, ONE MUST ADDRESS THE ENVIRONMENTAL FACTORS THAT INSPIRE STUPID IDEAS.
SO...
WHY ARE YOU A FASCIST?
...
IS SHE FOR REAL?

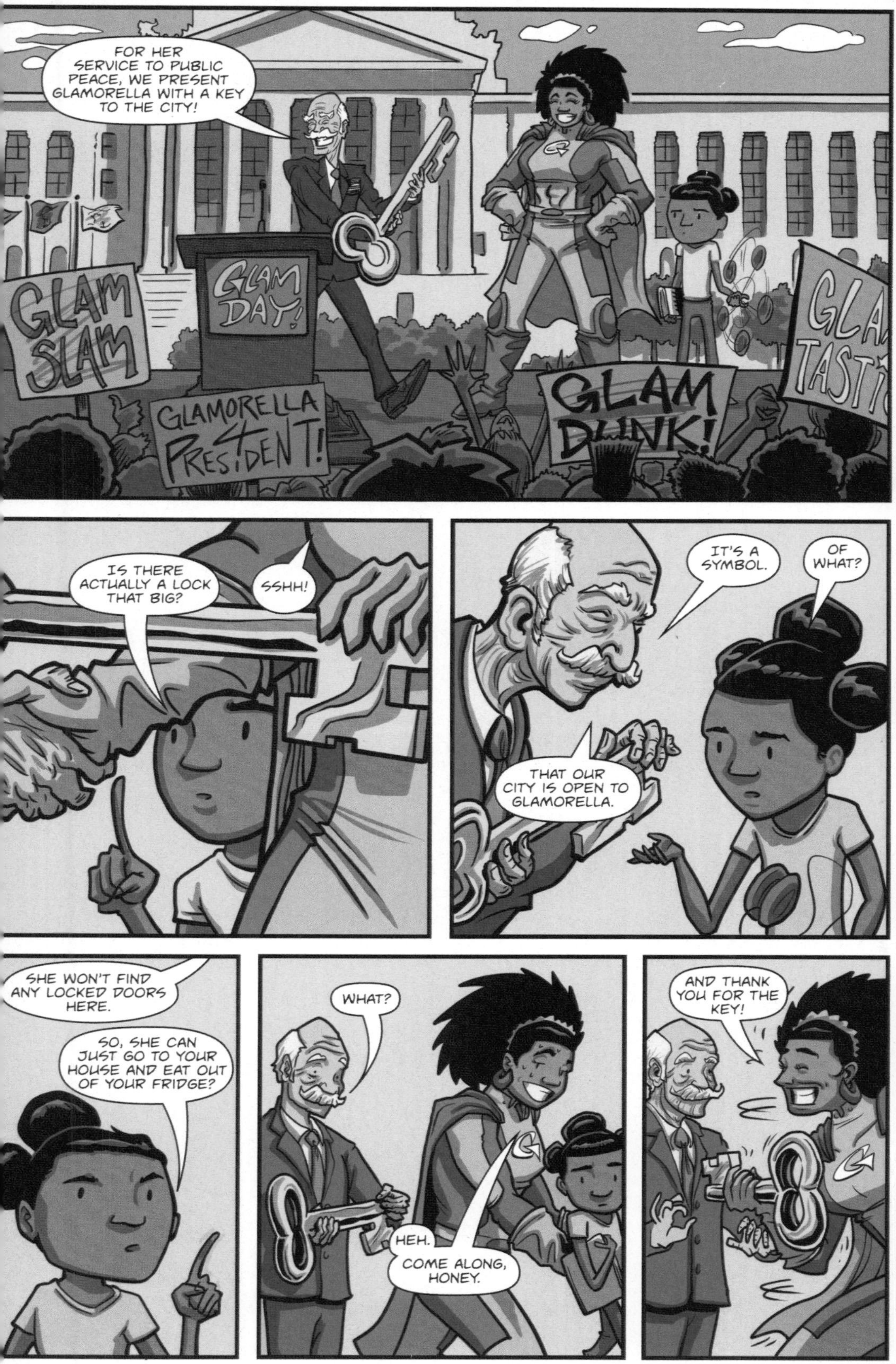
FOR HER SERVICE TO PUBLIC PEACE, WE PRESENT GLAMORELLA WITH A KEY TO THE CITY!
GLAM SLAM
GLAM DAY!
GLAMORELLA 4 PRESIDENT!
GLAM DUNK!
GLAMTASTIC
IS THERE ACTUALLY A LOCK THAT BIG?
SSHH!
IT'S A SYMBOL.
OF WHAT?
THAT OUR CITY IS OPEN TO GLAMORELLA.
SHE WON'T FIND ANY LOCKED DOORS HERE.
SO, SHE CAN JUST GO TO YOUR HOUSE AND EAT OUT OF YOUR FRIDGE?
WHAT?
HEH.
COME ALONG, HONEY.
AND THANK YOU FOR THE KEY!

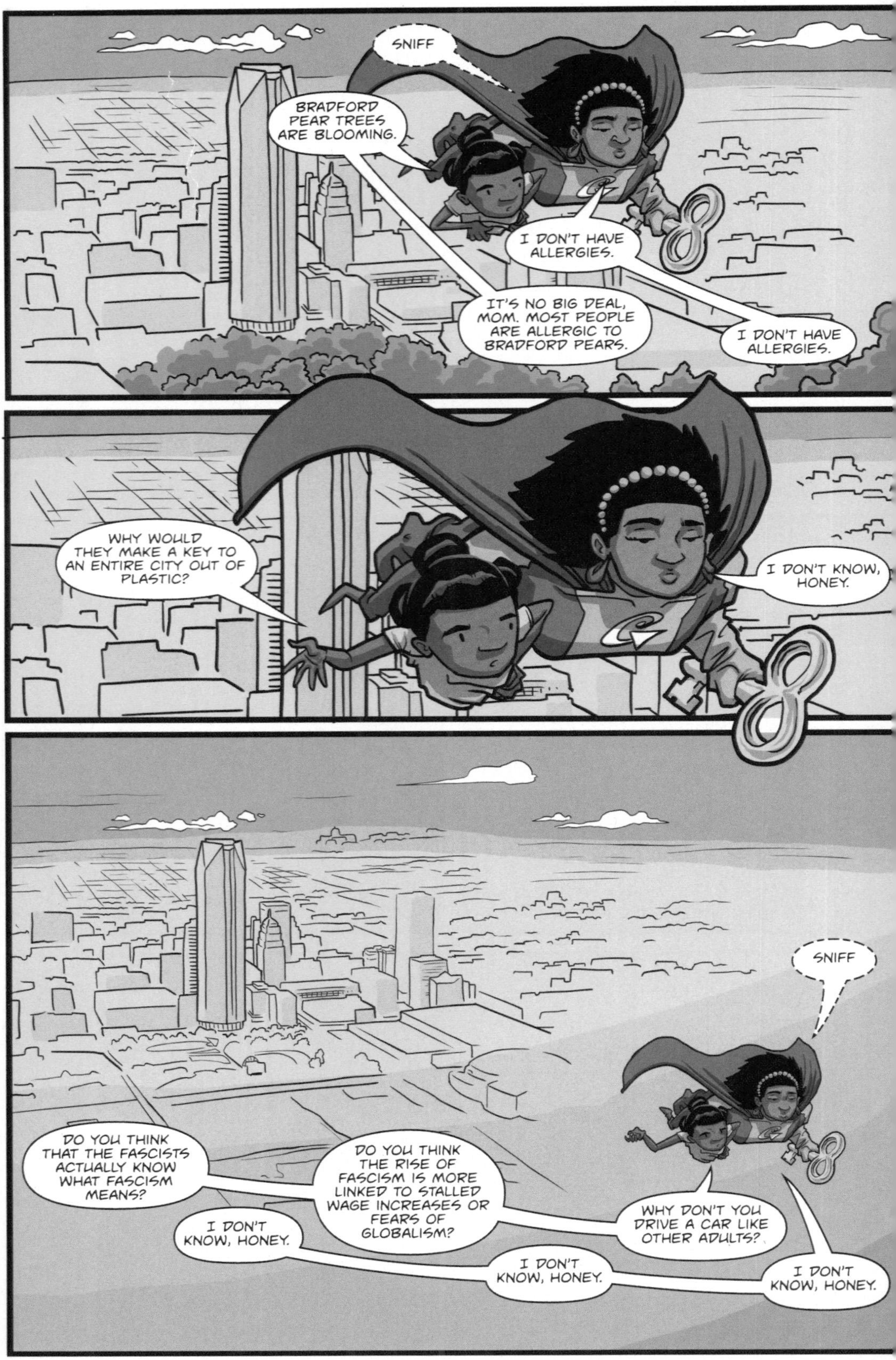
SNIFF
BRADFORD PEAR TREES ARE BLOOMING.
I DON'T HAVE ALLERGIES.
IT'S NO BIG DEAL, MOM. MOST PEOPLE ARE ALLERGIC TO BRADFORD PEARS.
I DON'T HAVE ALLERGIES.
WHY WOULD THEY MAKE A KEY TO AN ENTIRE CITY OUT OF PLASTIC?
I DON'T KNOW, HONEY.
SNIFF
DO YOU THINK THAT THE FASCISTS ACTUALLY KNOW WHAT FASCISM MEANS?
I DON'T KNOW, HONEY.
DO YOU THINK THE RISE OF FASCISM IS MORE LINKED TO STALLED WAGE INCREASES OR FEARS OF GLOBALISM?
I DON'T KNOW, HONEY.
WHY DON'T YOU DRIVE A CAR LIKE OTHER ADULTS?
I DON'T KNOW, HONEY.

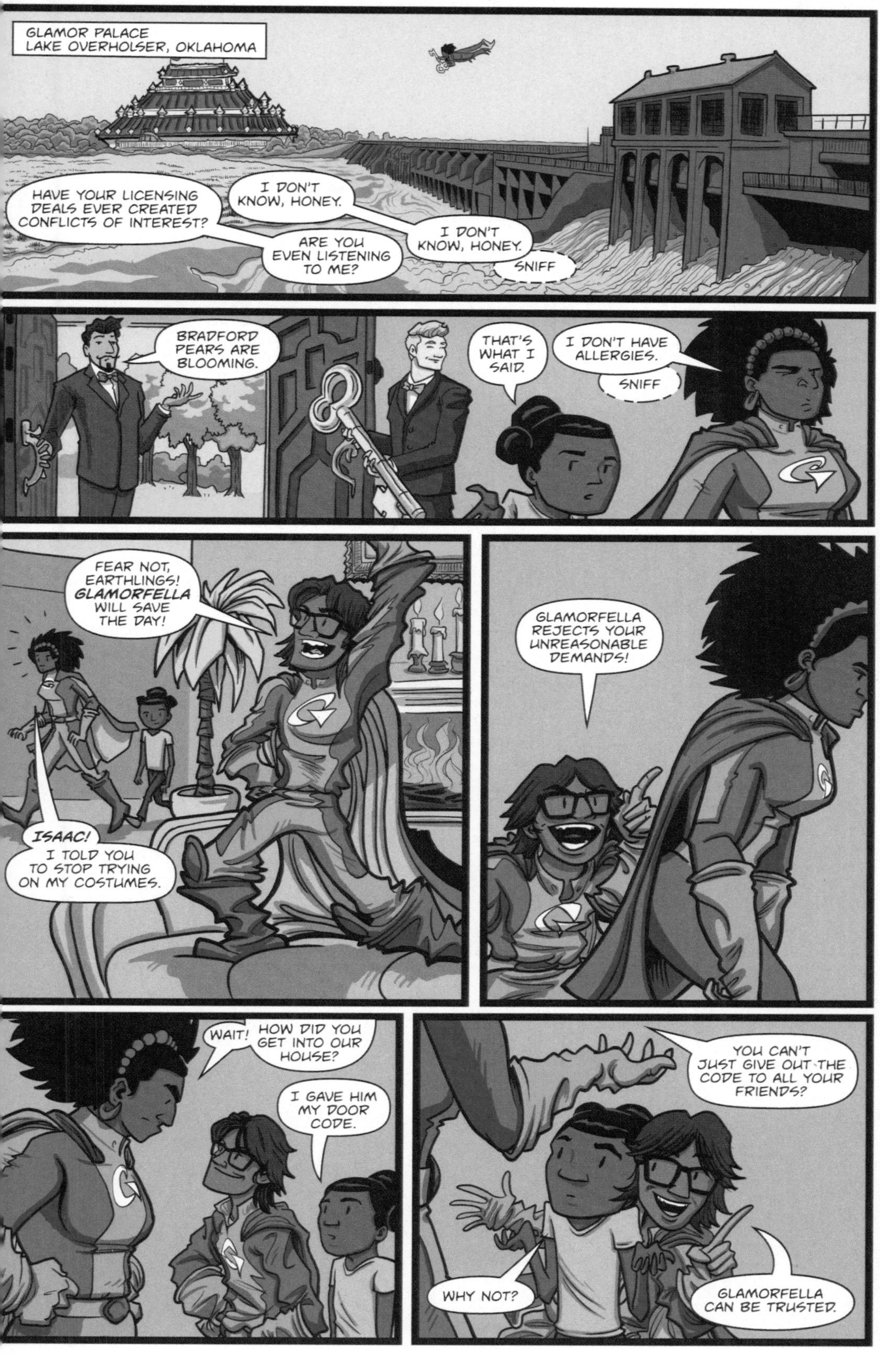
GLAMOR PALACE
LAKE OVERHOLSER, OKLAHOMA
HAVE YOUR LICENSING DEALS EVER CREATED CONFLICTS OF INTEREST?
I DON'T KNOW, HONEY.
ARE YOU EVEN LISTENING TO ME?
I DON'T KNOW, HONEY.
SNIFF
BRADFORD PEARS ARE BLOOMING.
THAT'S WHAT I SAID.
I DON'T HAVE ALLERGIES.
SNIFF
FEAR NOT, EARTHLINGS! GLAMORFELLA WILL SAVE THE DAY!
ISAAC! I TOLD YOU TO STOP TRYING ON MY COSTUMES.
GLAMORFELLA REJECTS YOUR UNREASONABLE DEMANDS!
WAIT!
HOW DID YOU GET INTO OUR HOUSE?
I GAVE HIM MY DOOR CODE.
YOU CAN'T JUST GIVE OUT THE CODE TO ALL YOUR FRIENDS?
WHY NOT?
GLAMORFELLA CAN BE TRUSTED.

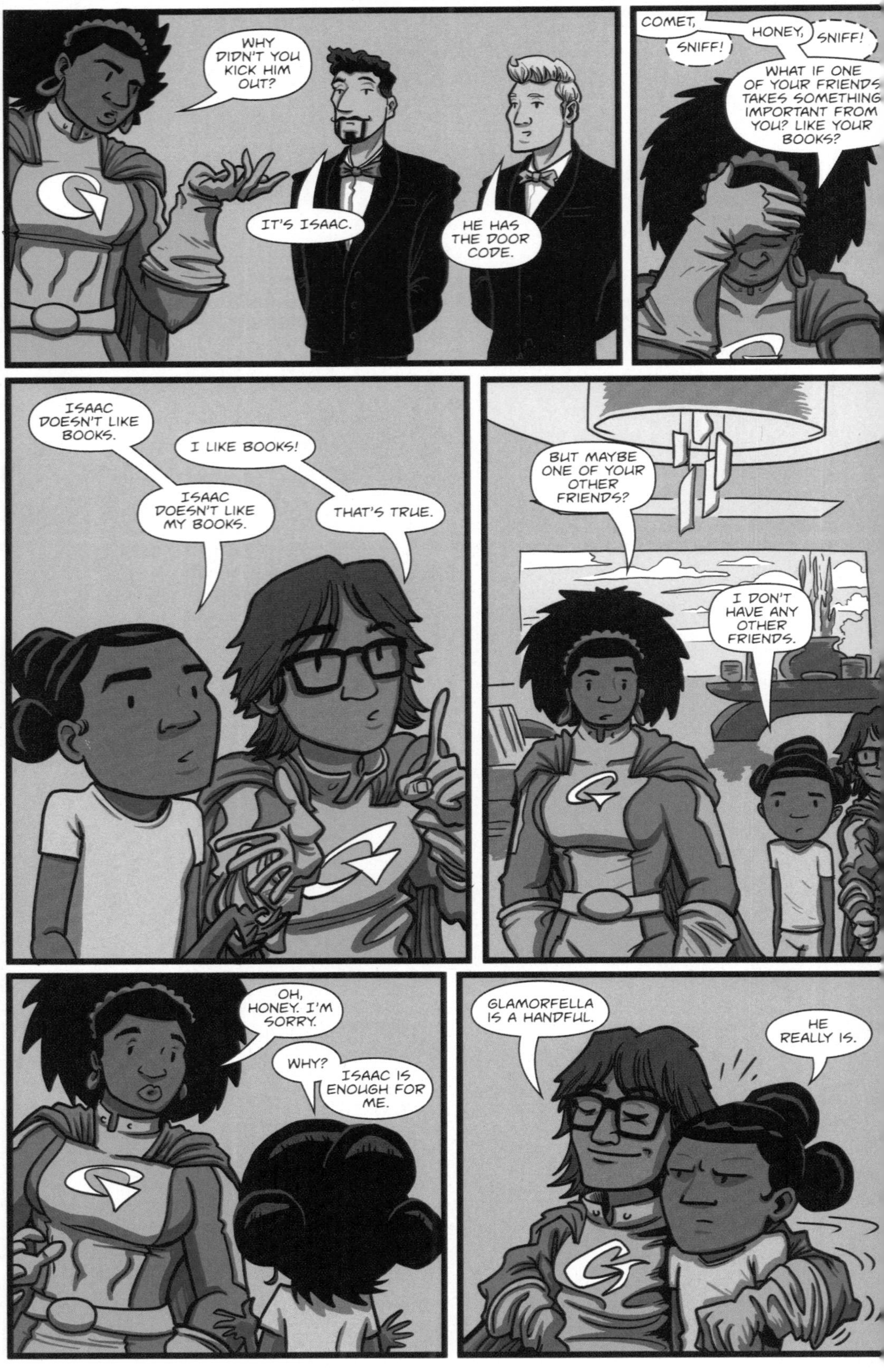
WHY DIDN'T YOU KICK HIM OUT?
IT'S ISAAC.
HE HAS THE DOOR CODE.
COMET,
SNIFF!
HONEY,
SNIFF!
WHAT IF ONE OF YOUR FRIENDS TAKES SOMETHING IMPORTANT FROM YOU? LIKE YOUR BOOKS?
ISAAC DOESN'T LIKE BOOKS.
I LIKE BOOKS!
ISAAC DOESN'T LIKE MY BOOKS.
THAT'S TRUE.
BUT MAYBE ONE OF YOUR OTHER FRIENDS?
I DON'T HAVE ANY OTHER FRIENDS.
OH, HONEY. I'M SORRY.
WHY?
ISAAC IS ENOUGH FOR ME.
GLAMORFELLA IS A HANDFUL.
HE REALLY IS.

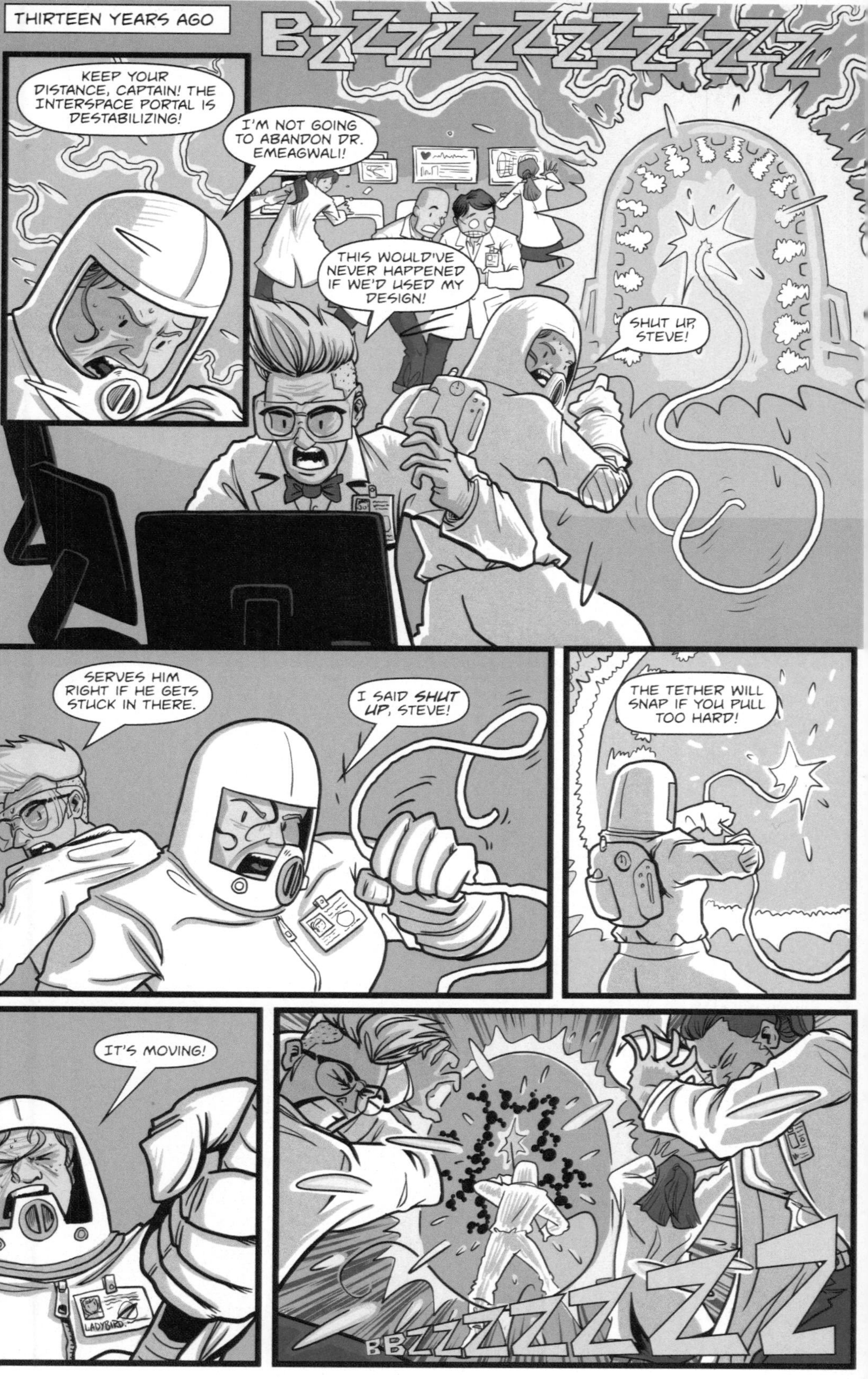
THIRTEEN YEARS AGO
BZZZZZZZZZZZZZZZ
KEEP YOUR DISTANCE, CAPTAIN! THE INTERSPACE PORTAL IS DESTABILIZING!
I'M NOT GOING TO ABANDON DR. EMEAGWALI!
THIS WOULD'VE NEVER HAPPENED IF WE'D USED MY DESIGN!
SHUT UP, STEVE!
SERVES HIM RIGHT IF HE GETS STUCK IN THERE.
I SAID SHUT UP, STEVE!
THE TETHER WILL SNAP IF YOU PULL TOO HARD!
IT'S MOVING!
LADYBIRD
BBZZZZZZZZ

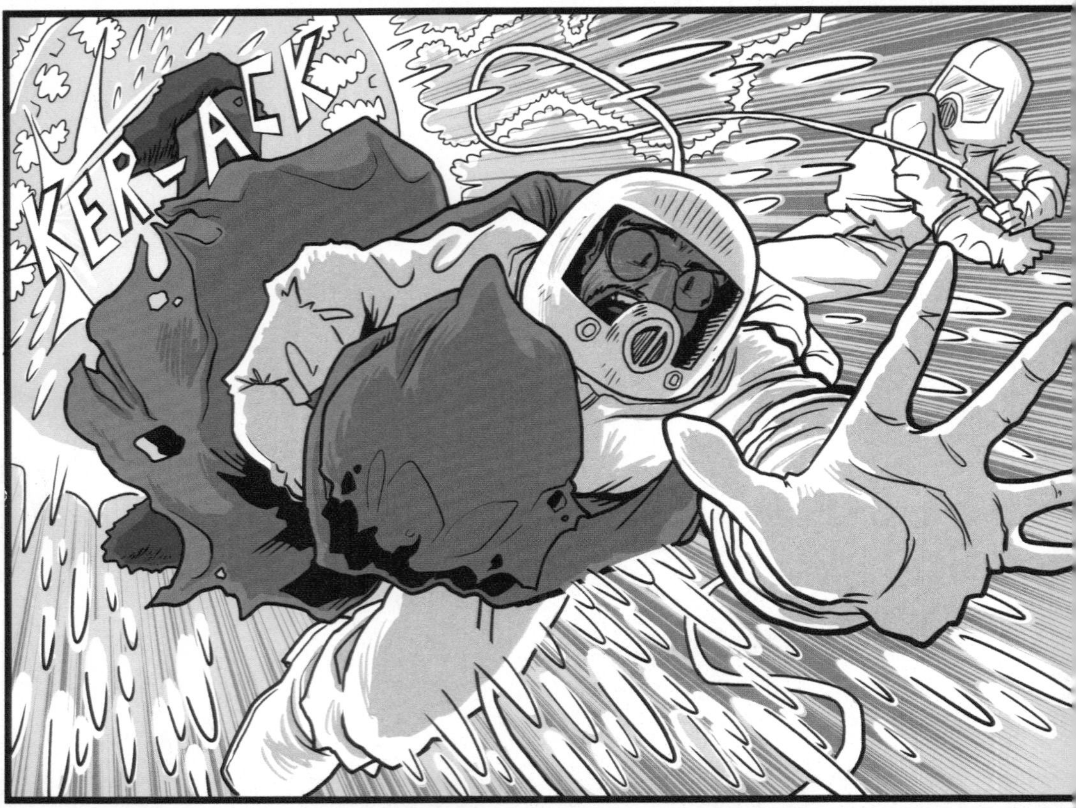
KER-ACK

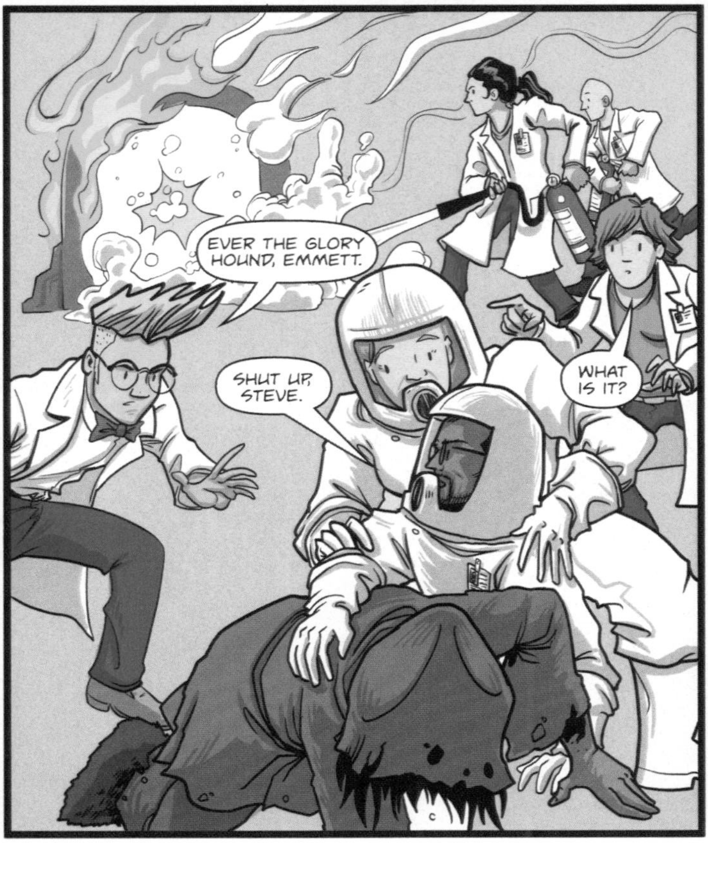
EVER THE GLORY HOUND, EMMETT.
SHUT UP, STEVE.
WHAT IS IT?

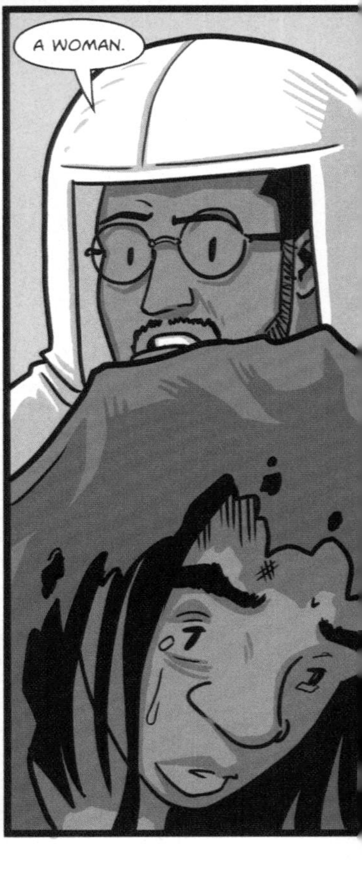
A WOMAN.

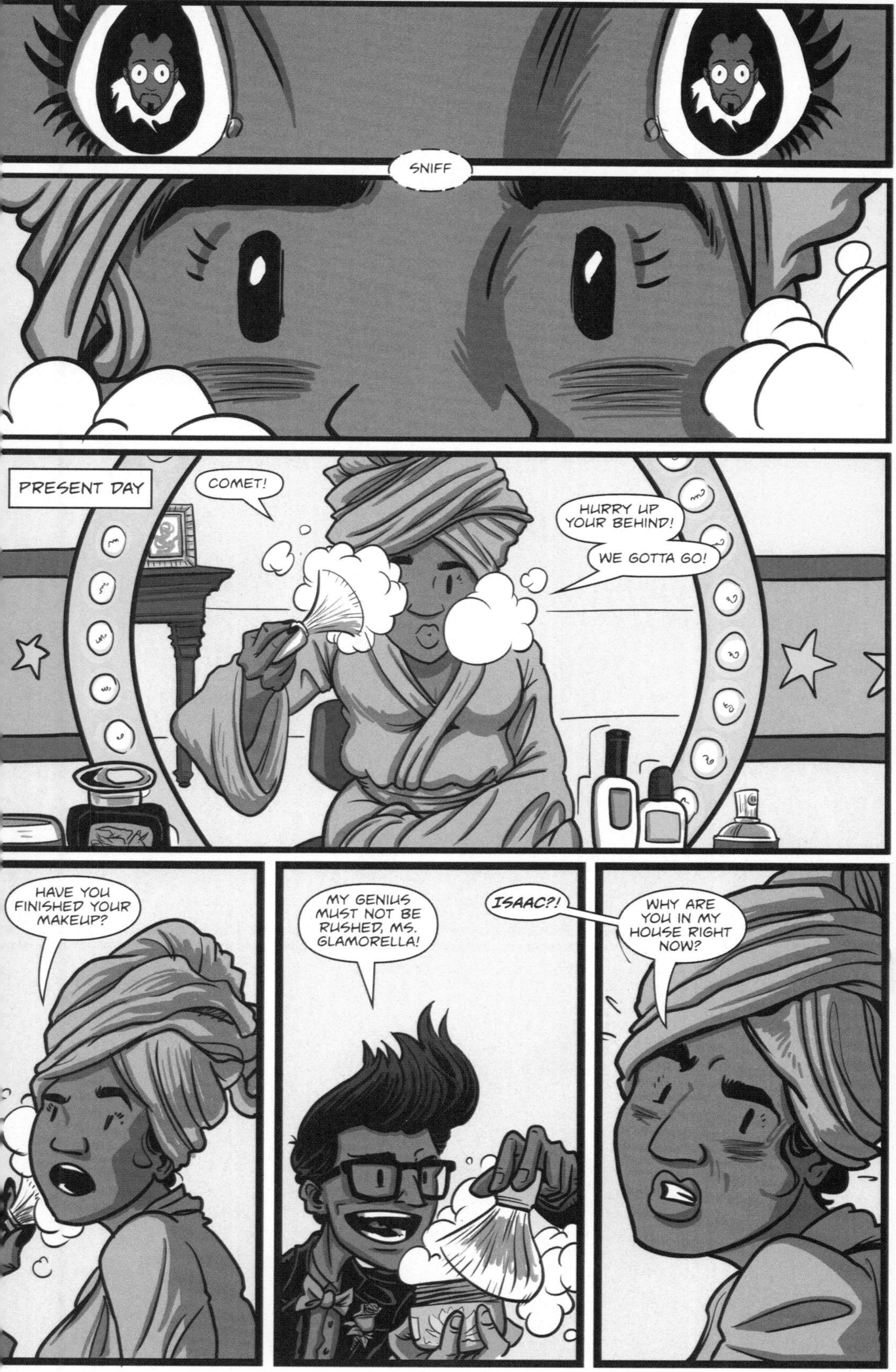
SNIFF
PRESENT DAY
COMET!
HURRY UP YOUR BEHIND!
WE GOTTA GO!
HAVE YOU FINISHED YOUR MAKEUP?
MY GENIUS MUST NOT BE RUSHED, MS. GLAMORELLA!
ISAAC?!
WHY ARE YOU IN MY HOUSE RIGHT NOW?

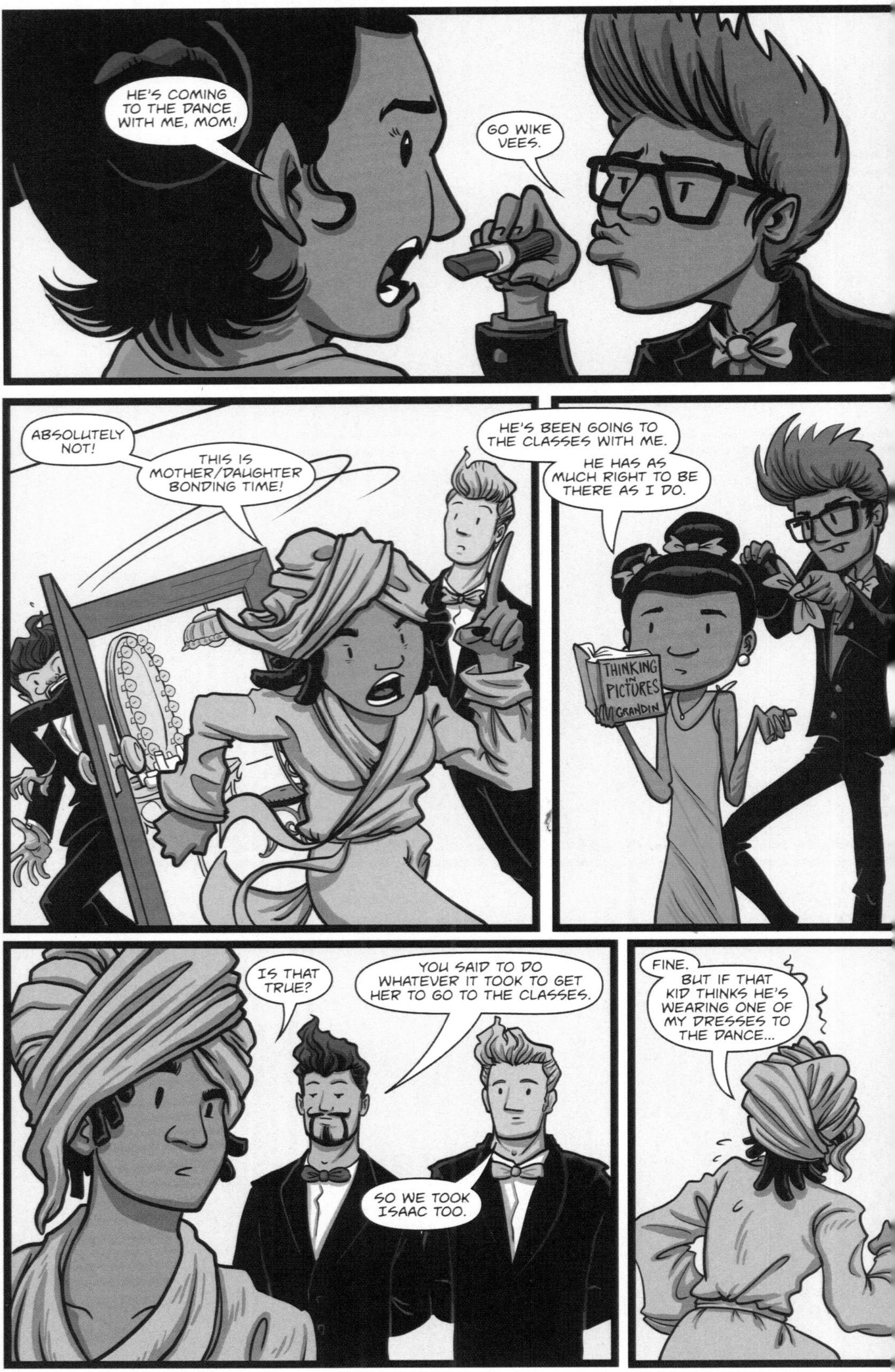
HE'S COMING TO THE DANCE WITH ME, MOM!
GO WIKE VEES.
ABSOLUTELY NOT!
THIS IS MOTHER/DAUGHTER BONDING TIME!
HE'S BEEN GOING TO THE CLASSES WITH ME.
HE HAS AS MUCH RIGHT TO BE THERE AS I DO.
THINKING IN PICTURES
GRANDIN
IS THAT TRUE?
YOU SAID TO DO WHATEVER IT TOOK TO GET HER TO GO TO THE CLASSES.
SO WE TOOK ISAAC TOO.
FINE.
BUT IF THAT KID THINKS HE'S WEARING ONE OF MY DRESSES TO THE DANCE...

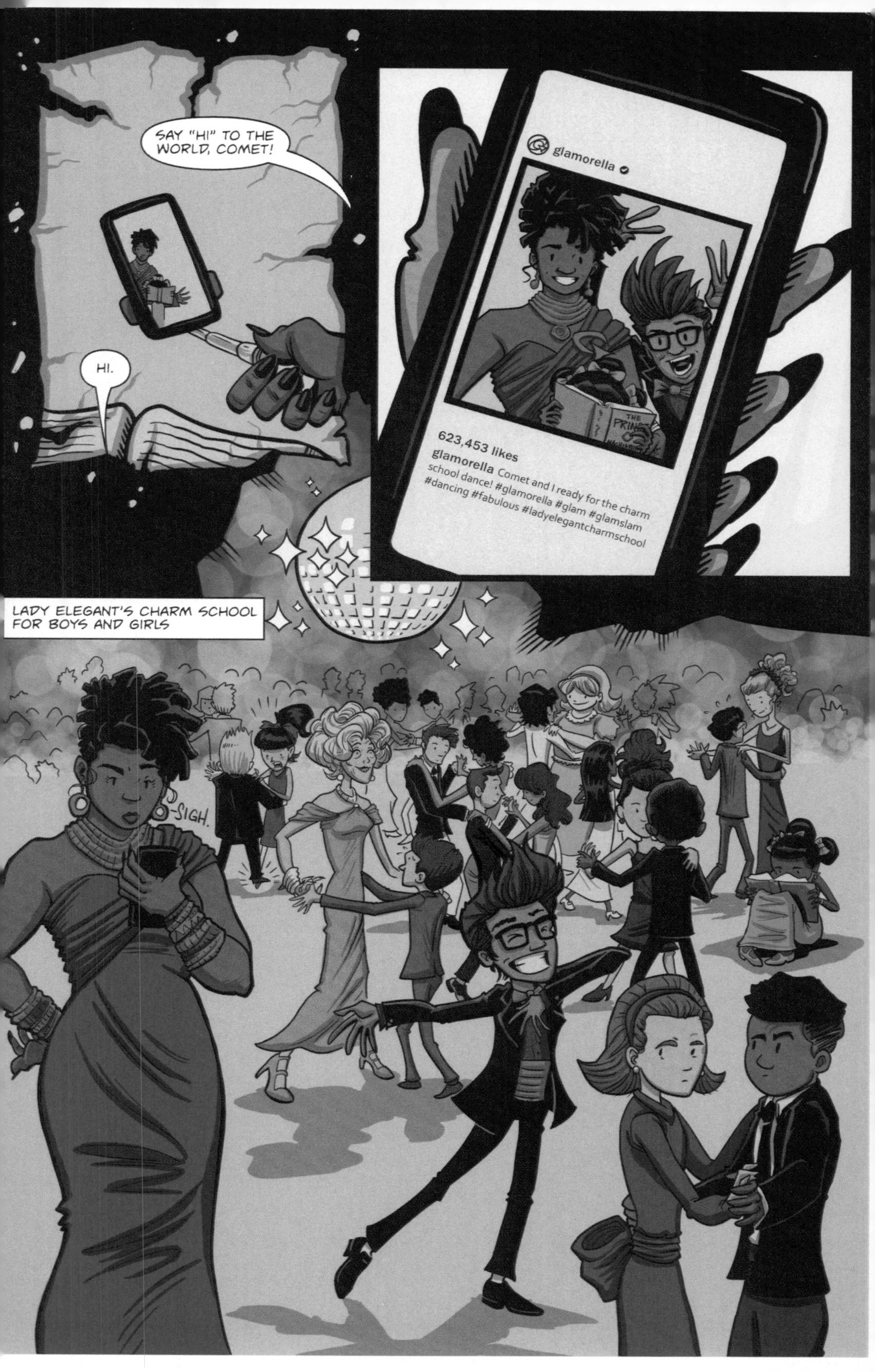
SAY "HI" TO THE WORLD, COMET!
HI.
glamorella
623,453 likes
glamorella Comet and I ready for the charm school dance! #glamorella #glam #glamslam #dancing #fabulous #ladyelegantcharmschool
THE PRINCE
LADY ELEGANT'S CHARM SCHOOL FOR BOYS AND GIRLS
SIGH.

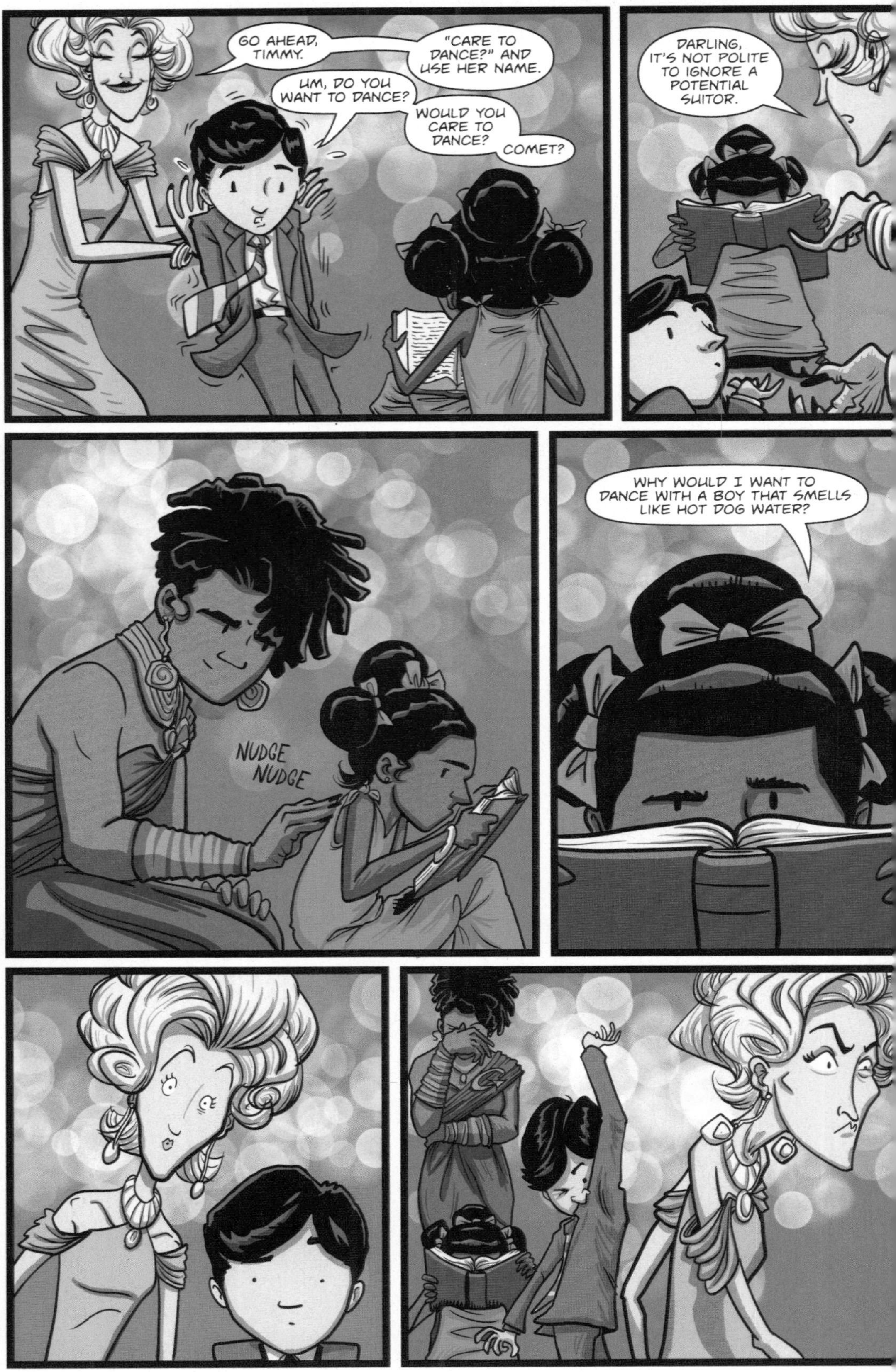
GO AHEAD, TIMMY.
"CARE TO DANCE?" AND USE HER NAME.
UM, DO YOU WANT TO DANCE?
WOULD YOU CARE TO DANCE?
COMET?
DARLING, IT'S NOT POLITE TO IGNORE A POTENTIAL SUITOR.
NUDGE NUDGE
WHY WOULD I WANT TO DANCE WITH A BOY THAT SMELLS LIKE HOT DOG WATER?

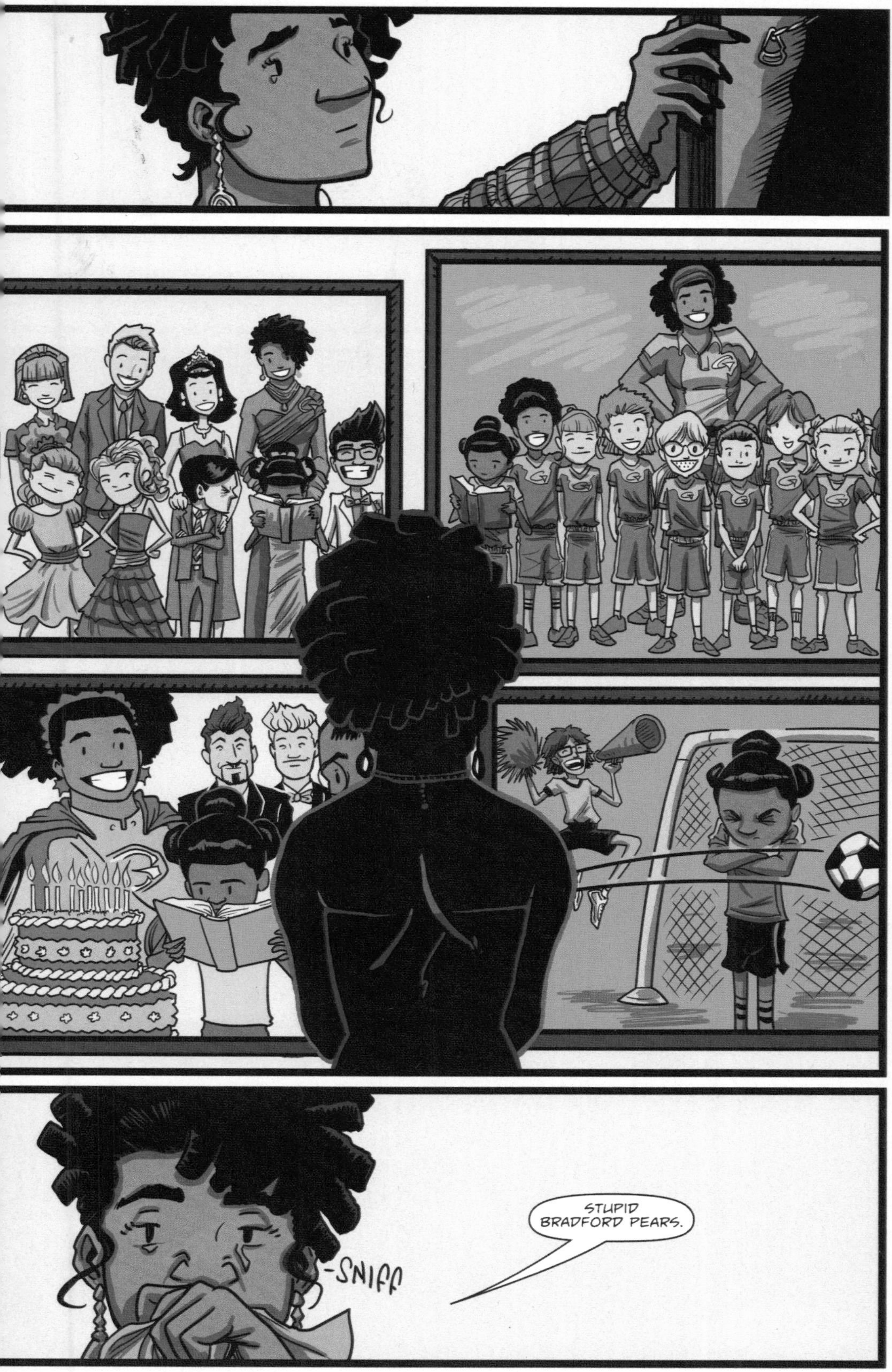
STUPID BRADFORD PEARS.
-SNIFF

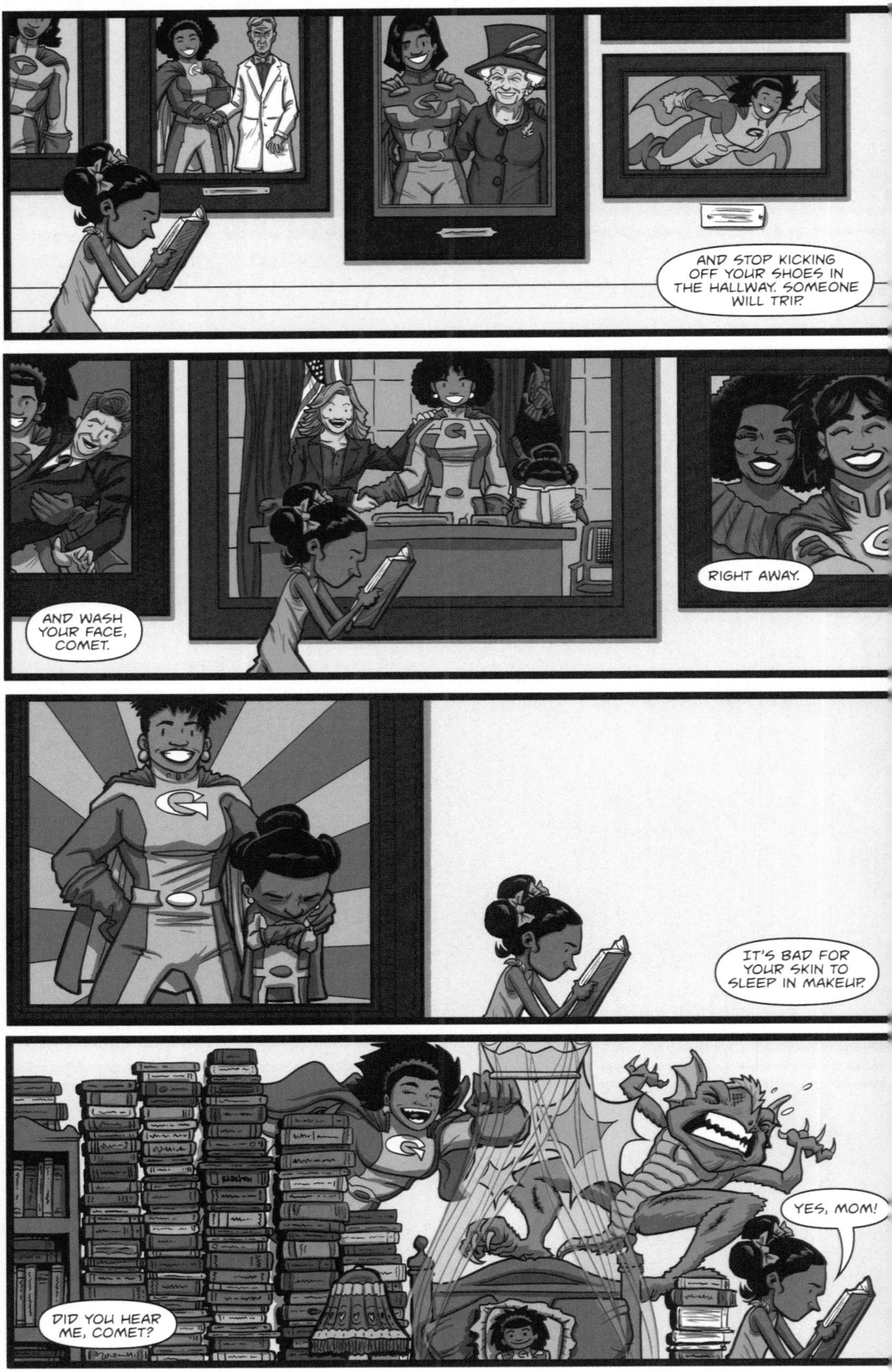
AND STOP KICKING OFF YOUR SHOES IN THE HALLWAY. SOMEONE WILL TRIP.
AND WASH YOUR FACE, COMET.
RIGHT AWAY.
IT'S BAD FOR YOUR SKIN TO SLEEP IN MAKEUP.
DID YOU HEAR ME, COMET?
YES, MOM!

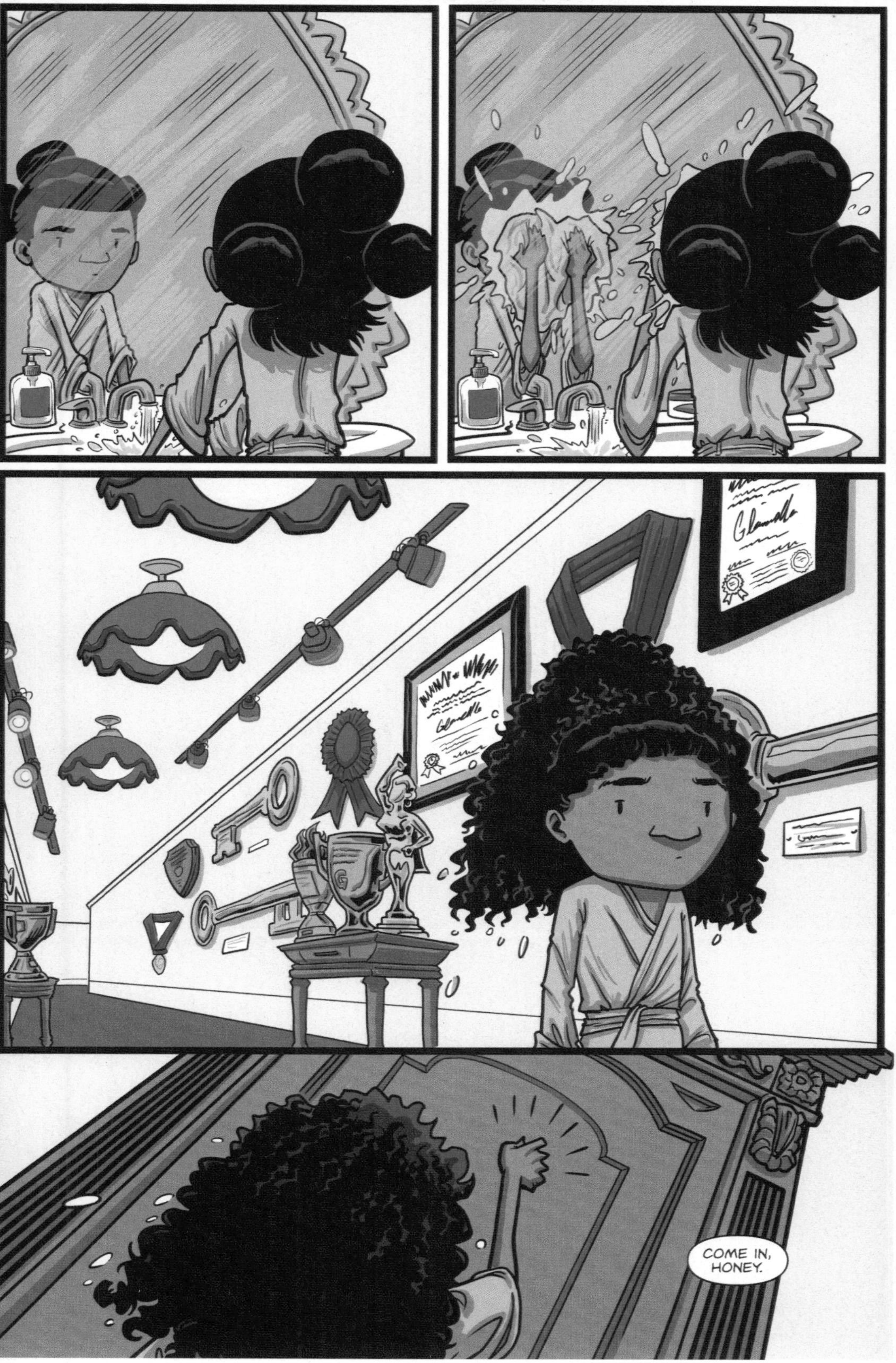
COME IN, HONEY.

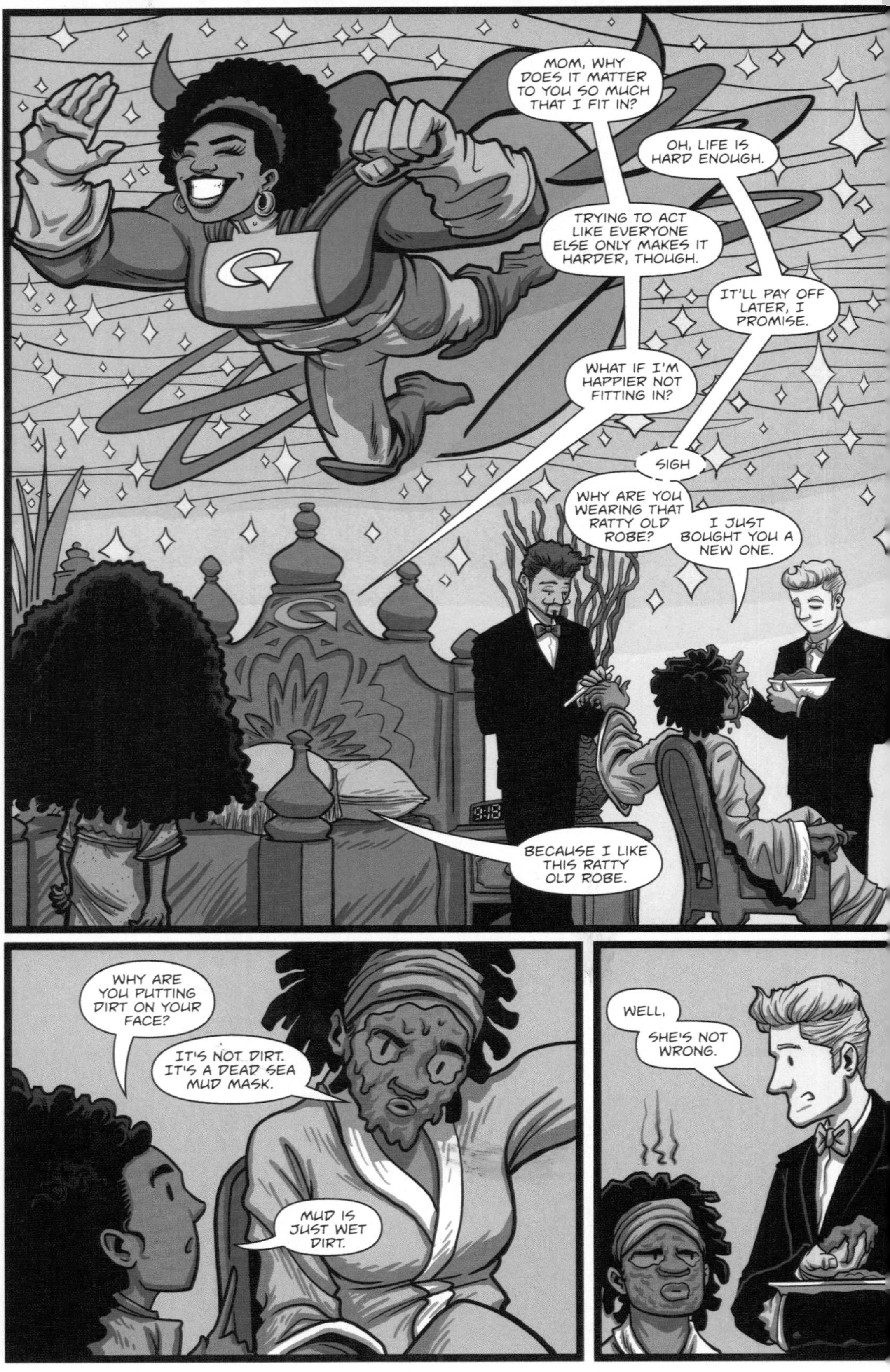
MOM, WHY DOES IT MATTER TO YOU SO MUCH THAT I FIT IN?
OH, LIFE IS HARD ENOUGH.
TRYING TO ACT LIKE EVERYONE ELSE ONLY MAKES IT HARDER, THOUGH.
IT'LL PAY OFF LATER, I PROMISE.
WHAT IF I'M HAPPIER NOT FITTING IN?
SIGH
WHY ARE YOU WEARING THAT RATTY OLD ROBE?
I JUST BOUGHT YOU A NEW ONE.
BECAUSE I LIKE THIS RATTY OLD ROBE.
WHY ARE YOU PUTTING DIRT ON YOUR FACE?
IT'S NOT DIRT. IT'S A DEAD SEA MUD MASK.
MUD IS JUST WET DIRT.
WELL,
SHE'S NOT WRONG.

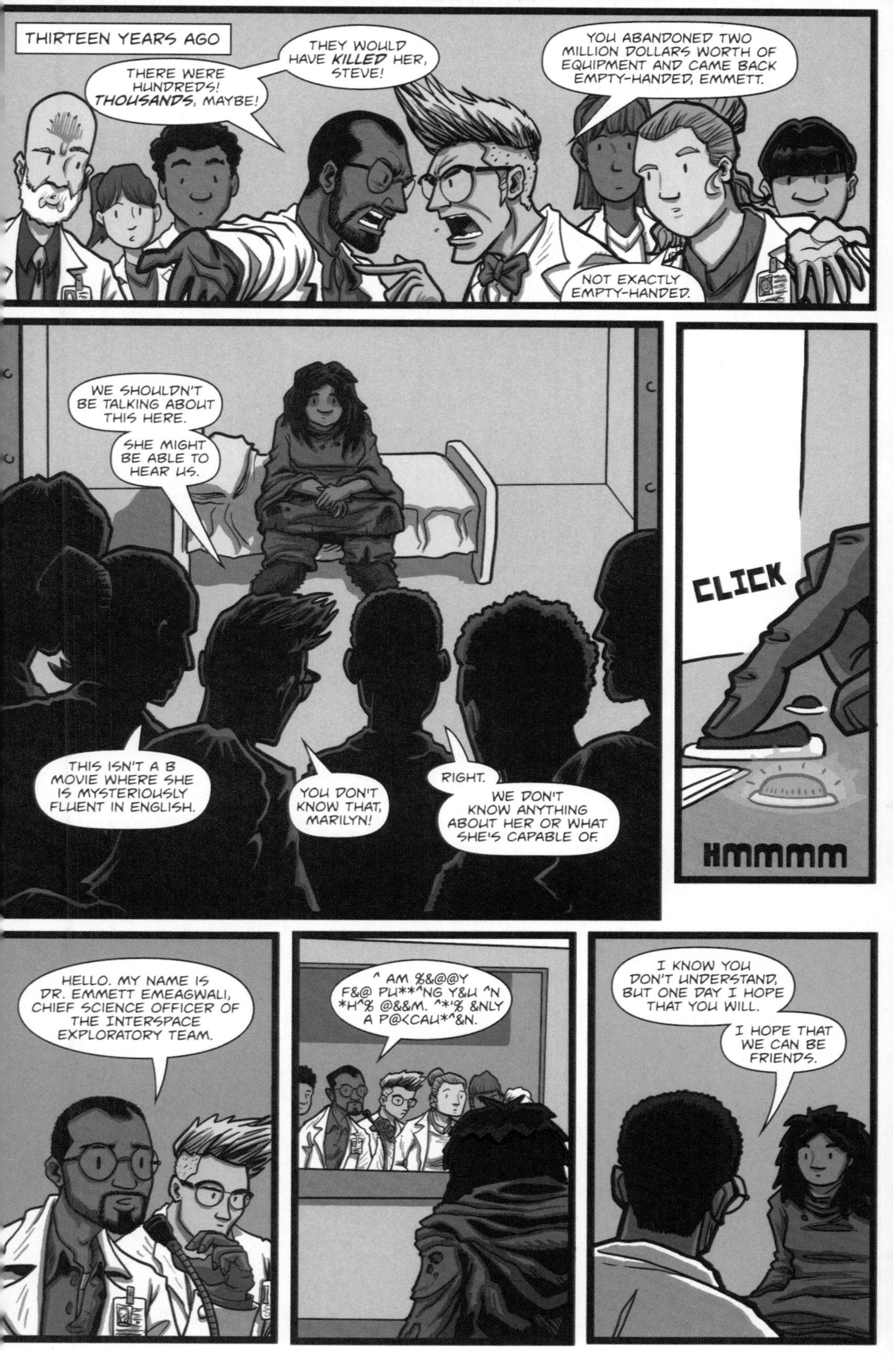
THIRTEEN YEARS AGO
THERE WERE HUNDREDS! THOUSANDS, MAYBE!
THEY WOULD HAVE KILLED HER, STEVE!
YOU ABANDONED TWO MILLION DOLLARS WORTH OF EQUIPMENT AND CAME BACK EMPTY-HANDED, EMMETT.
NOT EXACTLY EMPTY-HANDED.
WE SHOULDN'T BE TALKING ABOUT THIS HERE.
SHE MIGHT BE ABLE TO HEAR US.
THIS ISN'T A B MOVIE WHERE SHE IS MYSTERIOUSLY FLUENT IN ENGLISH.
YOU DON'T KNOW THAT, MARILYN!
RIGHT.
WE DON'T KNOW ANYTHING ABOUT HER OR WHAT SHE'S CAPABLE OF.
CLICK
HMMMM
HELLO. MY NAME IS DR. EMMETT EMEAGWALI, CHIEF SCIENCE OFFICER OF THE INTERSPACE EXPLORATORY TEAM.
^ AM %&@@Y F&@ PU**^NG Y&U ^N *H^% @&&M. ^*'% &NLY A P@<CAU*^&N.
I KNOW YOU DON'T UNDERSTAND, BUT ONE DAY I HOPE THAT YOU WILL.
I HOPE THAT WE CAN BE FRIENDS.

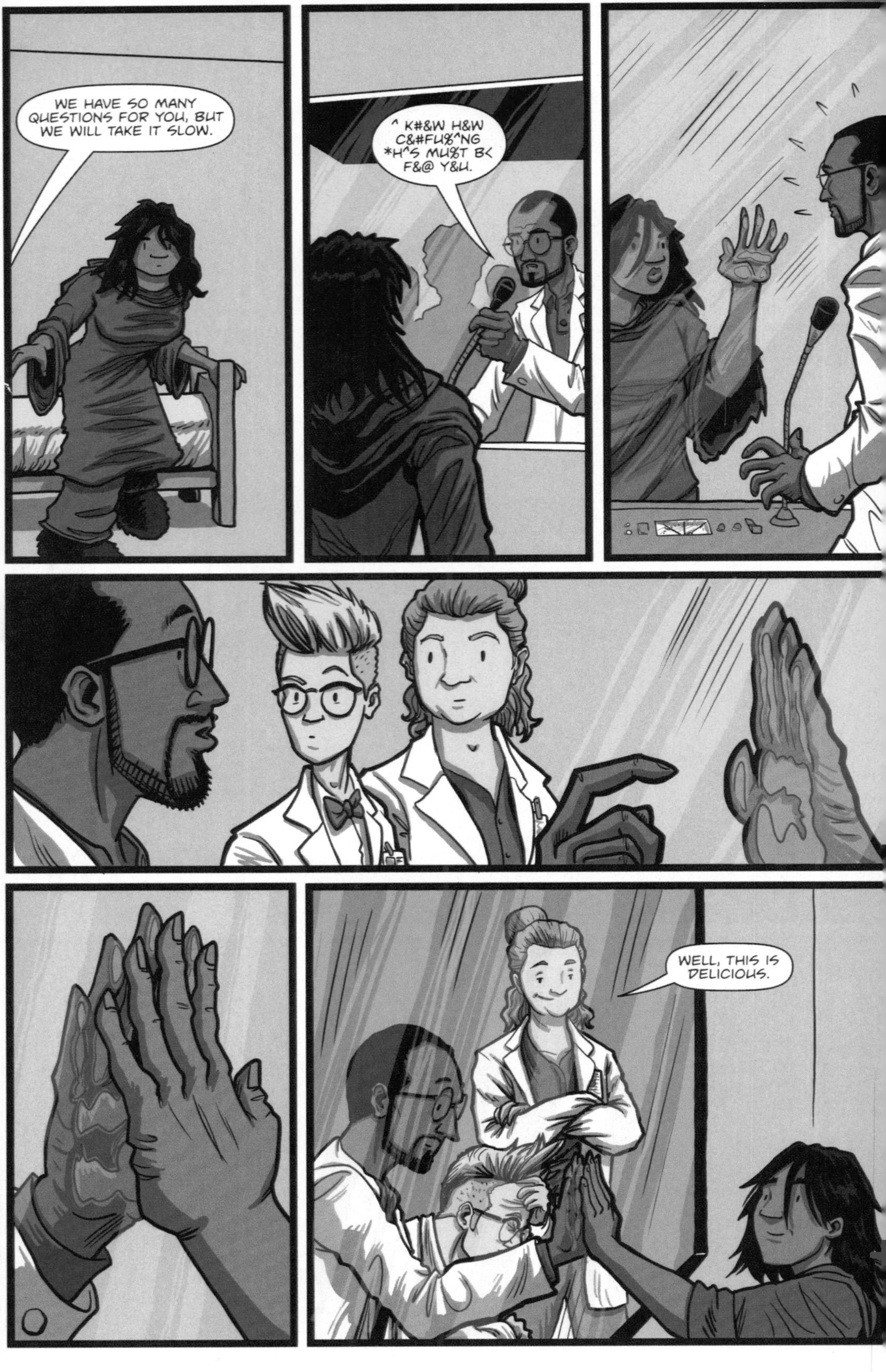
WE HAVE SO MANY QUESTIONS FOR YOU, BUT WE WILL TAKE IT SLOW.
^ K#&W H&W C&#FU%^NG *H^S MU%T B< F&@ Y&U.
WELL, THIS IS DELICIOUS.

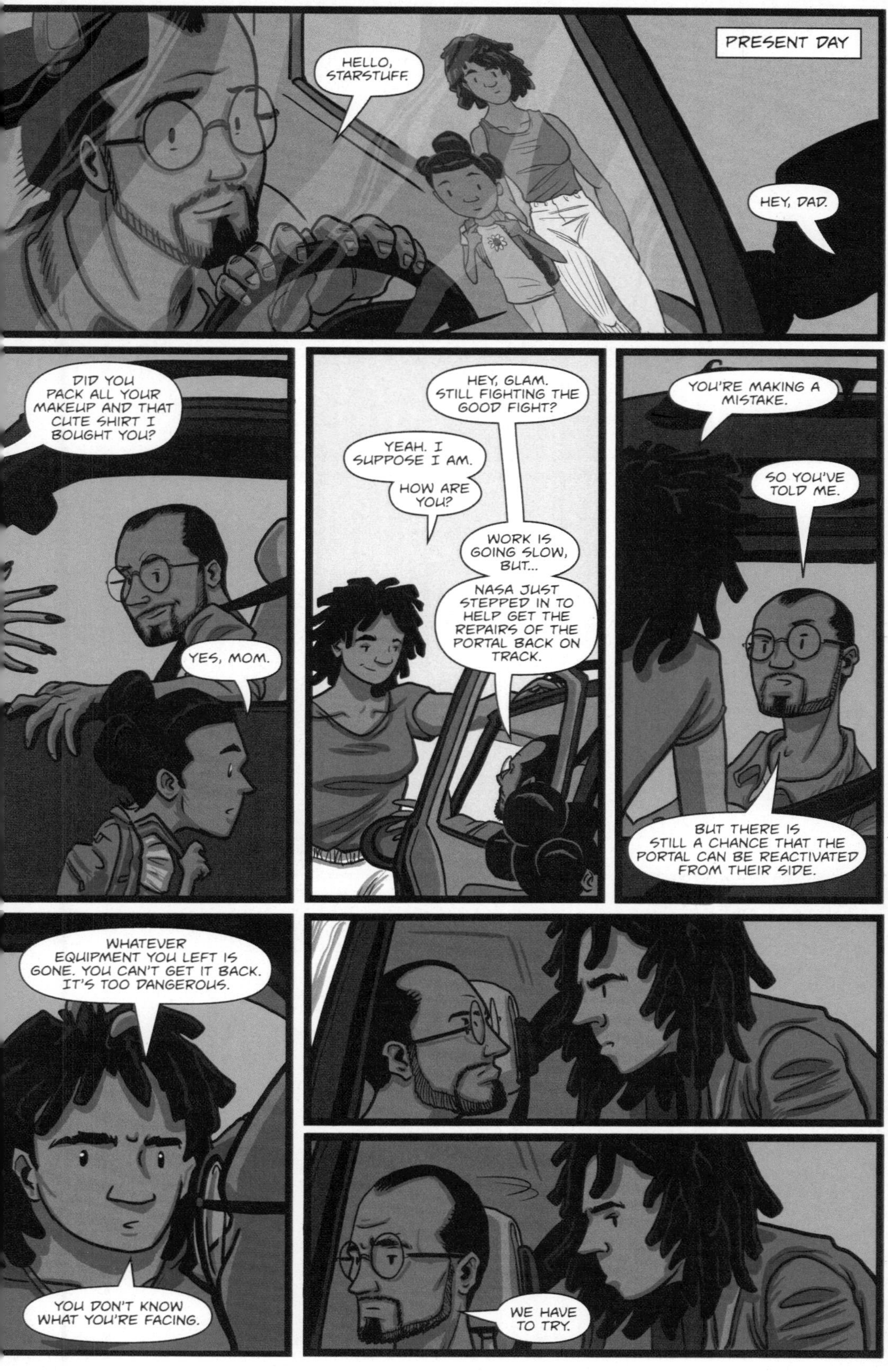
PRESENT DAY
HELLO, STARSTUFF.
HEY, DAD.
DID YOU PACK ALL YOUR MAKEUP AND THAT CUTE SHIRT I BOUGHT YOU?
YES, MOM.
HEY, GLAM. STILL FIGHTING THE GOOD FIGHT?
YEAH. I SUPPOSE I AM.
HOW ARE YOU?
WORK IS GOING SLOW, BUT...
NASA JUST STEPPED IN TO HELP GET THE REPAIRS OF THE PORTAL BACK ON TRACK.
YOU'RE MAKING A MISTAKE.
SO YOU'VE TOLD ME.
BUT THERE IS STILL A CHANCE THAT THE PORTAL CAN BE REACTIVATED FROM THEIR SIDE.
WHATEVER EQUIPMENT YOU LEFT IS GONE. YOU CAN'T GET IT BACK. IT'S TOO DANGEROUS.
YOU DON'T KNOW WHAT YOU'RE FACING.
WE HAVE TO TRY.

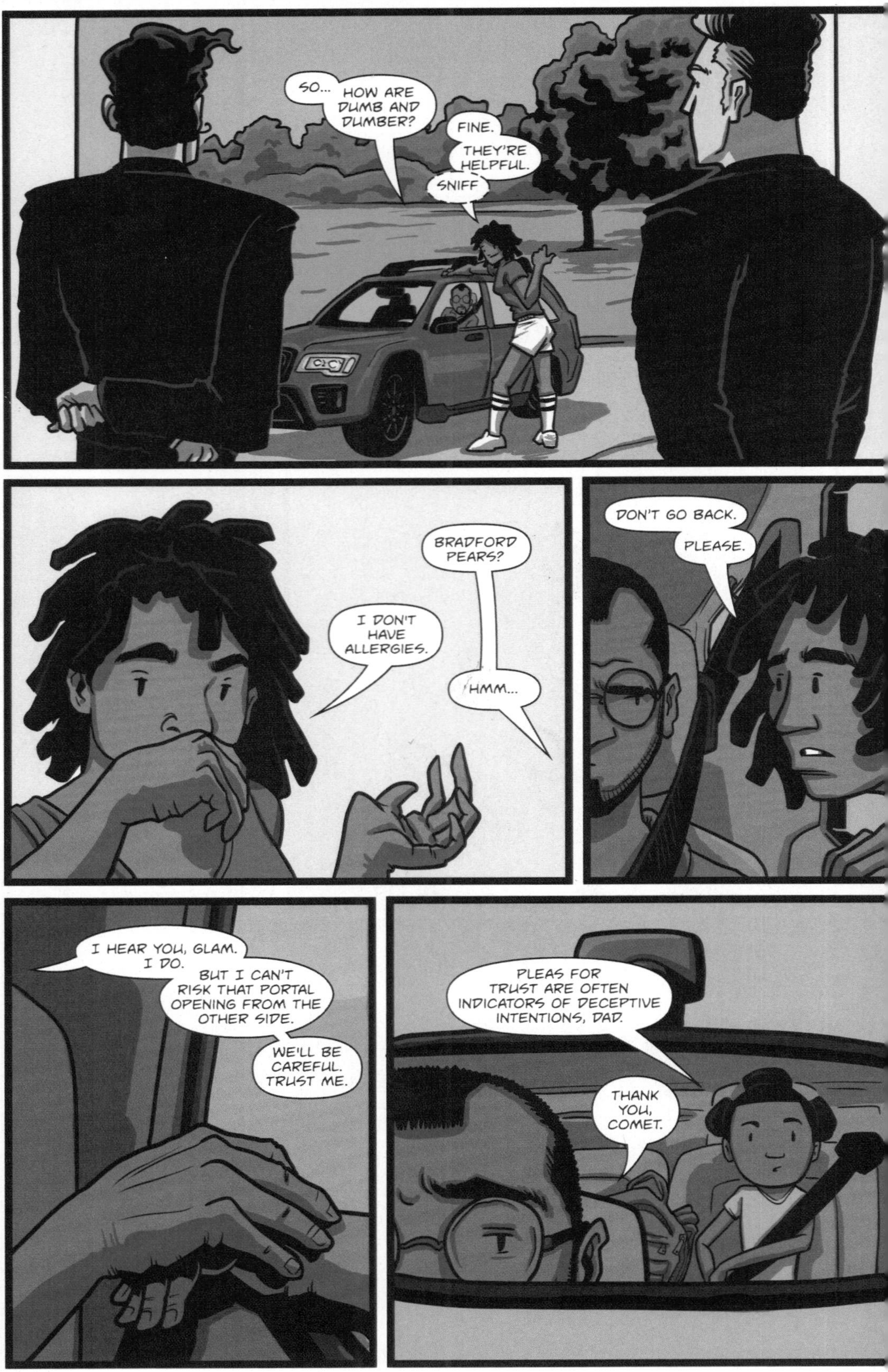

SO...
HOW ARE DUMB AND DUMBER?
FINE.
THEY'RE HELPFUL.
SNIFF
BRADFORD PEARS?
I DON'T HAVE ALLERGIES.
HMM...
DON'T GO BACK.
PLEASE.
I HEAR YOU, GLAM. I DO.
BUT I CAN'T RISK THAT PORTAL OPENING FROM THE OTHER SIDE.
WE'LL BE CAREFUL. TRUST ME.
PLEAS FOR TRUST ARE OFTEN INDICATORS OF DECEPTIVE INTENTIONS, DAD.
THANK YOU, COMET.

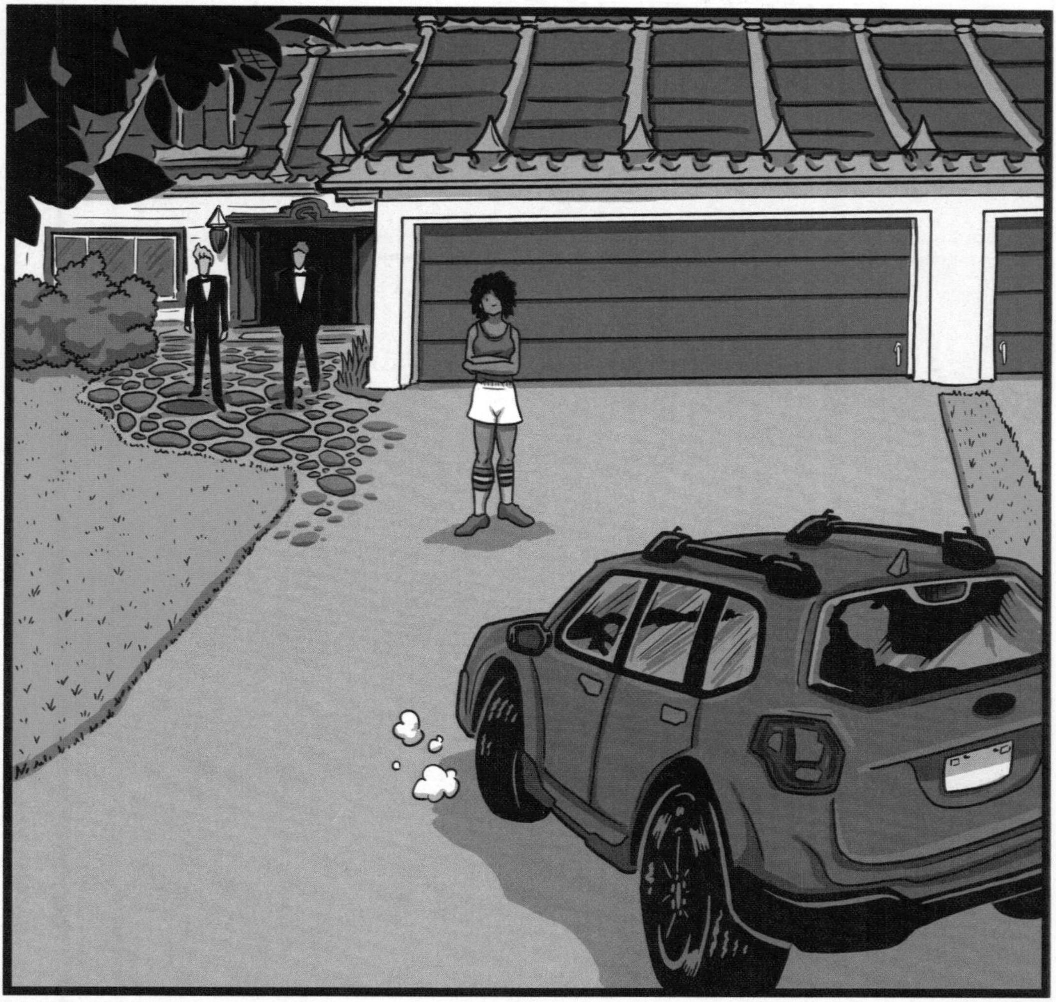

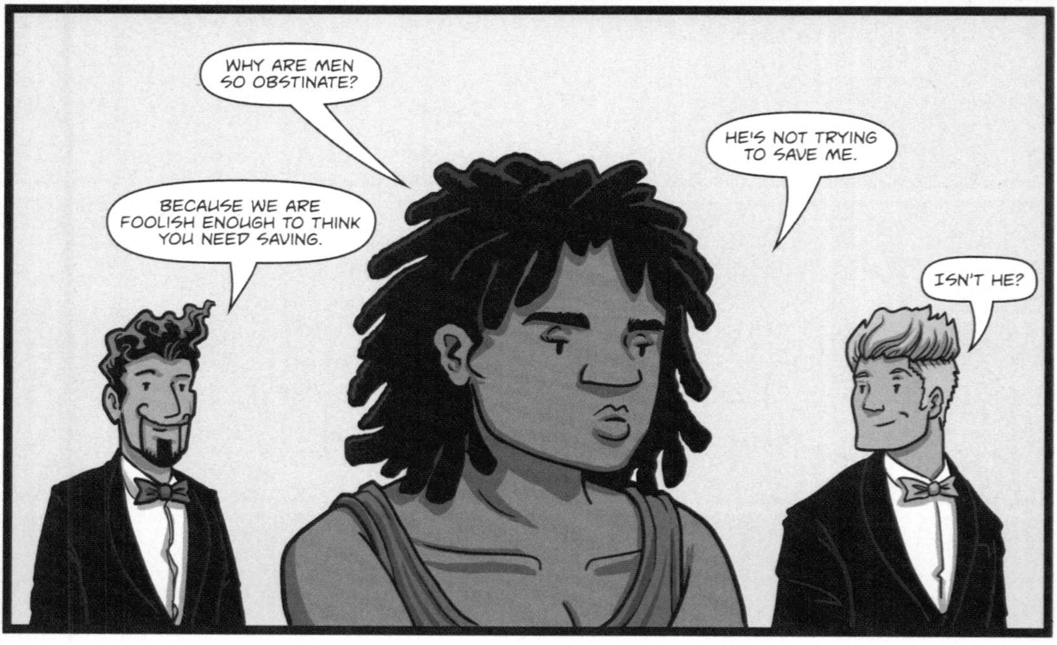
WHY ARE MEN SO OBSTINATE?
BECAUSE WE ARE FOOLISH ENOUGH TO THINK YOU NEED SAVING.
HE'S NOT TRYING TO SAVE ME.
ISN'T HE?

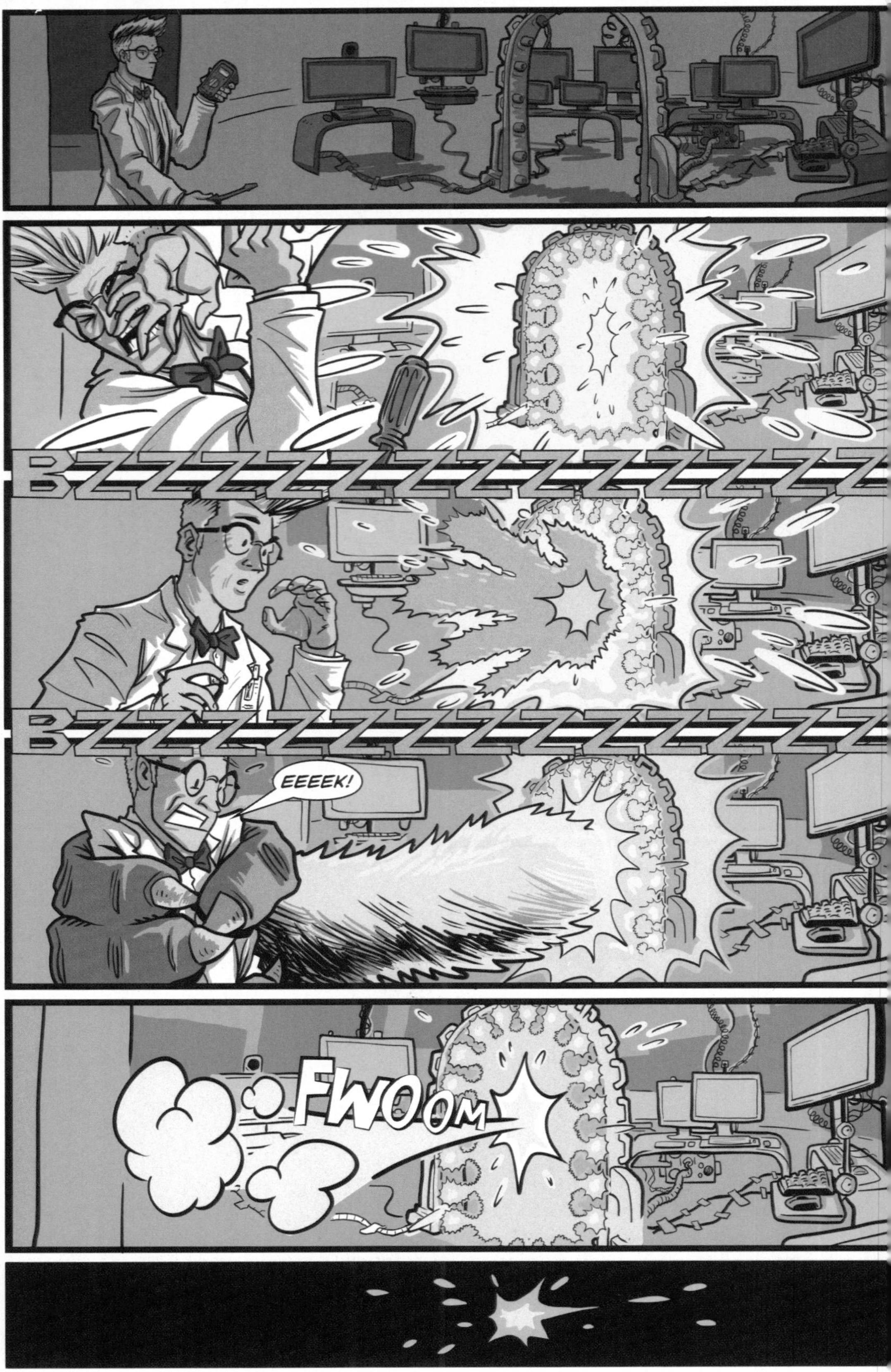
BZZZZZZZZZZZZZZZZZZ
BZZZZZZZZZZZZZZZZZZ
EEEEK!
FWOOM

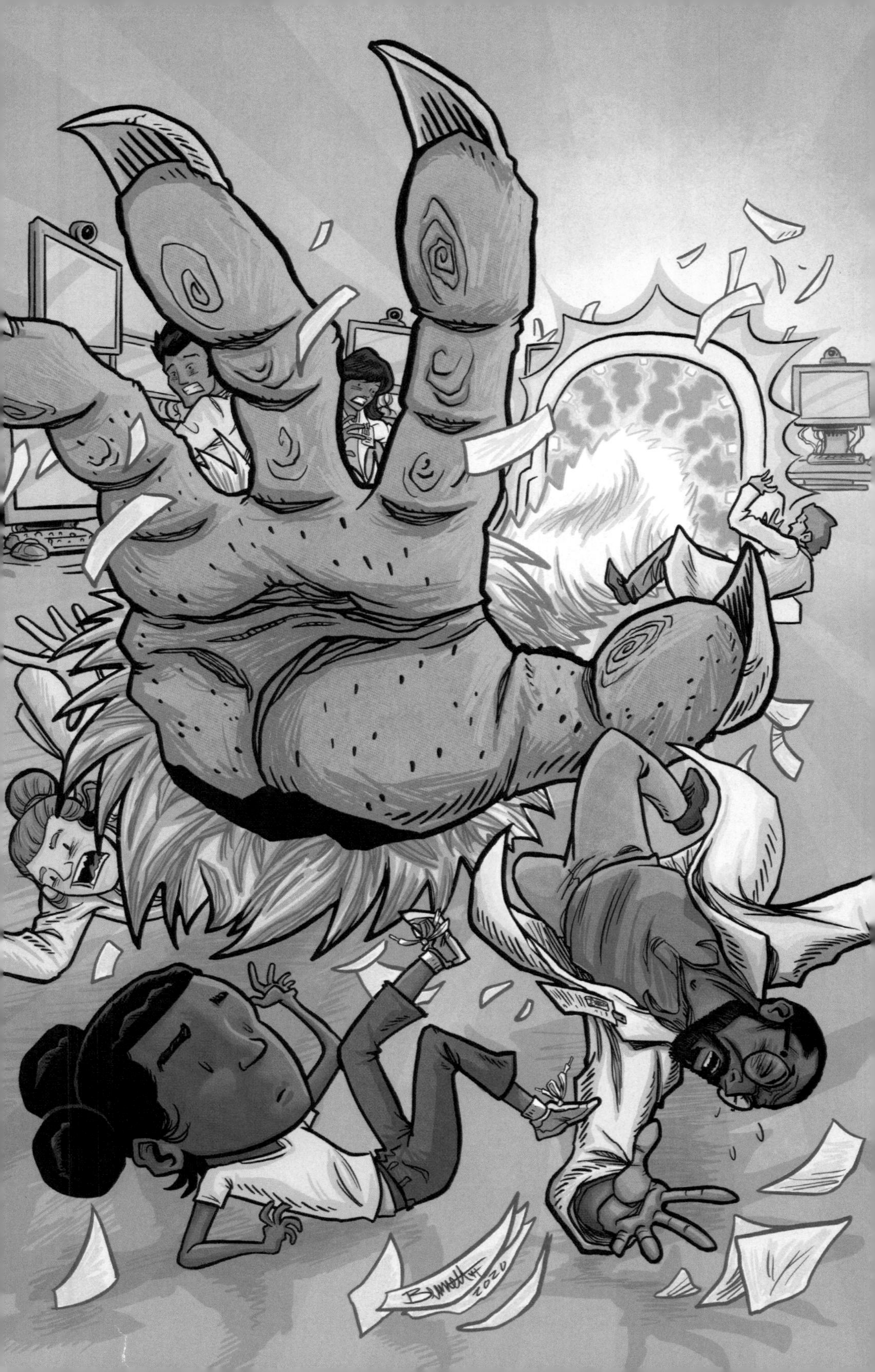

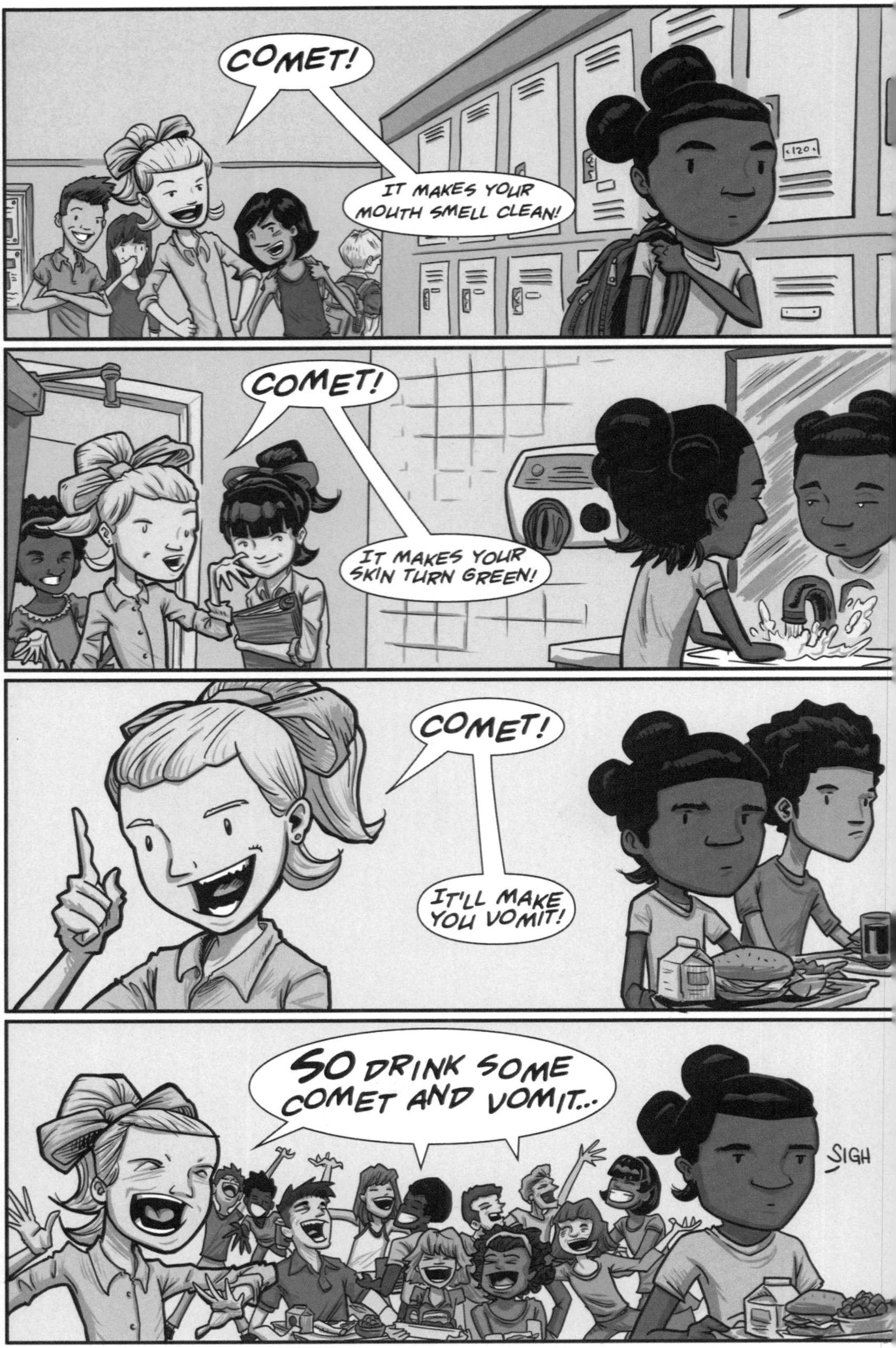
COMET!
IT MAKES YOUR MOUTH SMELL CLEAN!
COMET!
IT MAKES YOUR SKIN TURN GREEN!
COMET!
IT'LL MAKE YOU VOMIT!
SO DRINK SOME COMET AND VOMIT...
SIGH

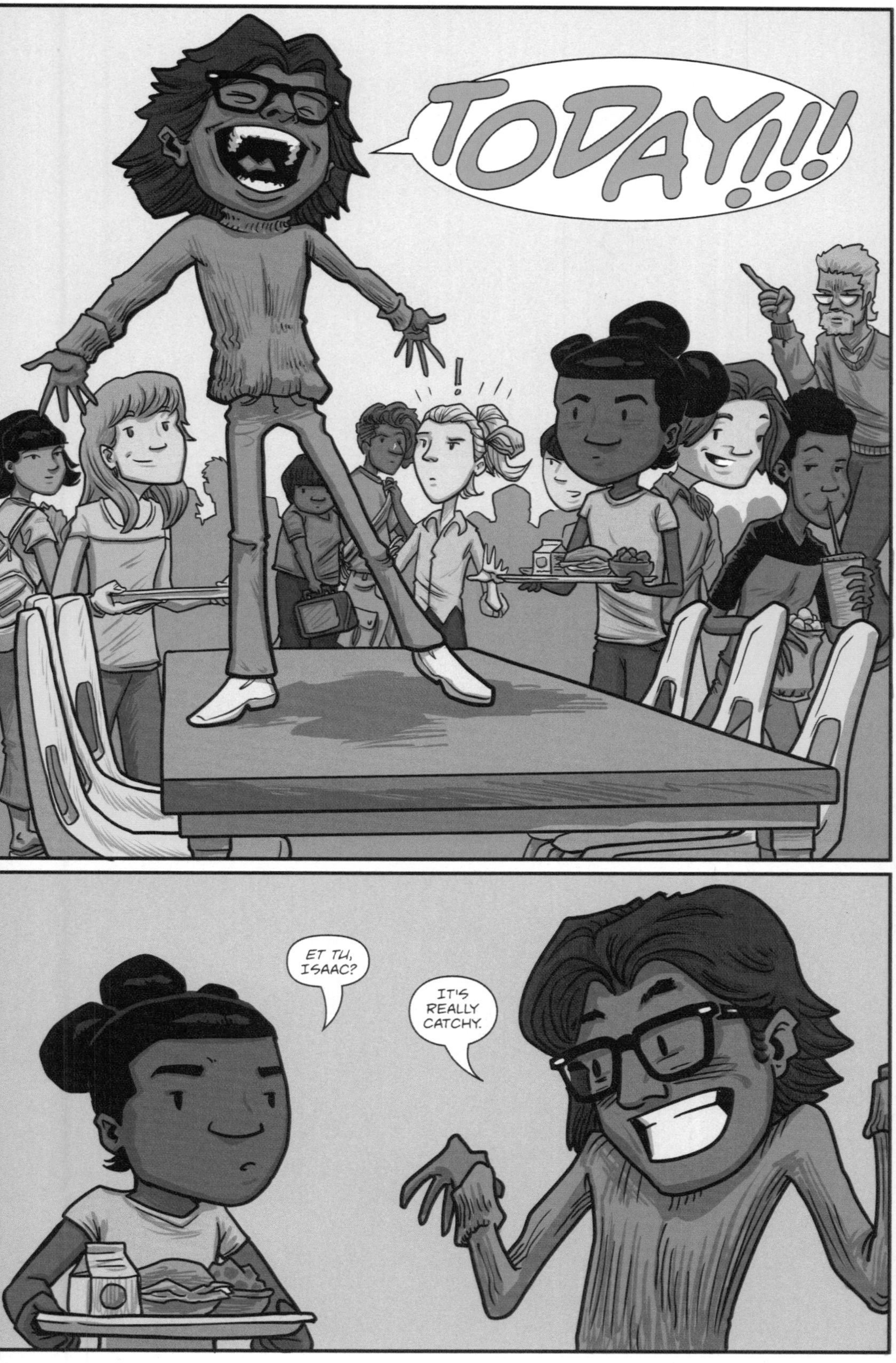
TODAY!!!
!
ET TU, ISAAC?
IT'S REALLY CATCHY.

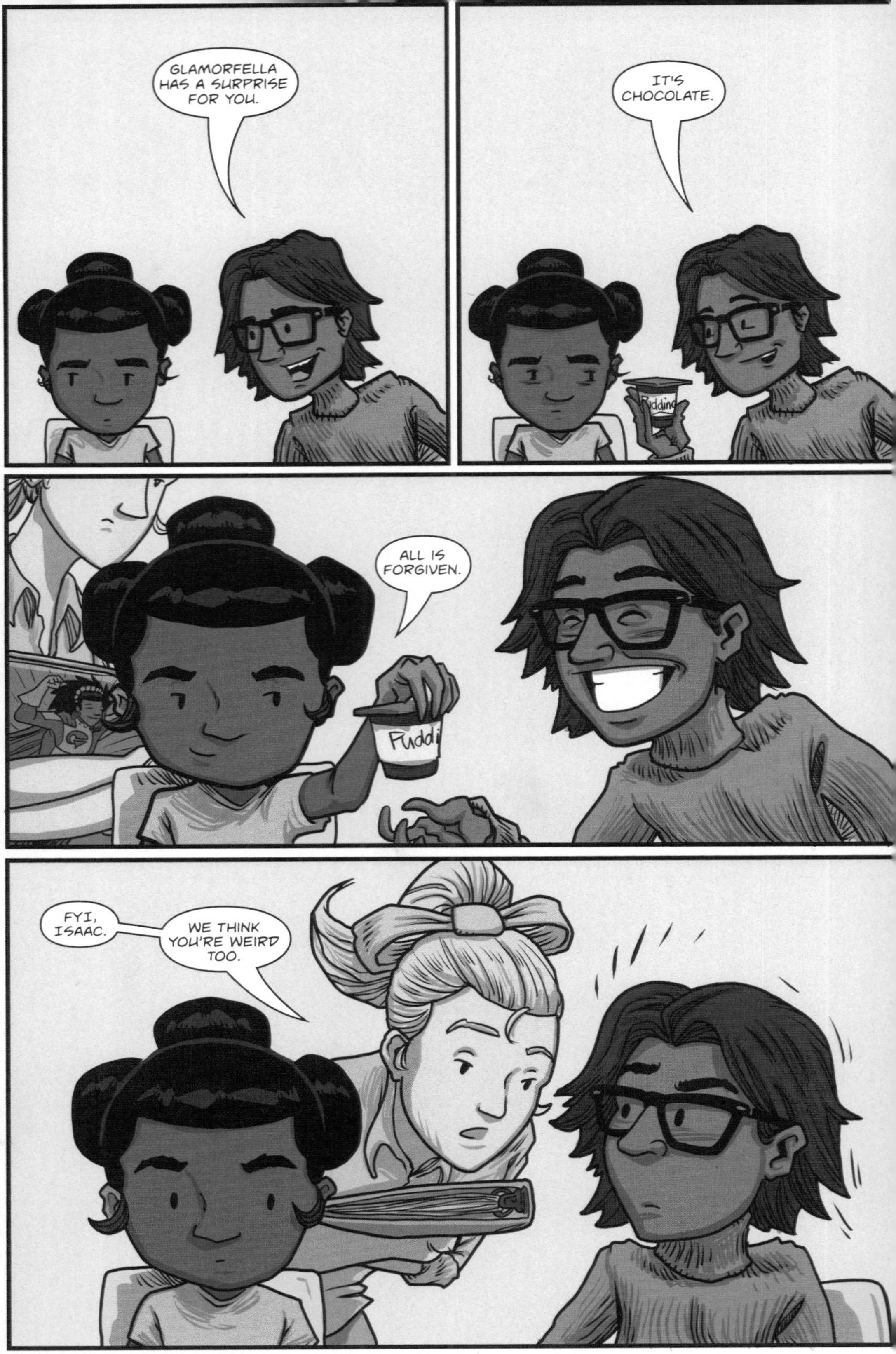
GLAMORFELLA HAS A SURPRISE FOR YOU.
IT'S CHOCOLATE.
Pudding
ALL IS FORGIVEN.
Puddi
FYI, ISAAC.
WE THINK YOU'RE WEIRD TOO.

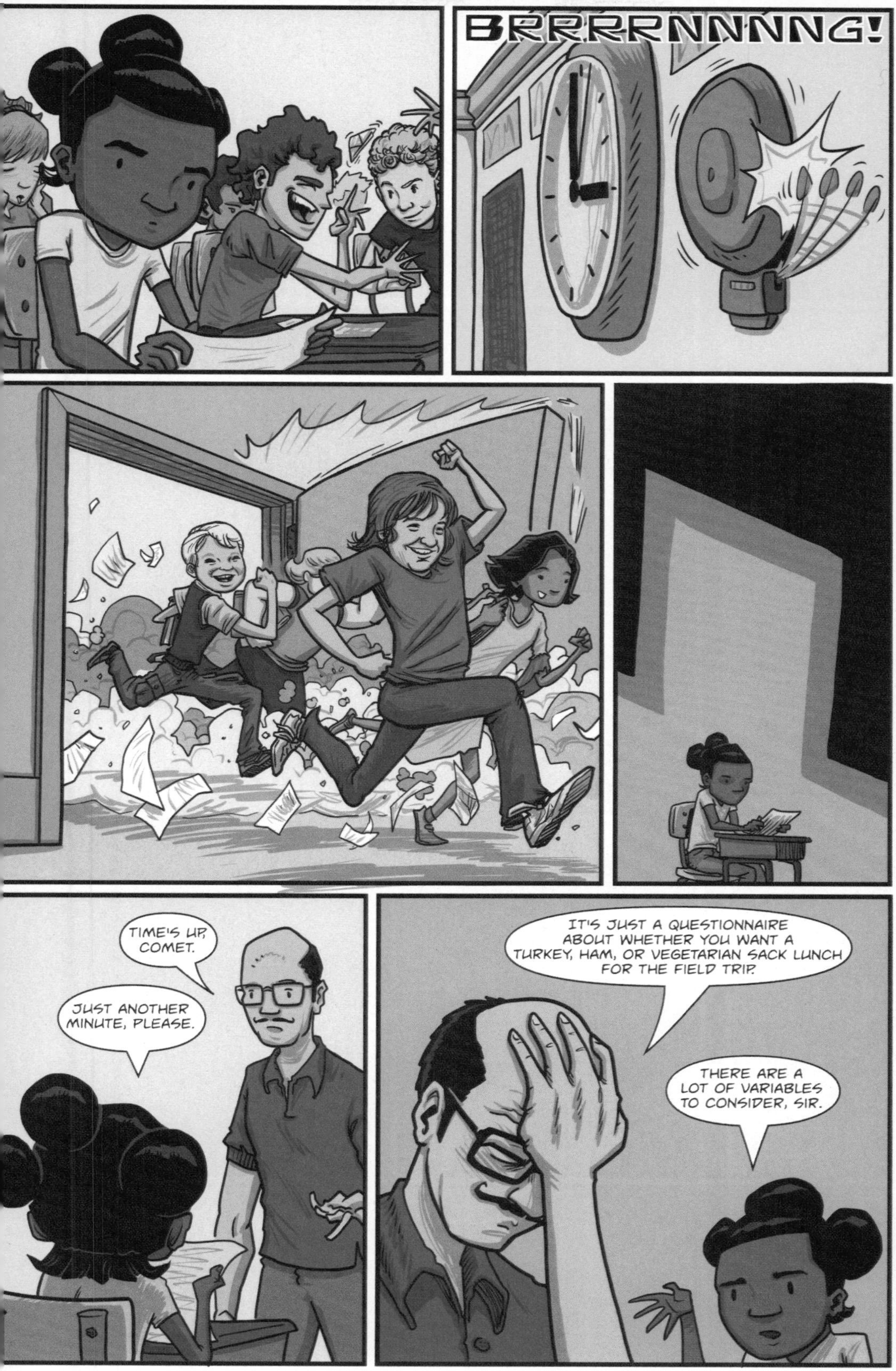
BRRRRRNNNNG!
TIME'S UP, COMET.
JUST ANOTHER MINUTE, PLEASE.
IT'S JUST A QUESTIONNAIRE ABOUT WHETHER YOU WANT A TURKEY, HAM, OR VEGETARIAN SACK LUNCH FOR THE FIELD TRIP.
THERE ARE A LOT OF VARIABLES TO CONSIDER, SIR.

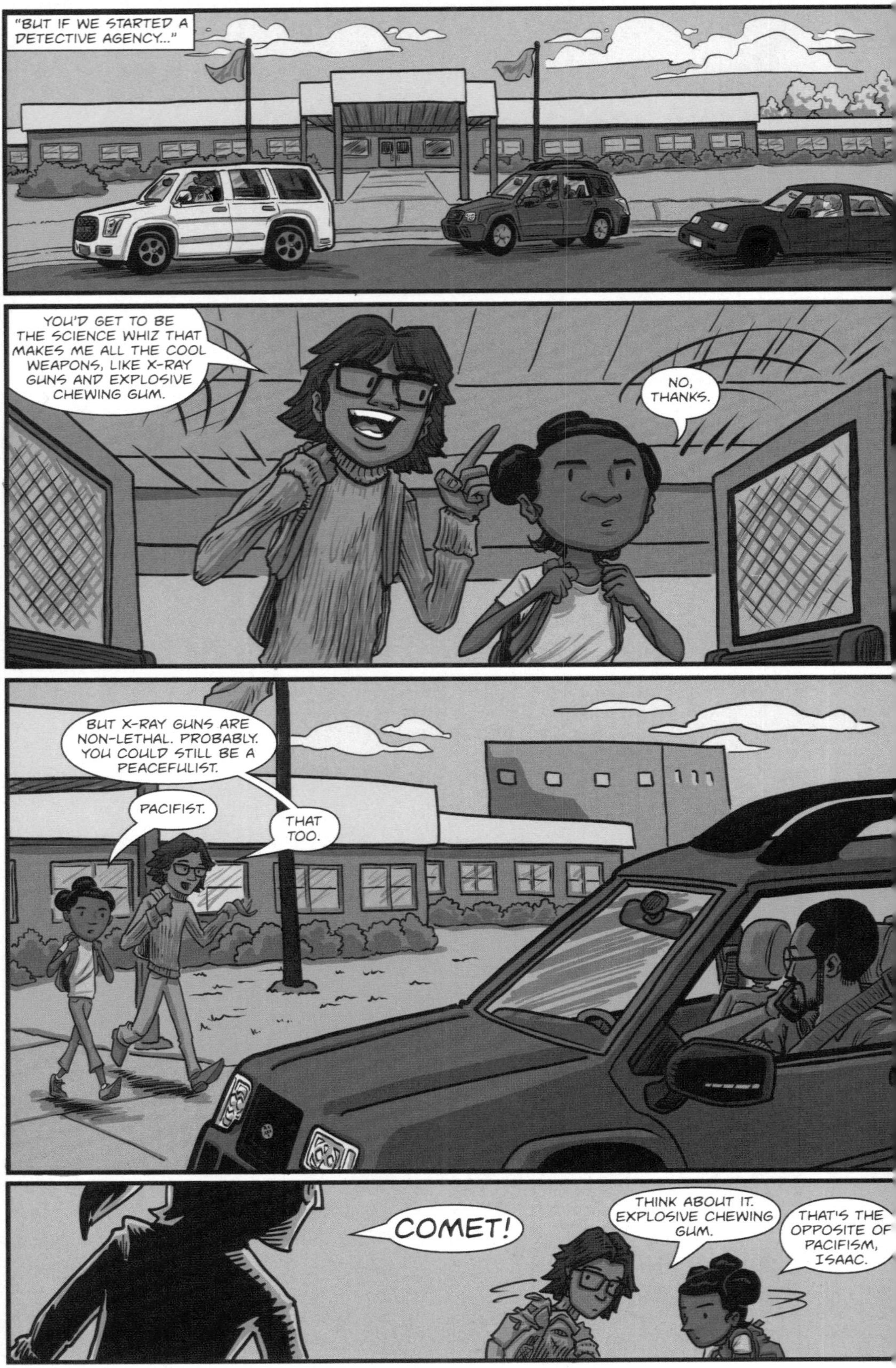
"BUT IF WE STARTED A DETECTIVE AGENCY..."
YOU'D GET TO BE THE SCIENCE WHIZ THAT MAKES ME ALL THE COOL WEAPONS, LIKE X-RAY GUNS AND EXPLOSIVE CHEWING GUM.
NO, THANKS.
BUT X-RAY GUNS ARE NON-LETHAL. PROBABLY. YOU COULD STILL BE A PEACEFULIST.
PACIFIST.
THAT TOO.
COMET!
THINK ABOUT IT. EXPLOSIVE CHEWING GUM.
THAT'S THE OPPOSITE OF PACIFISM, ISAAC.

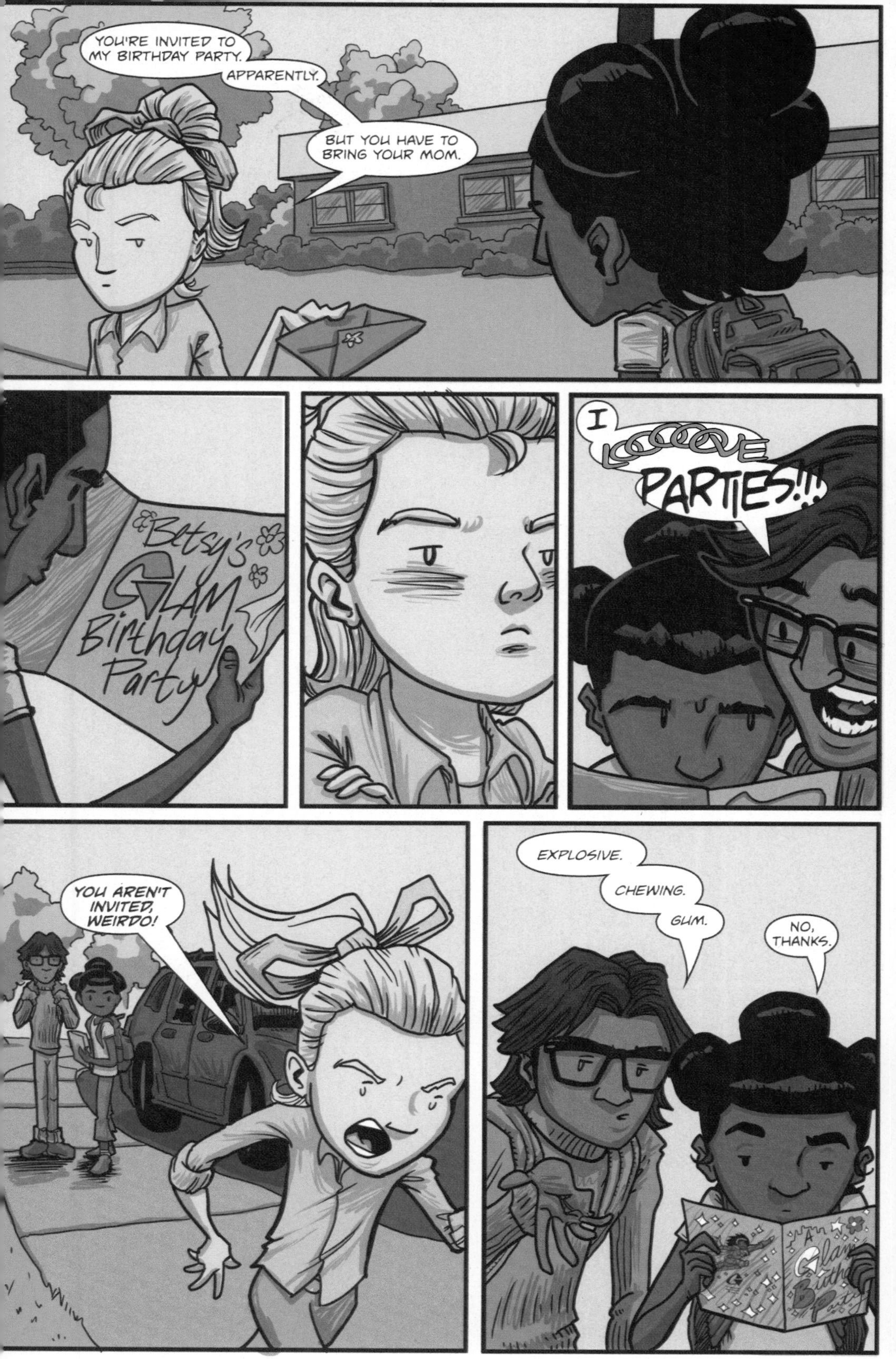
YOU'RE INVITED TO MY BIRTHDAY PARTY.
APPARENTLY.
BUT YOU HAVE TO BRING YOUR MOM.
Betsy's GLAM Birthday Party
I LOOOOOVE PARTIES!!!
YOU AREN'T INVITED, WEIRDO!
EXPLOSIVE.
CHEWING.
GUM.
NO, THANKS.

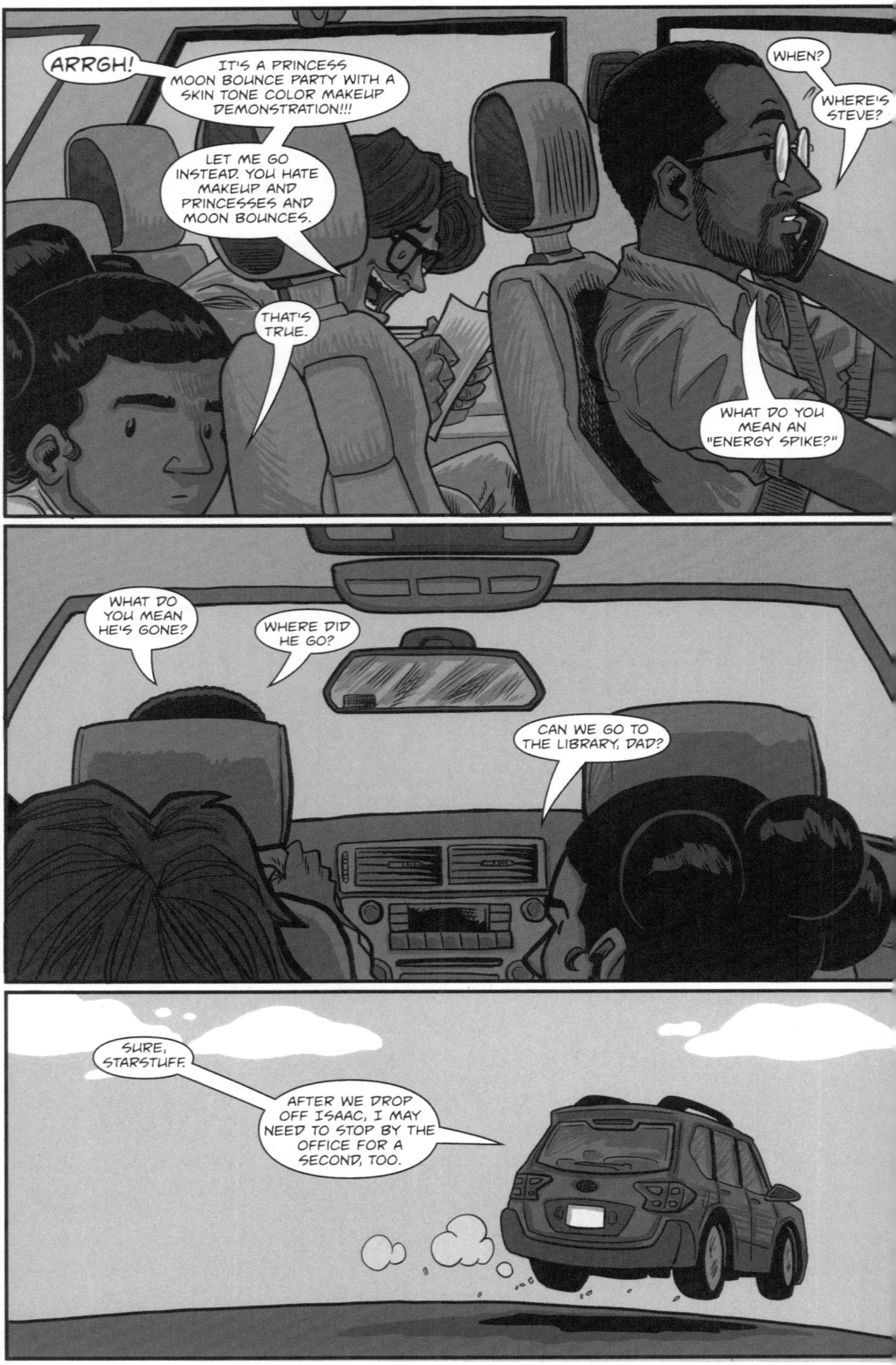
ARRGH!
IT'S A PRINCESS MOON BOUNCE PARTY WITH A SKIN TONE COLOR MAKEUP DEMONSTRATION!!!
LET ME GO INSTEAD. YOU HATE MAKEUP AND PRINCESSES AND MOON BOUNCES.
THAT'S TRUE.
WHEN?
WHERE'S STEVE?
WHAT DO YOU MEAN AN "ENERGY SPIKE?"
WHAT DO YOU MEAN HE'S GONE?
WHERE DID HE GO?
CAN WE GO TO THE LIBRARY, DAD?
SURE, STARSTUFF.
AFTER WE DROP OFF ISAAC, I MAY NEED TO STOP BY THE OFFICE FOR A SECOND, TOO.

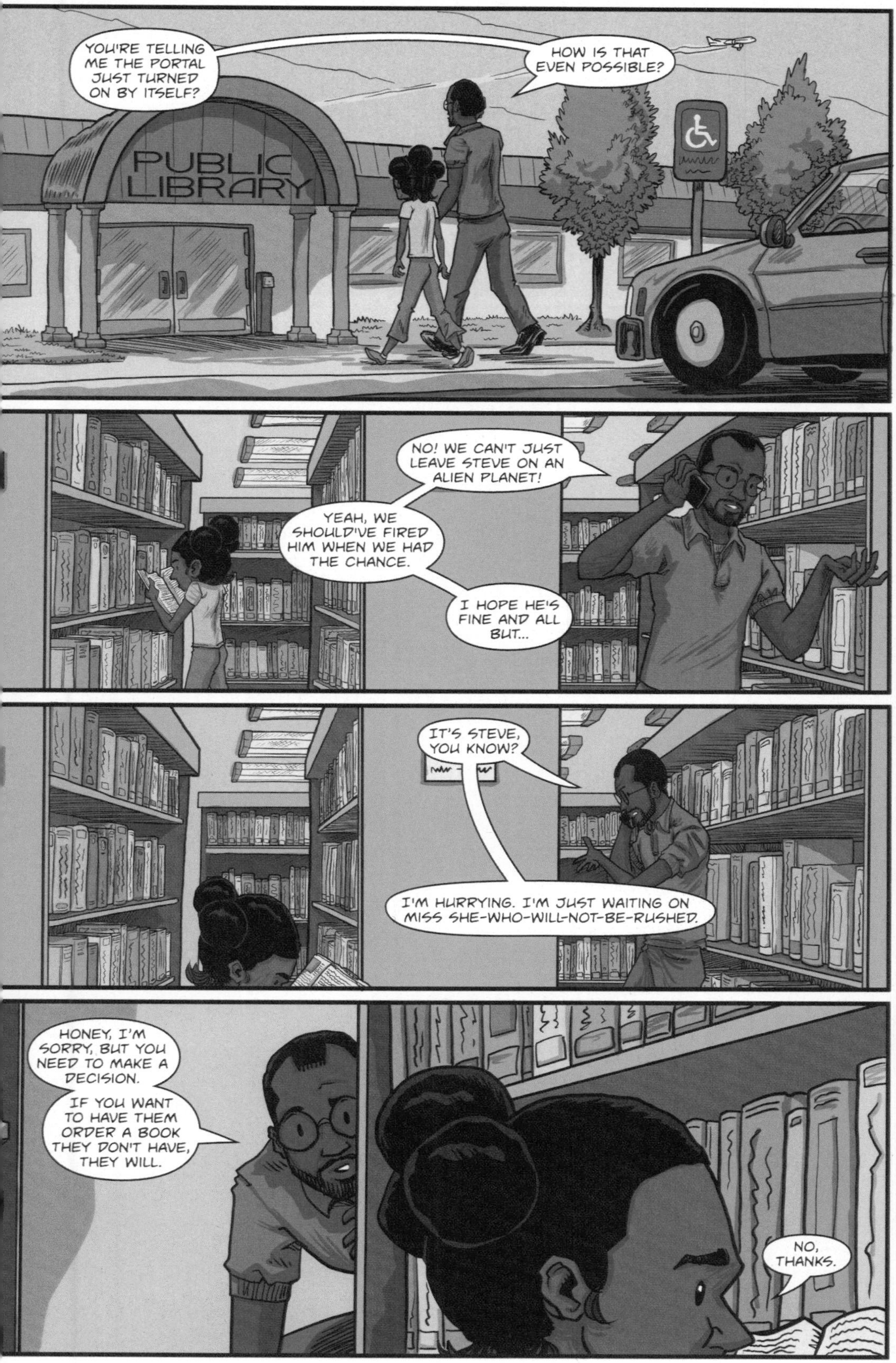
YOU'RE TELLING ME THE PORTAL JUST TURNED ON BY ITSELF?
HOW IS THAT EVEN POSSIBLE?
PUBLIC LIBRARY
NO! WE CAN'T JUST LEAVE STEVE ON AN ALIEN PLANET!
YEAH, WE SHOULD'VE FIRED HIM WHEN WE HAD THE CHANCE.
I HOPE HE'S FINE AND ALL BUT...
IT'S STEVE, YOU KNOW?
I'M HURRYING. I'M JUST WAITING ON MISS SHE-WHO-WILL-NOT-BE-RUSHED.
HONEY, I'M SORRY, BUT YOU NEED TO MAKE A DECISION.
IF YOU WANT TO HAVE THEM ORDER A BOOK THEY DON'T HAVE, THEY WILL.
NO, THANKS.

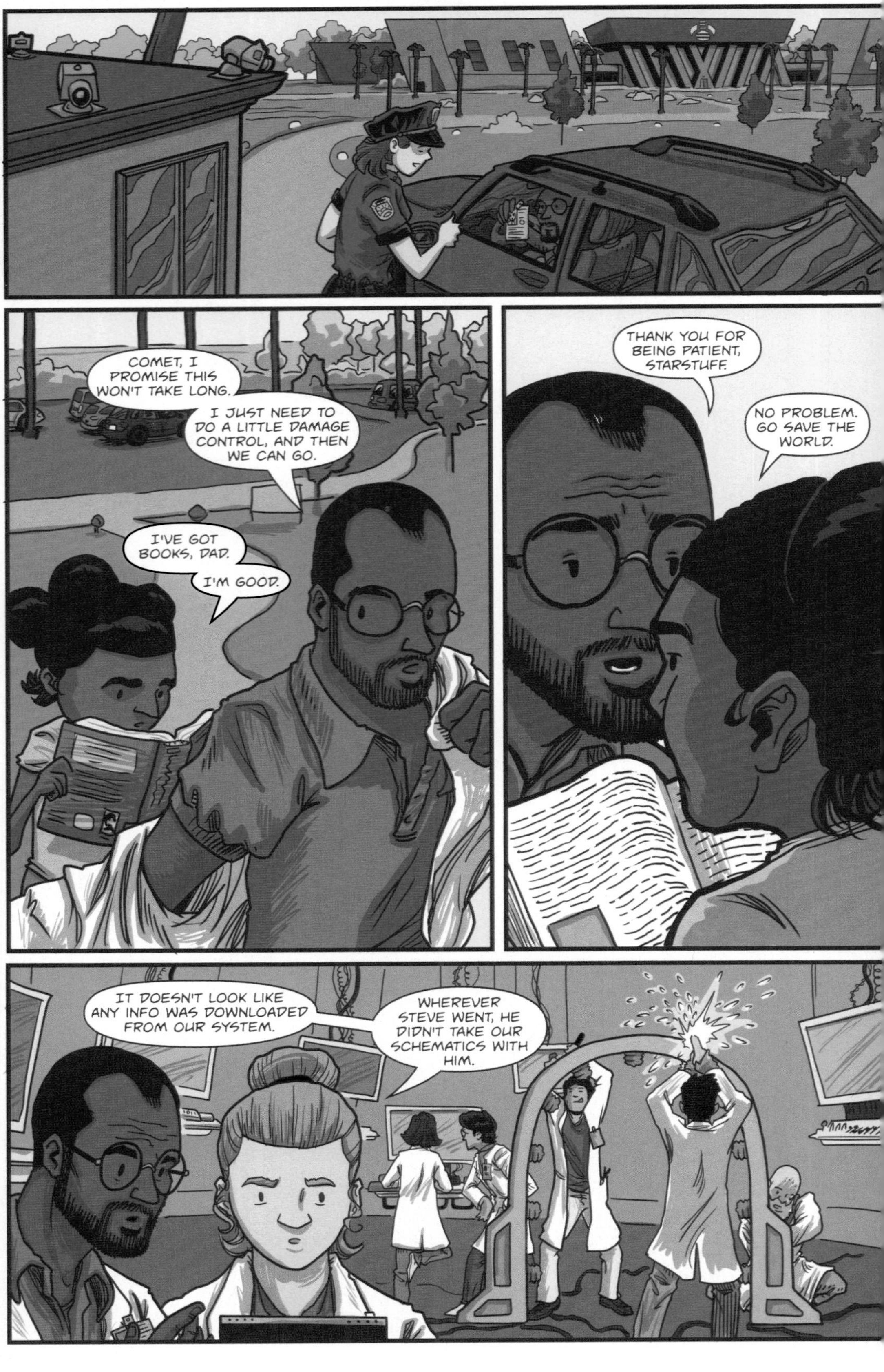
COMET, I PROMISE THIS WON'T TAKE LONG.
I JUST NEED TO DO A LITTLE DAMAGE CONTROL, AND THEN WE CAN GO.
I'VE GOT BOOKS, DAD.
I'M GOOD.
THANK YOU FOR BEING PATIENT, STARSTUFF.
NO PROBLEM. GO SAVE THE WORLD.
IT DOESN'T LOOK LIKE ANY INFO WAS DOWNLOADED FROM OUR SYSTEM.
WHEREVER STEVE WENT, HE DIDN'T TAKE OUR SCHEMATICS WITH HIM.

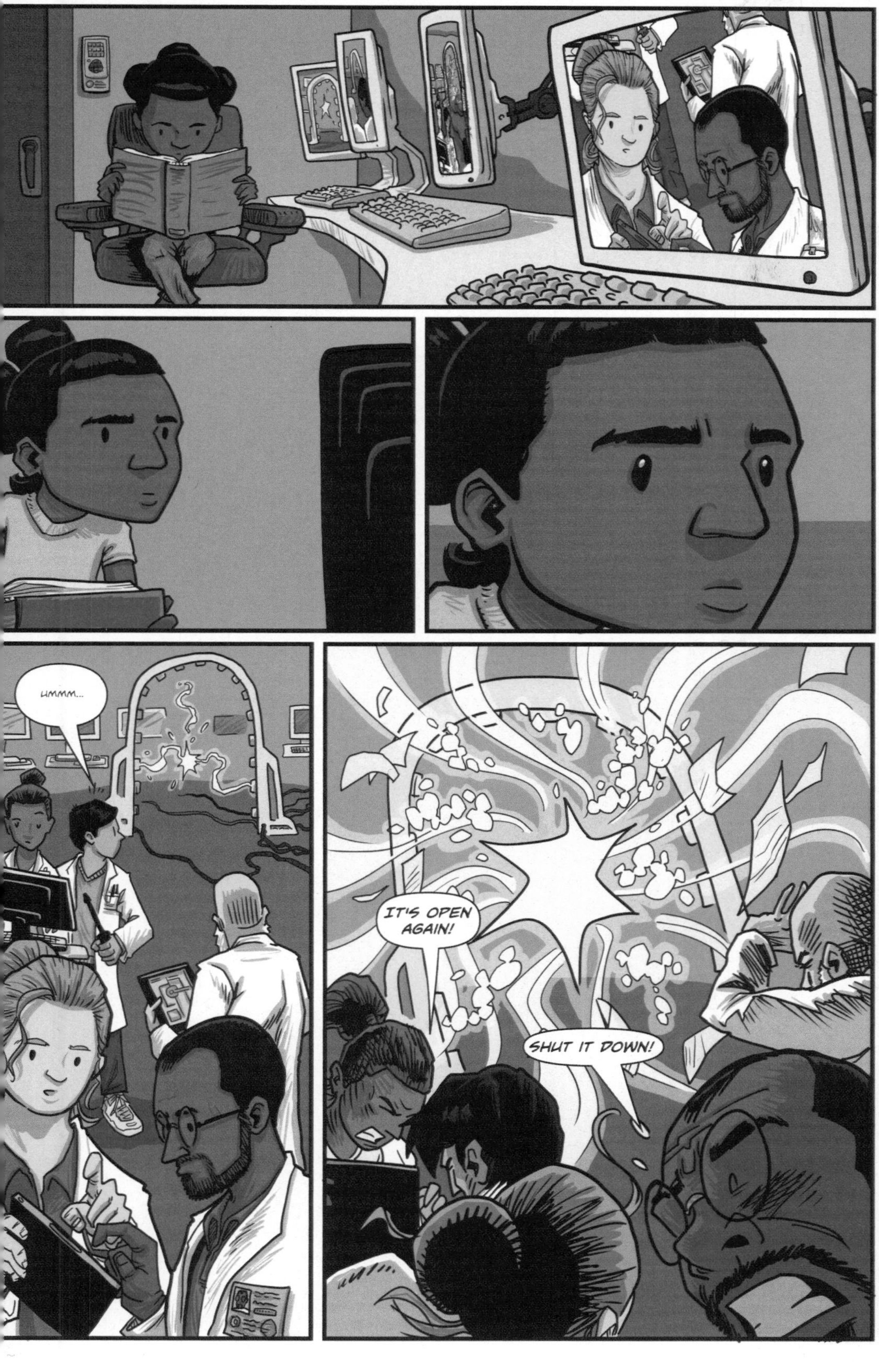
UMMM...
IT'S OPEN AGAIN!
SHUT IT DOWN!

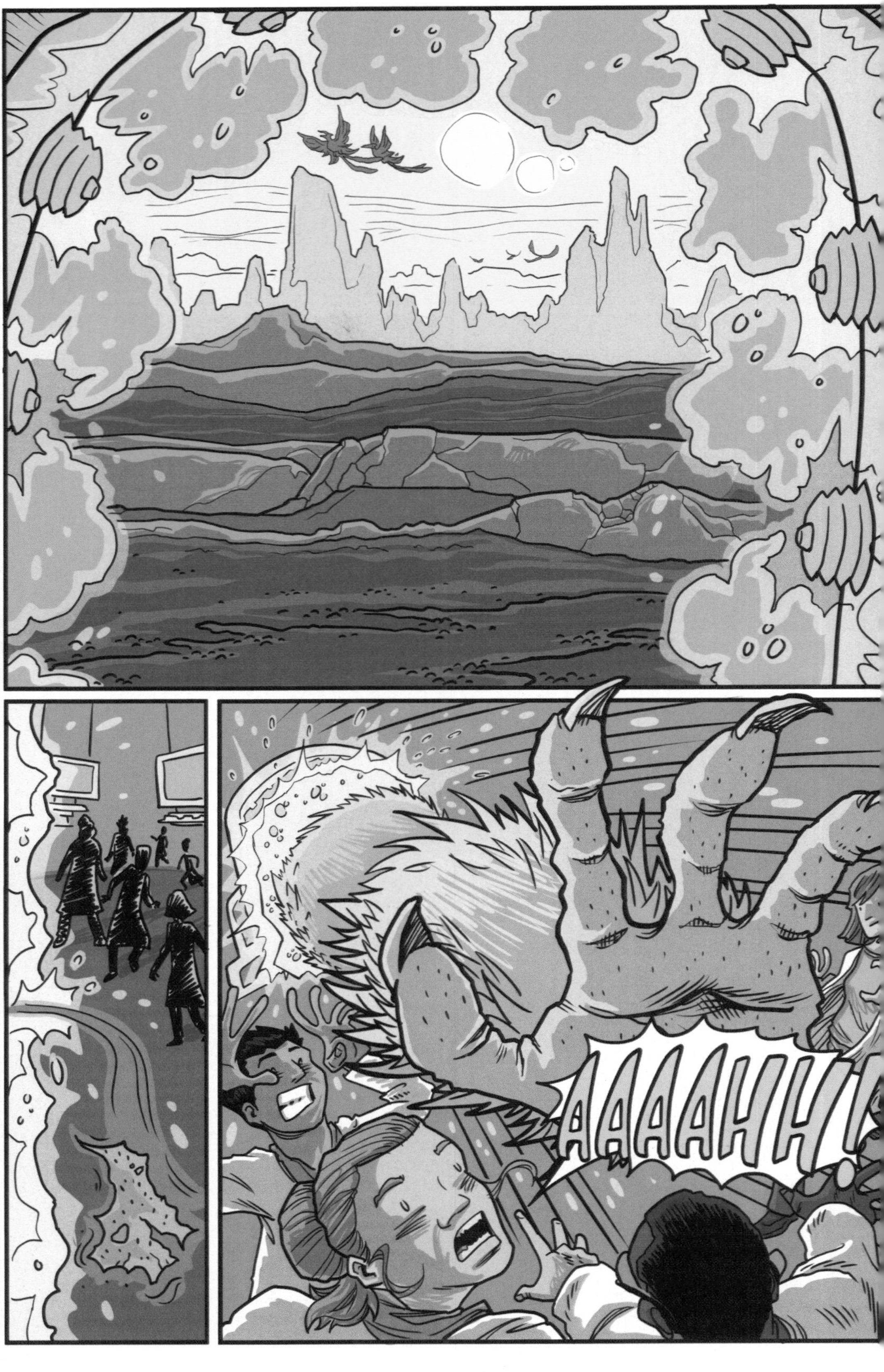
AAAAHH!

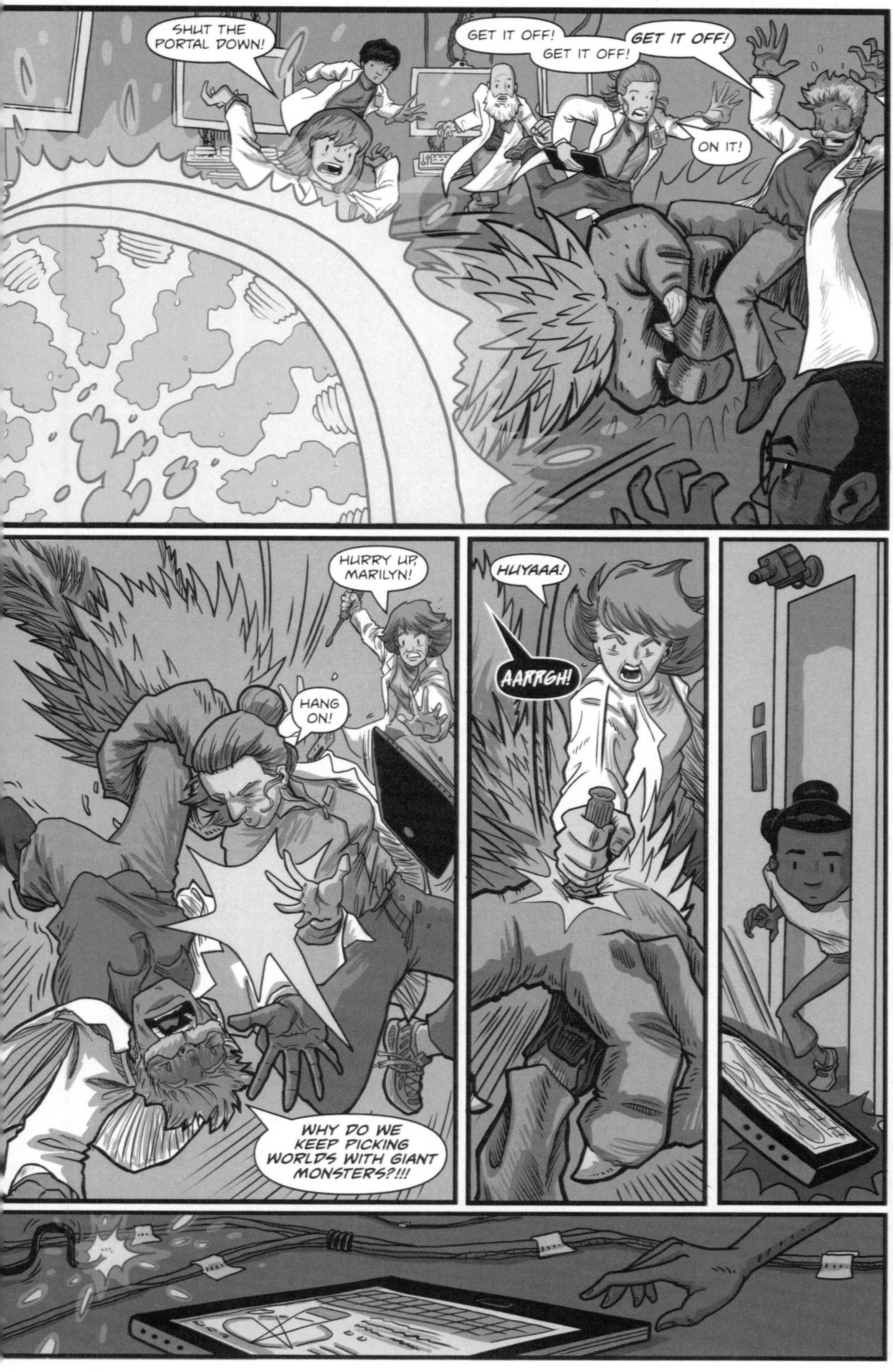
SHUT THE PORTAL DOWN!
GET IT OFF!
GET IT OFF!
GET IT OFF!
ON IT!
HURRY UP, MARILYN!
HANG ON!
WHY DO WE KEEP PICKING WORLDS WITH GIANT MONSTERS?!!!
HUYAAA!
AARRGH!

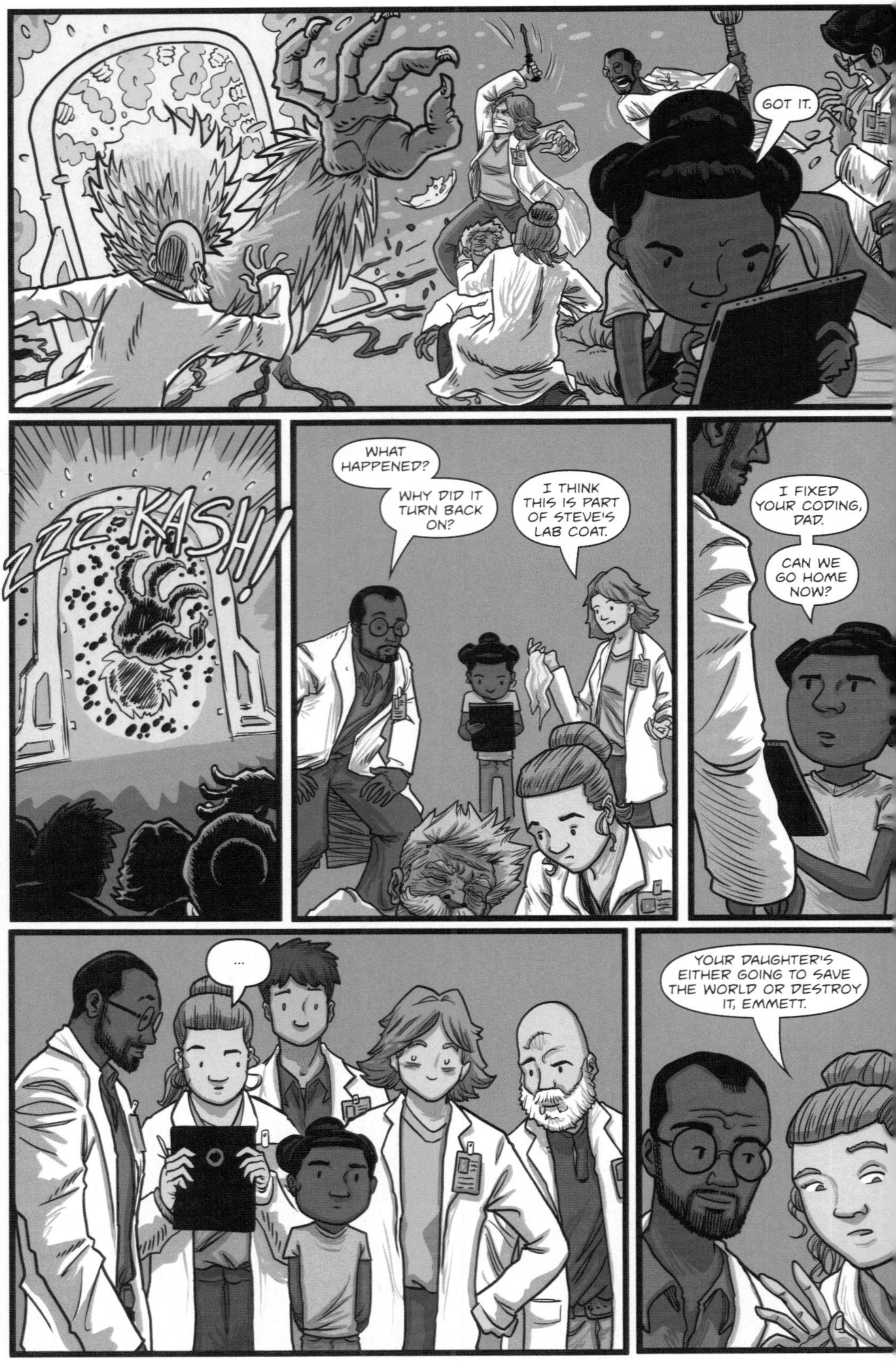
GOT IT.
ZZZZ-KASH!!
WHAT HAPPENED?
WHY DID IT TURN BACK ON?
I THINK THIS IS PART OF STEVE'S LAB COAT.
I FIXED YOUR CODING, DAD.
CAN WE GO HOME NOW?
...
YOUR DAUGHTER'S EITHER GOING TO SAVE THE WORLD OR DESTROY IT, EMMETT.

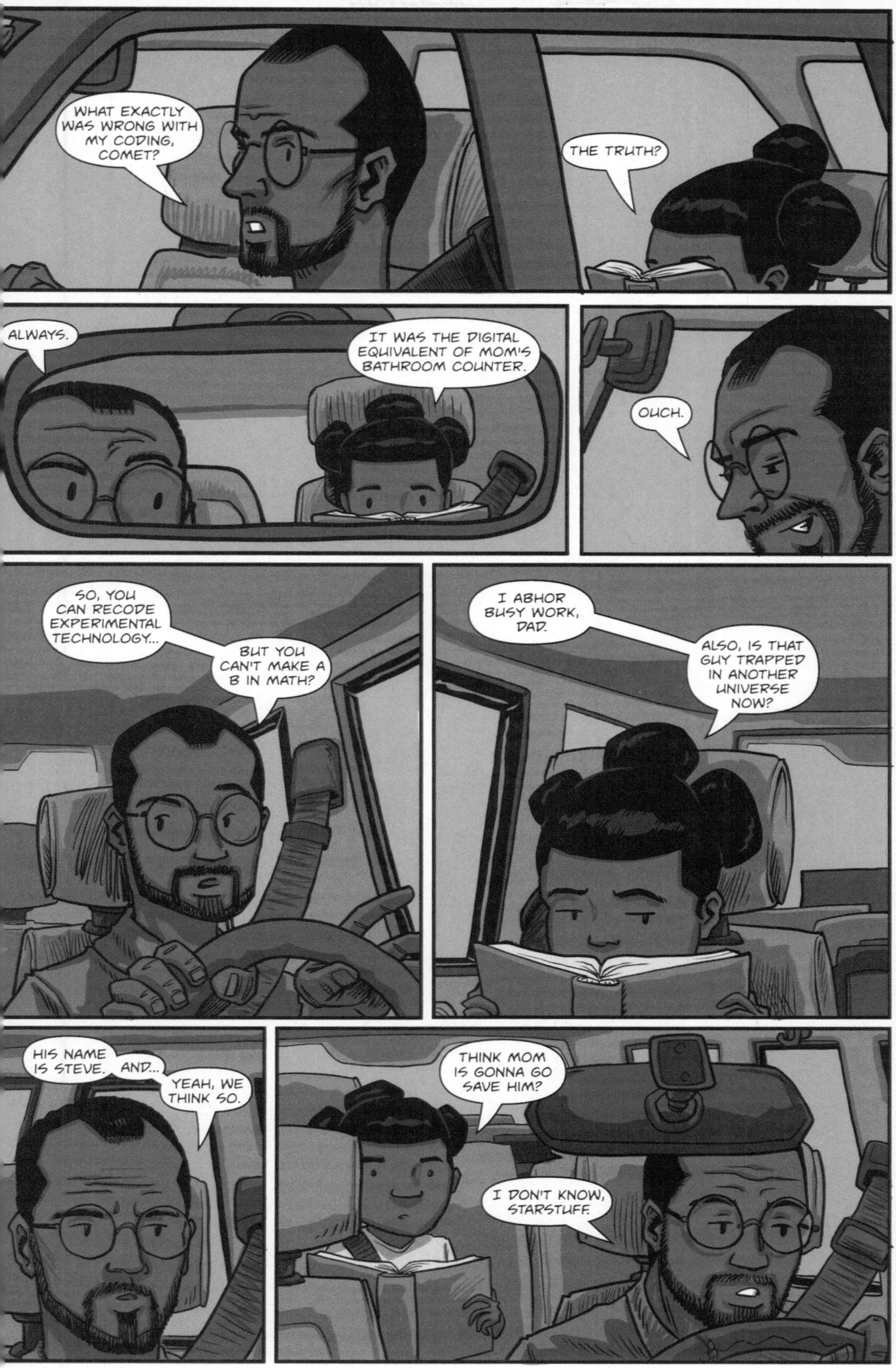
WHAT EXACTLY WAS WRONG WITH MY CODING, COMET?
THE TRUTH?
ALWAYS.
IT WAS THE DIGITAL EQUIVALENT OF MOM'S BATHROOM COUNTER.
OUCH.
SO, YOU CAN RECODE EXPERIMENTAL TECHNOLOGY...
BUT YOU CAN'T MAKE A B IN MATH?
I ABHOR BUSY WORK, DAD.
ALSO, IS THAT GUY TRAPPED IN ANOTHER UNIVERSE NOW?
HIS NAME IS STEVE.
AND...
YEAH, WE THINK SO.
THINK MOM IS GONNA GO SAVE HIM?
I DON'T KNOW, STARSTUFF.

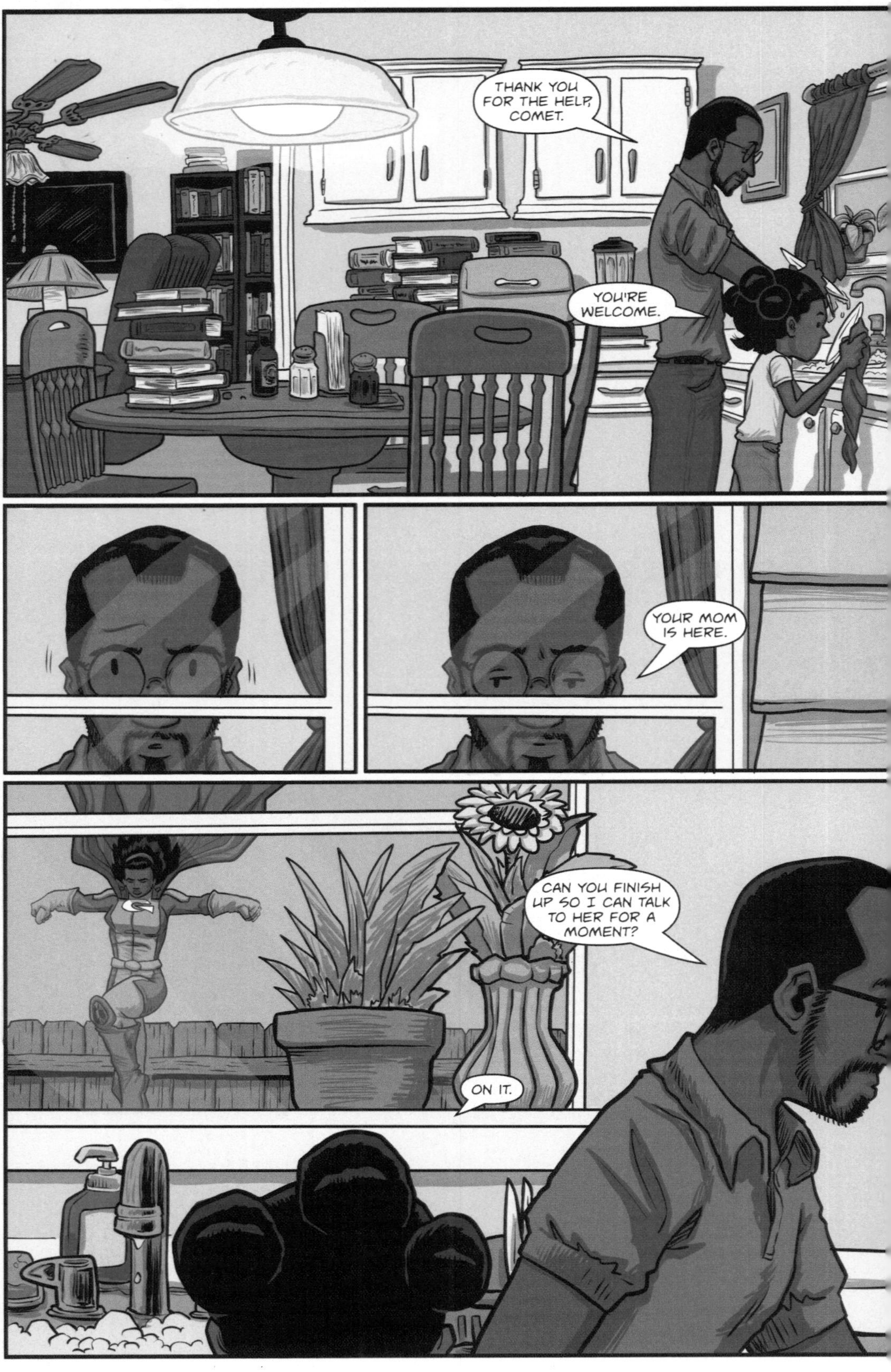
THANK YOU FOR THE HELP, COMET.
YOU'RE WELCOME.
YOUR MOM IS HERE.
CAN YOU FINISH UP SO I CAN TALK TO HER FOR A MOMENT?
ON IT.

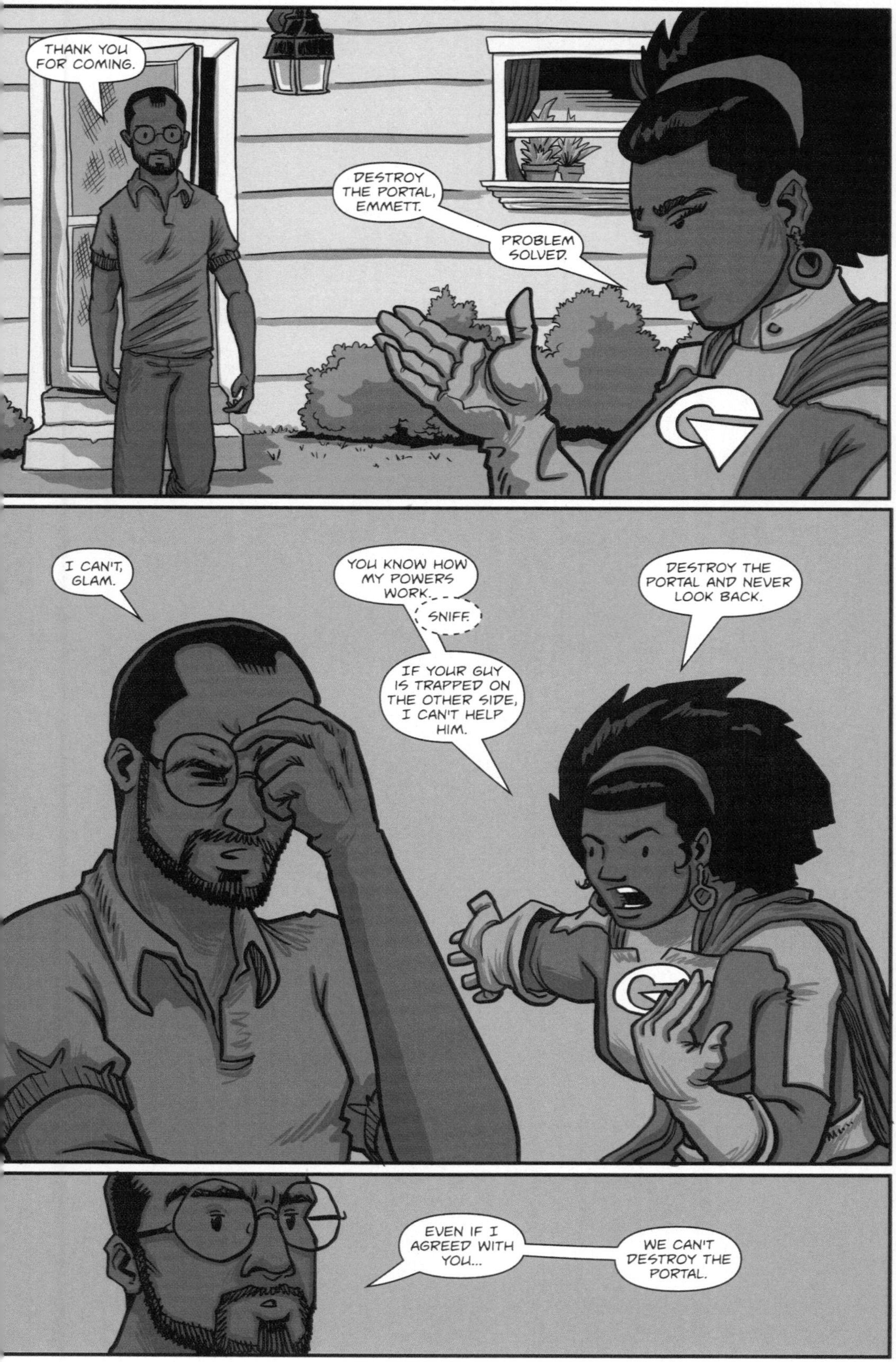

THANK YOU FOR COMING.
DESTROY THE PORTAL, EMMETT.
PROBLEM SOLVED.
I CAN'T, GLAM.
YOU KNOW HOW MY POWERS WORK.
SNIFF.
IF YOUR GUY IS TRAPPED ON THE OTHER SIDE, I CAN'T HELP HIM.
DESTROY THE PORTAL AND NEVER LOOK BACK.
EVEN IF I AGREED WITH YOU...
WE CAN'T DESTROY THE PORTAL.

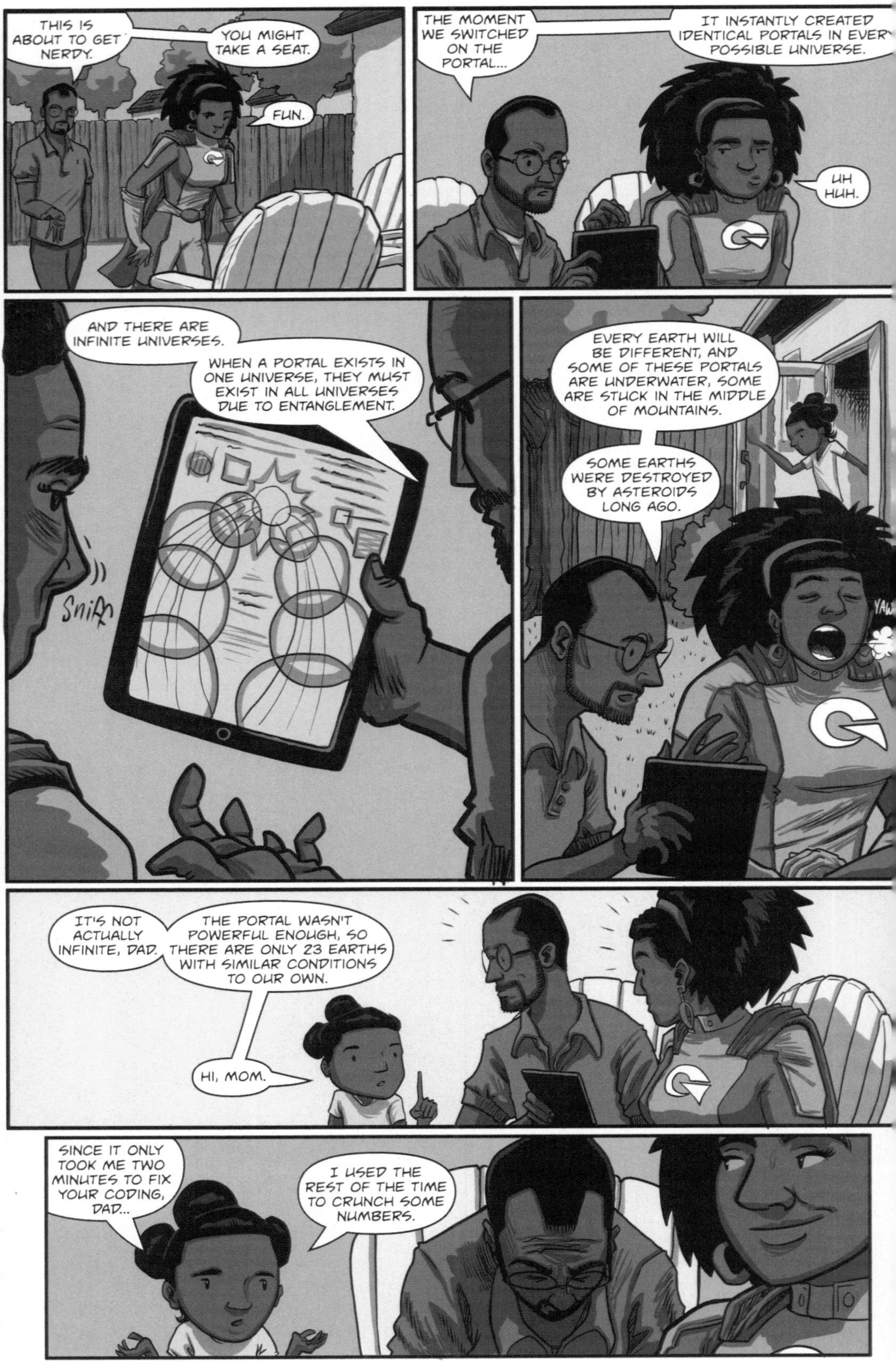

THIS IS ABOUT TO GET NERDY.
YOU MIGHT TAKE A SEAT.
FUN.
THE MOMENT WE SWITCHED ON THE PORTAL...
IT INSTANTLY CREATED IDENTICAL PORTALS IN EVERY POSSIBLE UNIVERSE.
UH HUH.
AND THERE ARE INFINITE UNIVERSES.
WHEN A PORTAL EXISTS IN ONE UNIVERSE, THEY MUST EXIST IN ALL UNIVERSES DUE TO ENTANGLEMENT.
SNIFF
EVERY EARTH WILL BE DIFFERENT, AND SOME OF THESE PORTALS ARE UNDERWATER, SOME ARE STUCK IN THE MIDDLE OF MOUNTAINS.
SOME EARTHS WERE DESTROYED BY ASTEROIDS LONG AGO.
IT'S NOT ACTUALLY INFINITE, DAD.
THE PORTAL WASN'T POWERFUL ENOUGH, SO THERE ARE ONLY 23 EARTHS WITH SIMILAR CONDITIONS TO OUR OWN.
HI, MOM.
SINCE IT ONLY TOOK ME TWO MINUTES TO FIX YOUR CODING, DAD...
I USED THE REST OF THE TIME TO CRUNCH SOME NUMBERS.

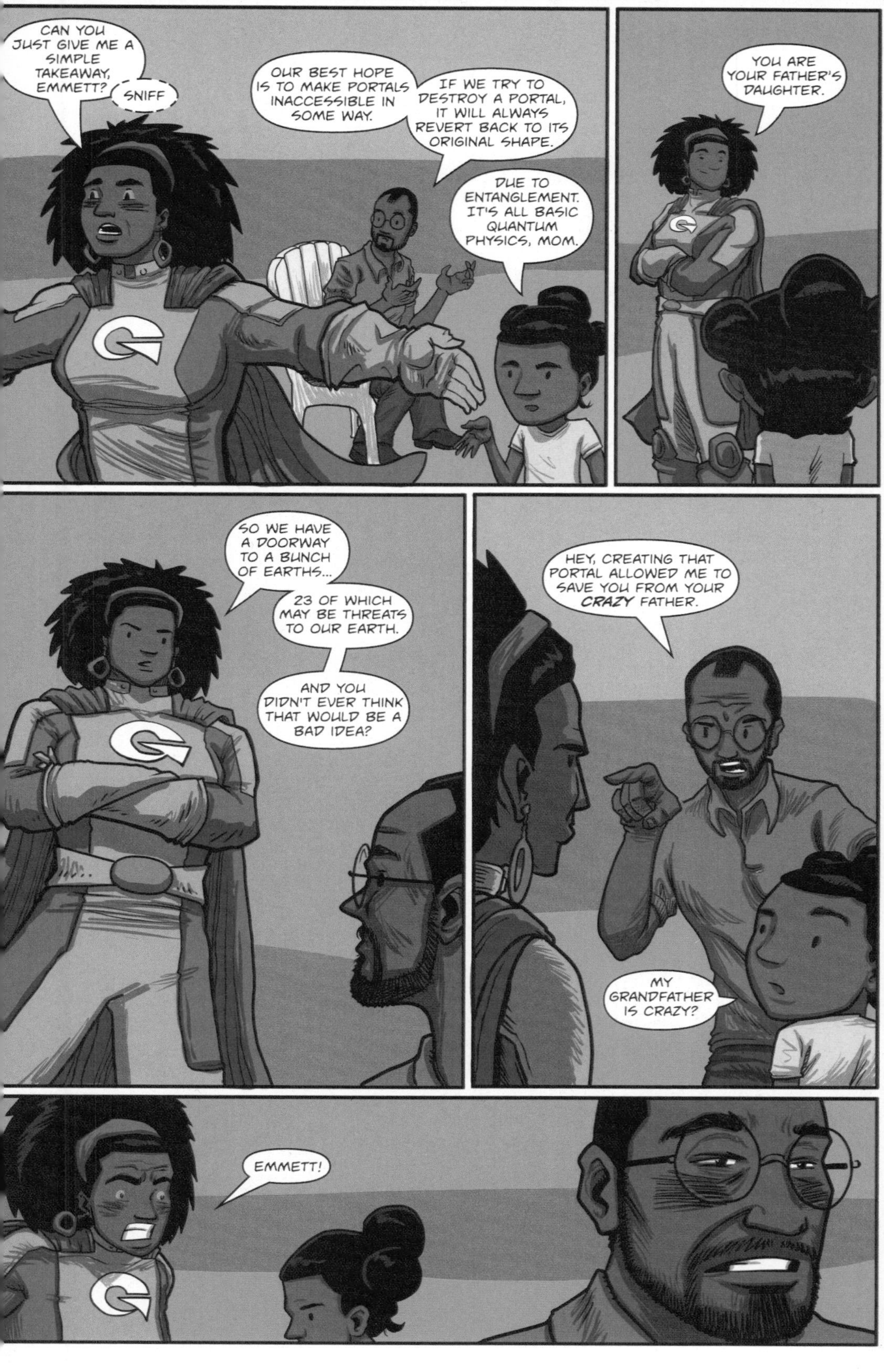
CAN YOU JUST GIVE ME A SIMPLE TAKEAWAY, EMMETT?
SNIFF
OUR BEST HOPE IS TO MAKE PORTALS INACCESSIBLE IN SOME WAY.
IF WE TRY TO DESTROY A PORTAL, IT WILL ALWAYS REVERT BACK TO ITS ORIGINAL SHAPE.
DUE TO ENTANGLEMENT. IT'S ALL BASIC QUANTUM PHYSICS, MOM.
YOU ARE YOUR FATHER'S DAUGHTER.
SO WE HAVE A DOORWAY TO A BUNCH OF EARTHS...
23 OF WHICH MAY BE THREATS TO OUR EARTH.
AND YOU DIDN'T EVER THINK THAT WOULD BE A BAD IDEA?
HEY, CREATING THAT PORTAL ALLOWED ME TO SAVE YOU FROM YOUR *CRAZY* FATHER.
MY GRANDFATHER IS CRAZY?
EMMETT!

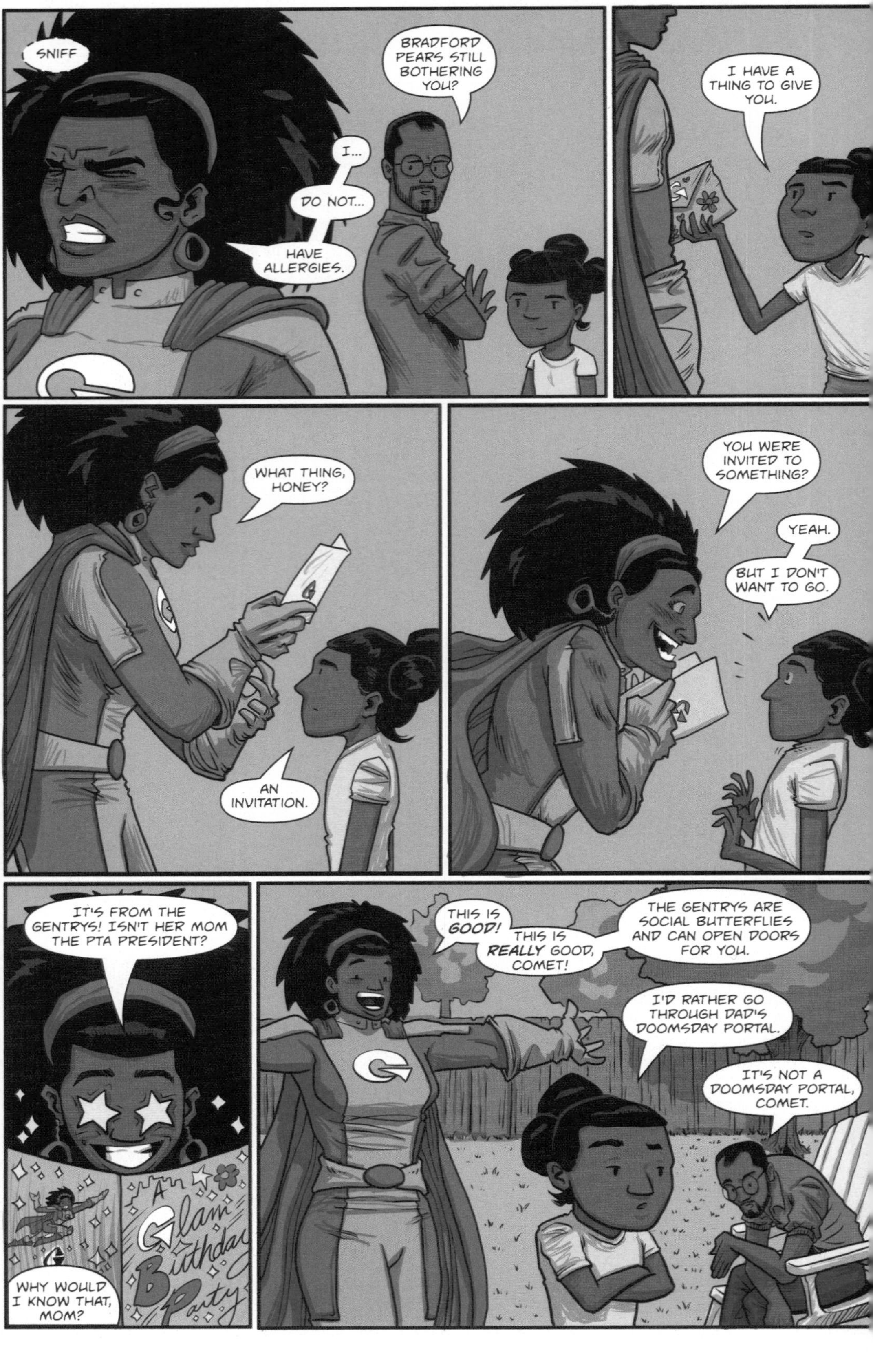
SNIFF
BRADFORD PEARS STILL BOTHERING YOU?
I...
DO NOT...
HAVE ALLERGIES.
I HAVE A THING TO GIVE YOU.
WHAT THING, HONEY?
AN INVITATION.
YOU WERE INVITED TO SOMETHING?
YEAH.
BUT I DON'T WANT TO GO.
IT'S FROM THE GENTRYS! ISN'T HER MOM THE PTA PRESIDENT?
A Glam Birthday Party
WHY WOULD I KNOW THAT, MOM?
THIS IS GOOD!
THIS IS REALLY GOOD, COMET!
THE GENTRYS ARE SOCIAL BUTTERFLIES AND CAN OPEN DOORS FOR YOU.
I'D RATHER GO THROUGH DAD'S DOOMSDAY PORTAL.
IT'S NOT A DOOMSDAY PORTAL, COMET.

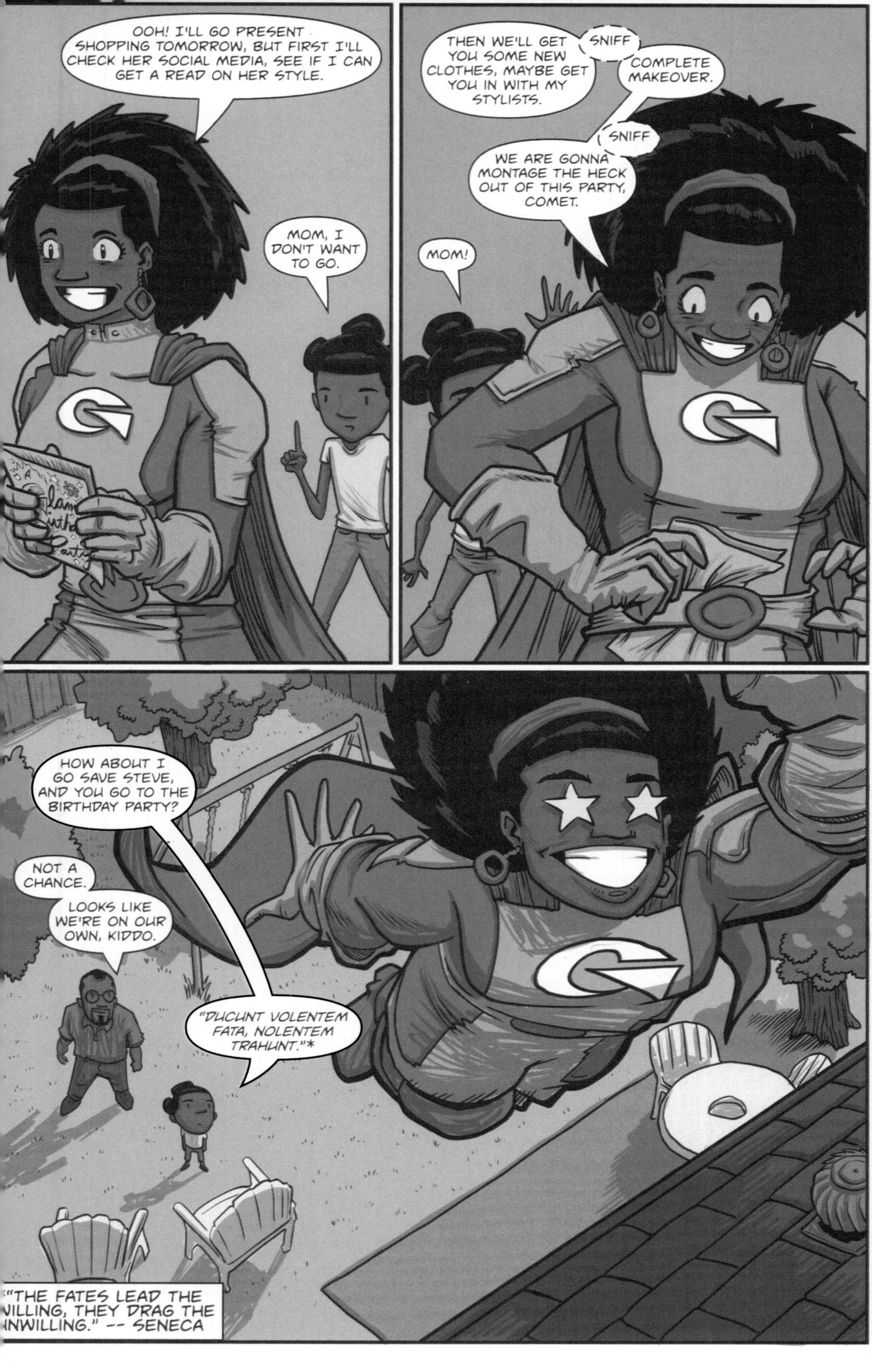
OOH! I'LL GO PRESENT SHOPPING TOMORROW, BUT FIRST I'LL CHECK HER SOCIAL MEDIA, SEE IF I CAN GET A READ ON HER STYLE.
MOM, I DON'T WANT TO GO.
THEN WE'LL GET YOU SOME NEW CLOTHES, MAYBE GET YOU IN WITH MY STYLISTS.
SNIFF
COMPLETE MAKEOVER.
SNIFF
WE ARE GONNA MONTAGE THE HECK OUT OF THIS PARTY, COMET.
MOM!
HOW ABOUT I GO SAVE STEVE, AND YOU GO TO THE BIRTHDAY PARTY?
NOT A CHANCE.
LOOKS LIKE WE'RE ON OUR OWN, KIDDO.
"DUCUNT VOLENTEM FATA, NOLENTEM TRAHUNT."*
*"THE FATES LEAD THE WILLING, THEY DRAG THE UNWILLING." -- SENECA

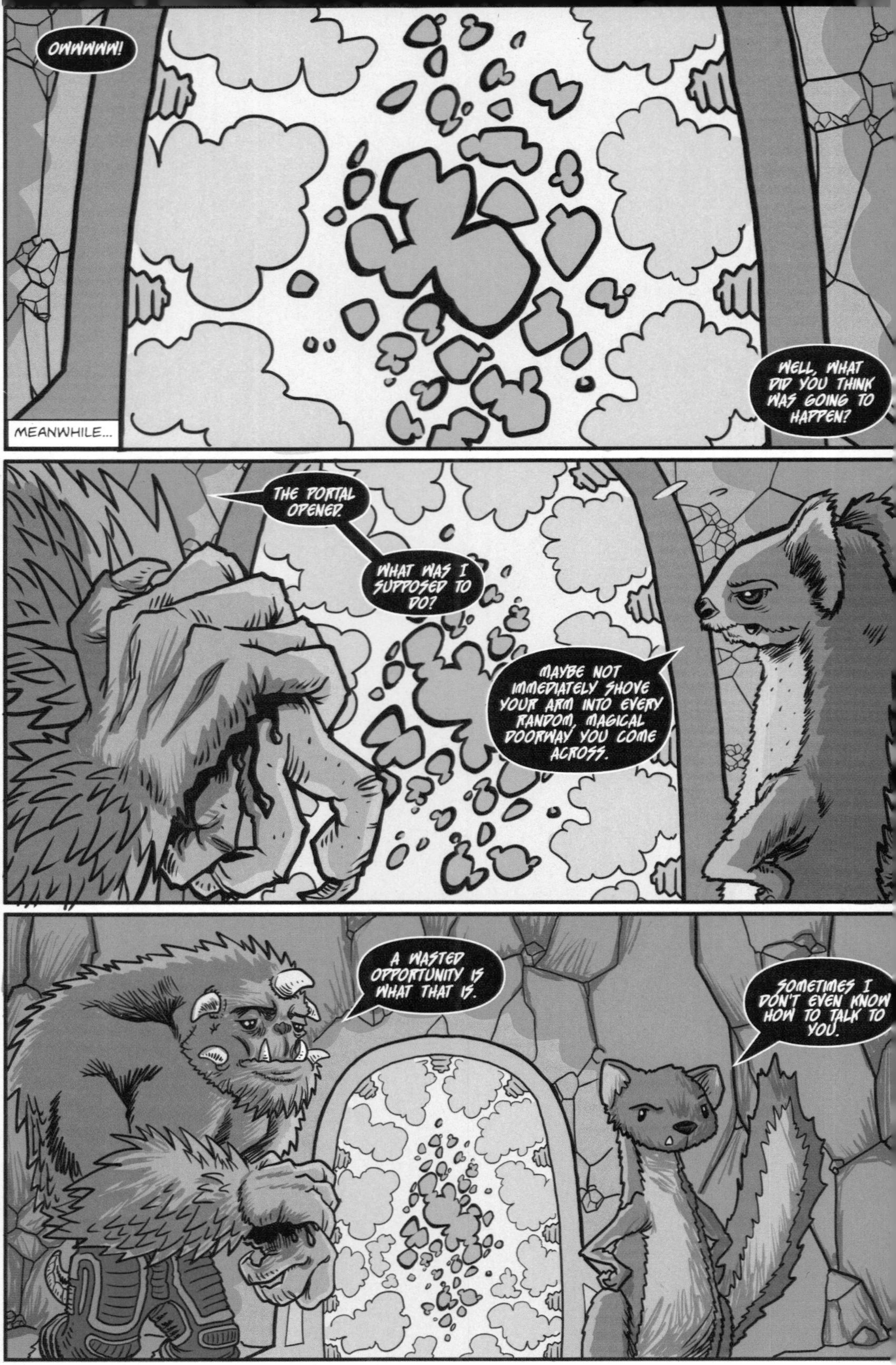
OWWWWW!
MEANWHILE...
WELL, WHAT DID YOU THINK WAS GOING TO HAPPEN?
THE PORTAL OPENED.
WHAT WAS I SUPPOSED TO DO?
MAYBE NOT IMMEDIATELY SHOVE YOUR ARM INTO EVERY RANDOM, MAGICAL DOORWAY YOU COME ACROSS.
A WASTED OPPORTUNITY IS WHAT THAT IS.
SOMETIMES I DON'T EVEN KNOW HOW TO TALK TO YOU.

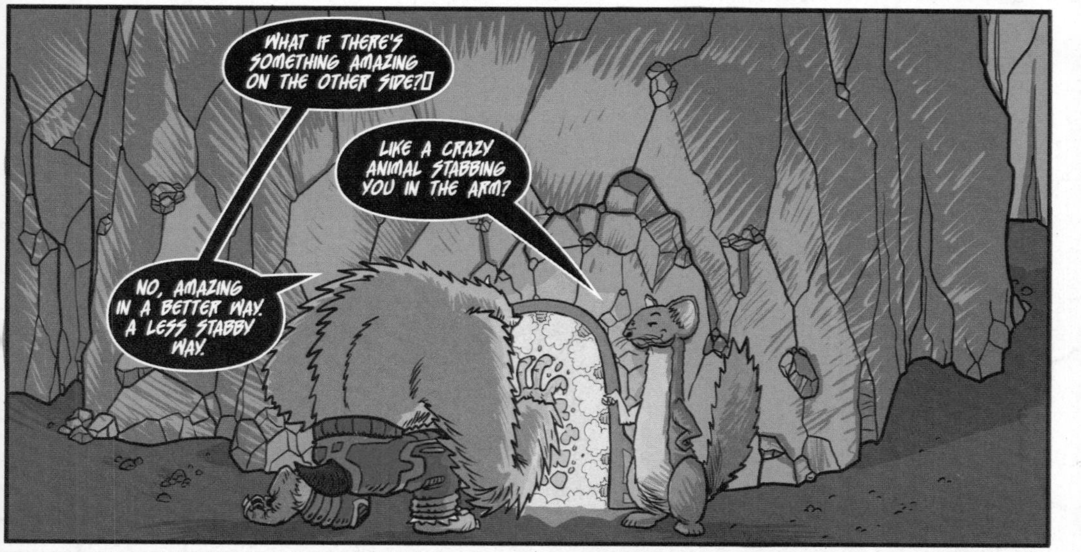
WHAT IF THERE'S SOMETHING AMAZING ON THE OTHER SIDE?
LIKE A CRAZY ANIMAL STABBING YOU IN THE ARM?
NO, AMAZING IN A BETTER WAY. A LESS STABBY WAY.

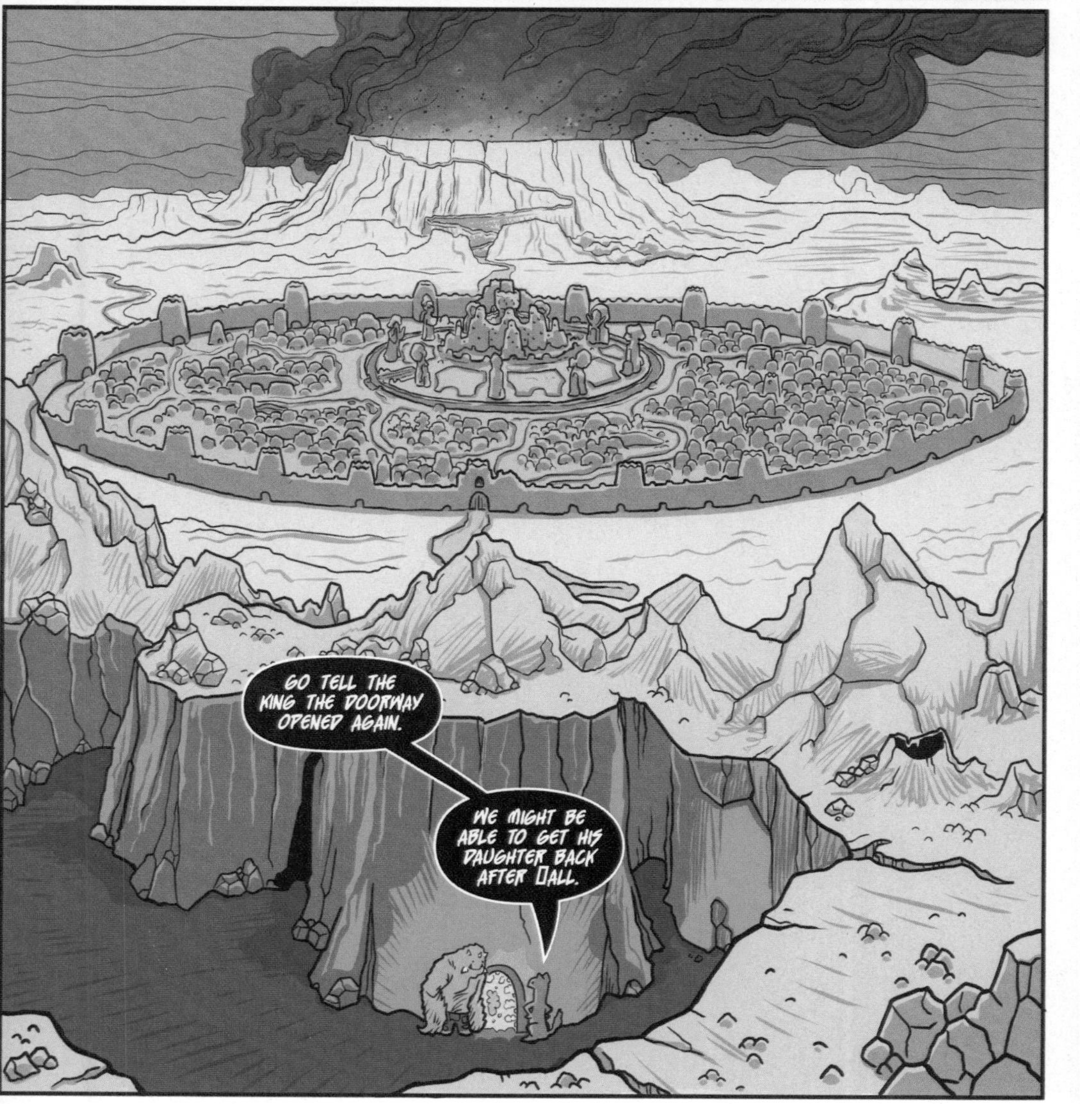
GO TELL THE KING THE DOORWAY OPENED AGAIN.
WE MIGHT BE ABLE TO GET HIS DAUGHTER BACK AFTER ALL.

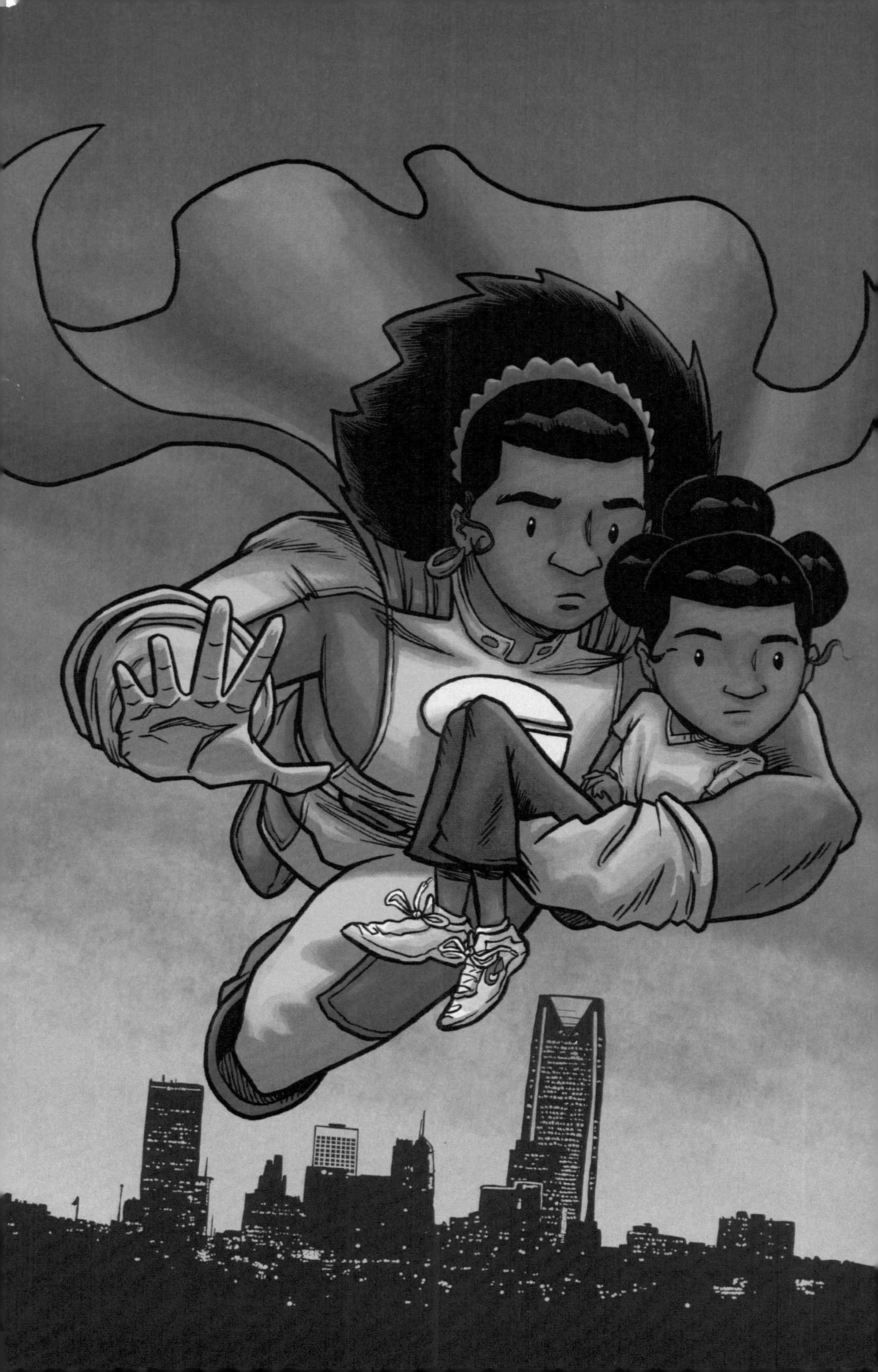

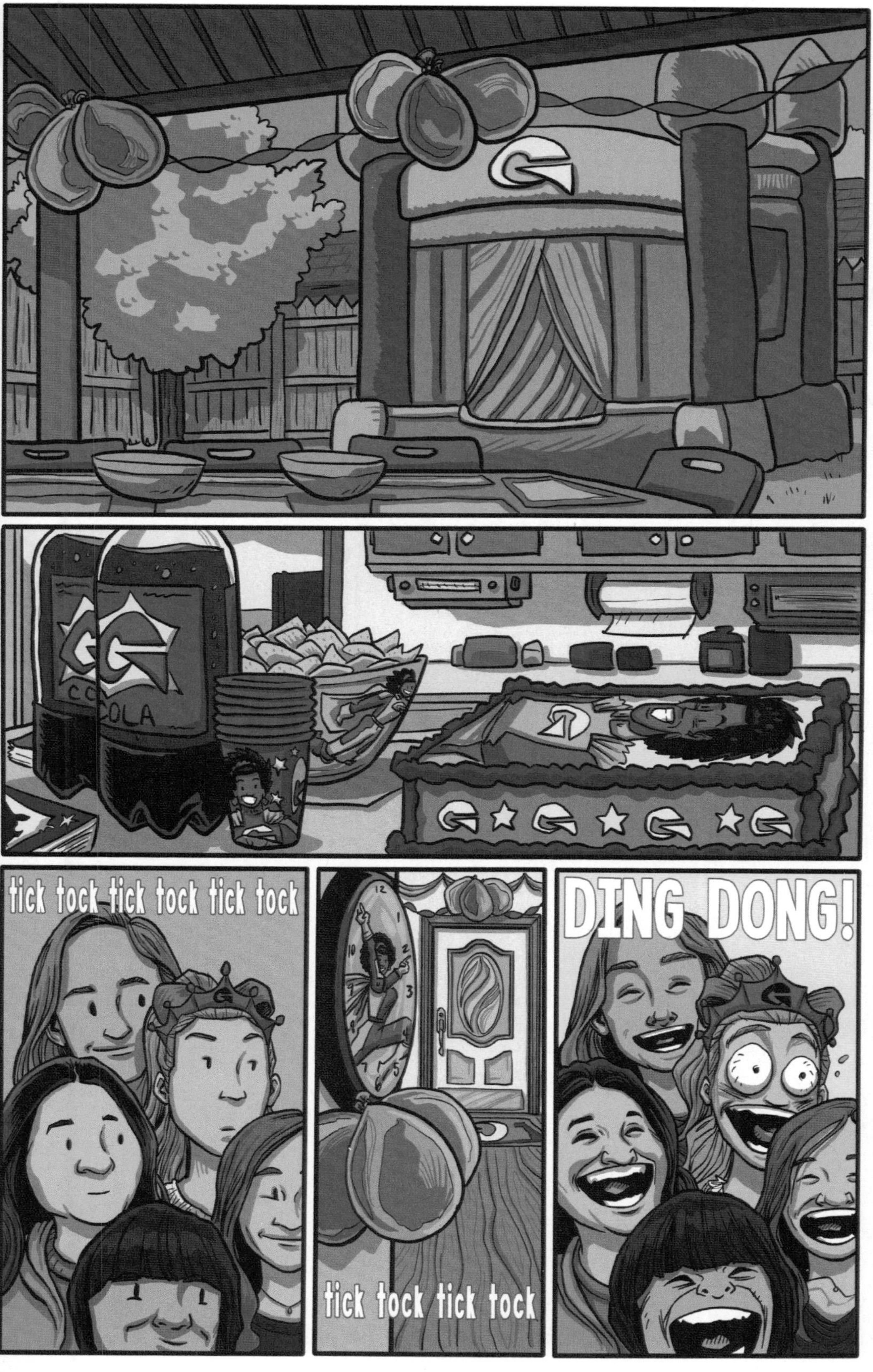

G
G COLA
COLA
tick tock tick tock tick tock
tick tock tick tock
DING DONG!

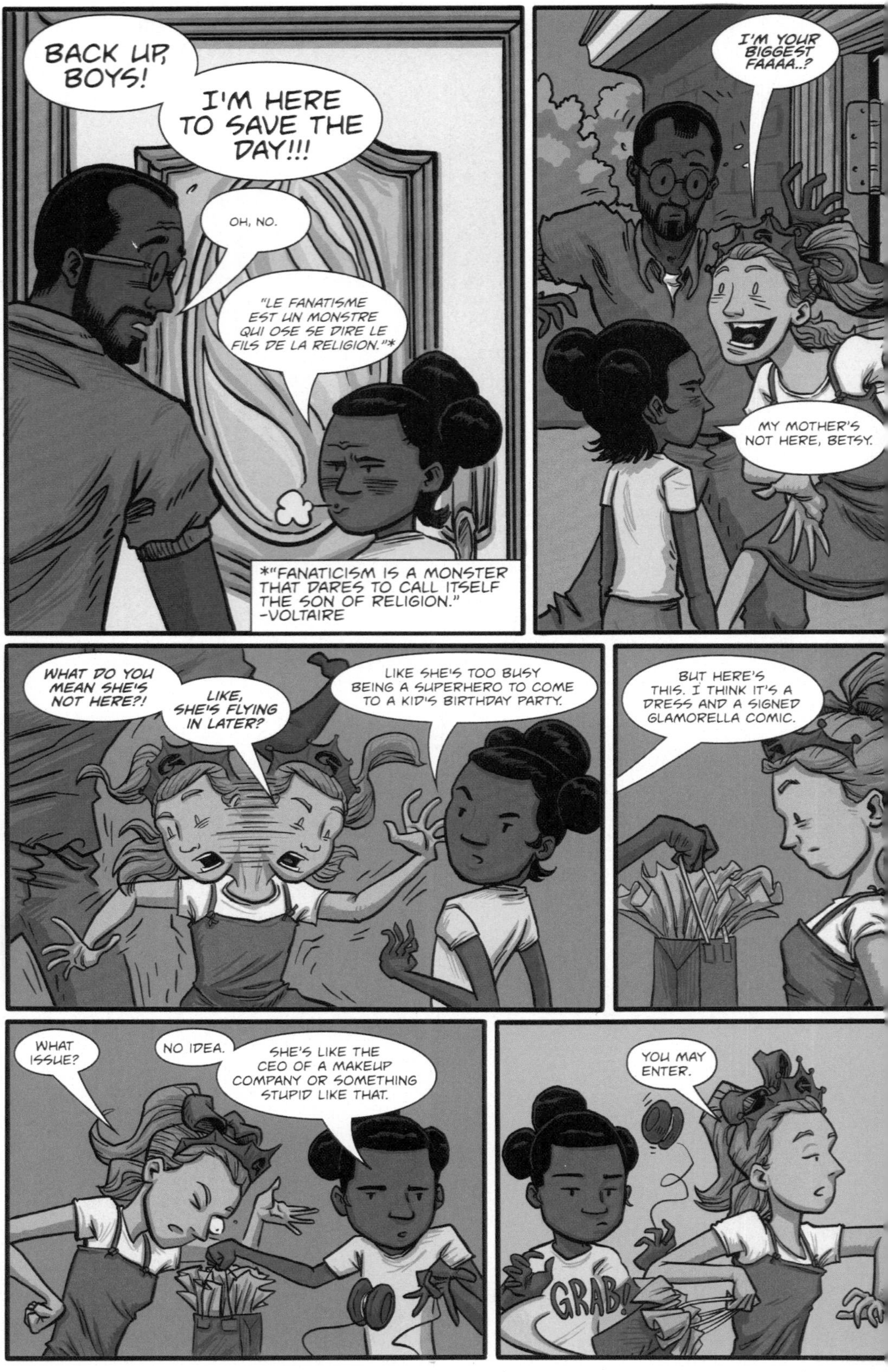
BACK UP, BOYS!
I'M HERE TO SAVE THE DAY!!!
OH, NO.
"LE FANATISME EST UN MONSTRE QUI OSE SE DIRE LE FILS DE LA RELIGION."*
*"FANATICISM IS A MONSTER THAT DARES TO CALL ITSELF THE SON OF RELIGION." -VOLTAIRE
I'M YOUR BIGGEST FAAAA..?
MY MOTHER'S NOT HERE, BETSY.
WHAT DO YOU MEAN SHE'S NOT HERE?!
LIKE, SHE'S FLYING IN LATER?
LIKE SHE'S TOO BUSY BEING A SUPERHERO TO COME TO A KID'S BIRTHDAY PARTY.
BUT HERE'S THIS. I THINK IT'S A DRESS AND A SIGNED GLAMORELLA COMIC.
WHAT ISSUE?
NO IDEA.
SHE'S LIKE THE CEO OF A MAKEUP COMPANY OR SOMETHING STUPID LIKE THAT.
YOU MAY ENTER.
GRAB!

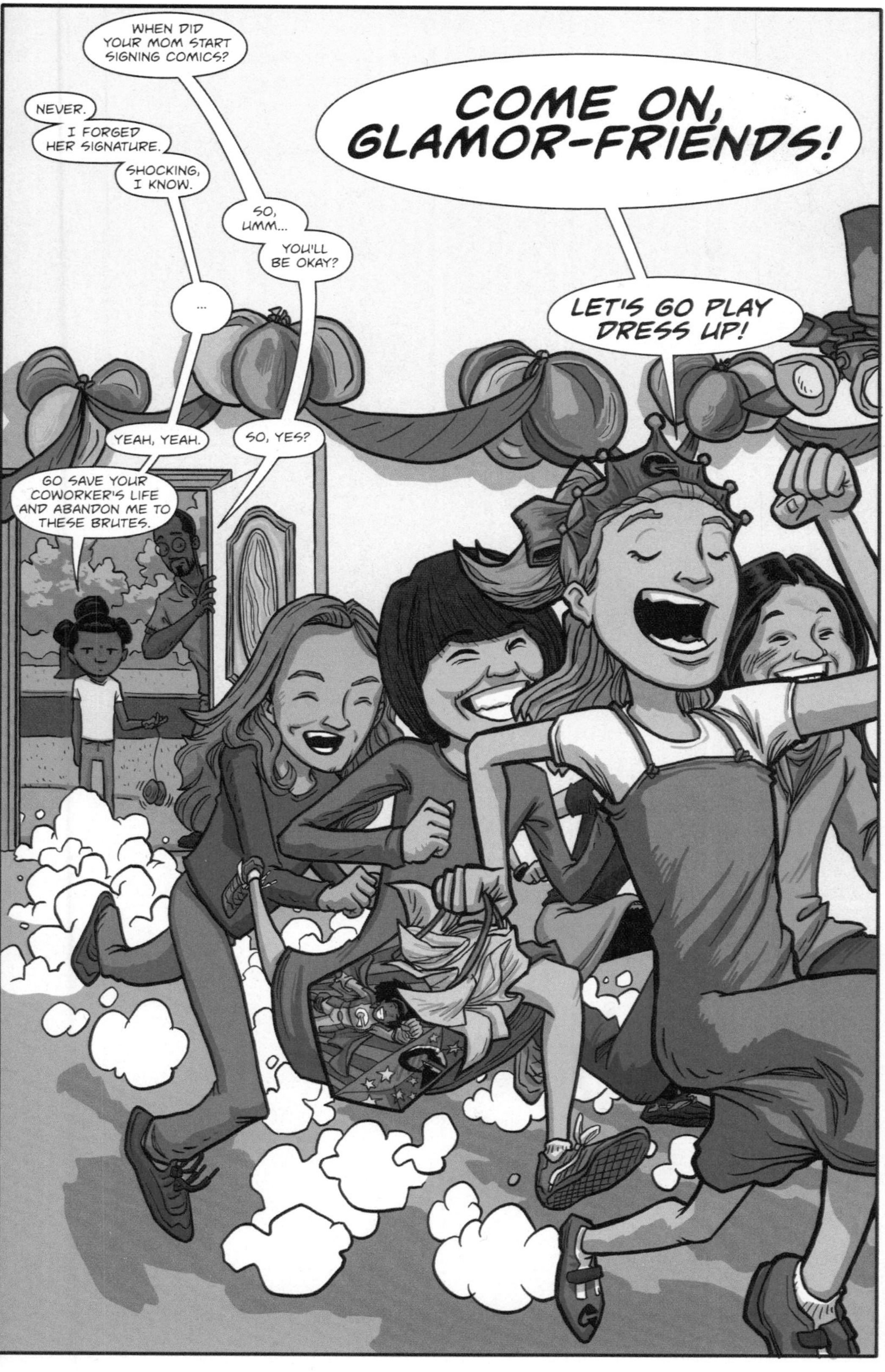

WHEN DID YOUR MOM START SIGNING COMICS?
NEVER.
I FORGED HER SIGNATURE.
SHOCKING, I KNOW.
SO, UMM...
YOU'LL BE OKAY?
...
YEAH, YEAH.
GO SAVE YOUR COWORKER'S LIFE AND ABANDON ME TO THESE BRUTES.
SO, YES?
COME ON, GLAMOR-FRIENDS!
LET'S GO PLAY DRESS UP!

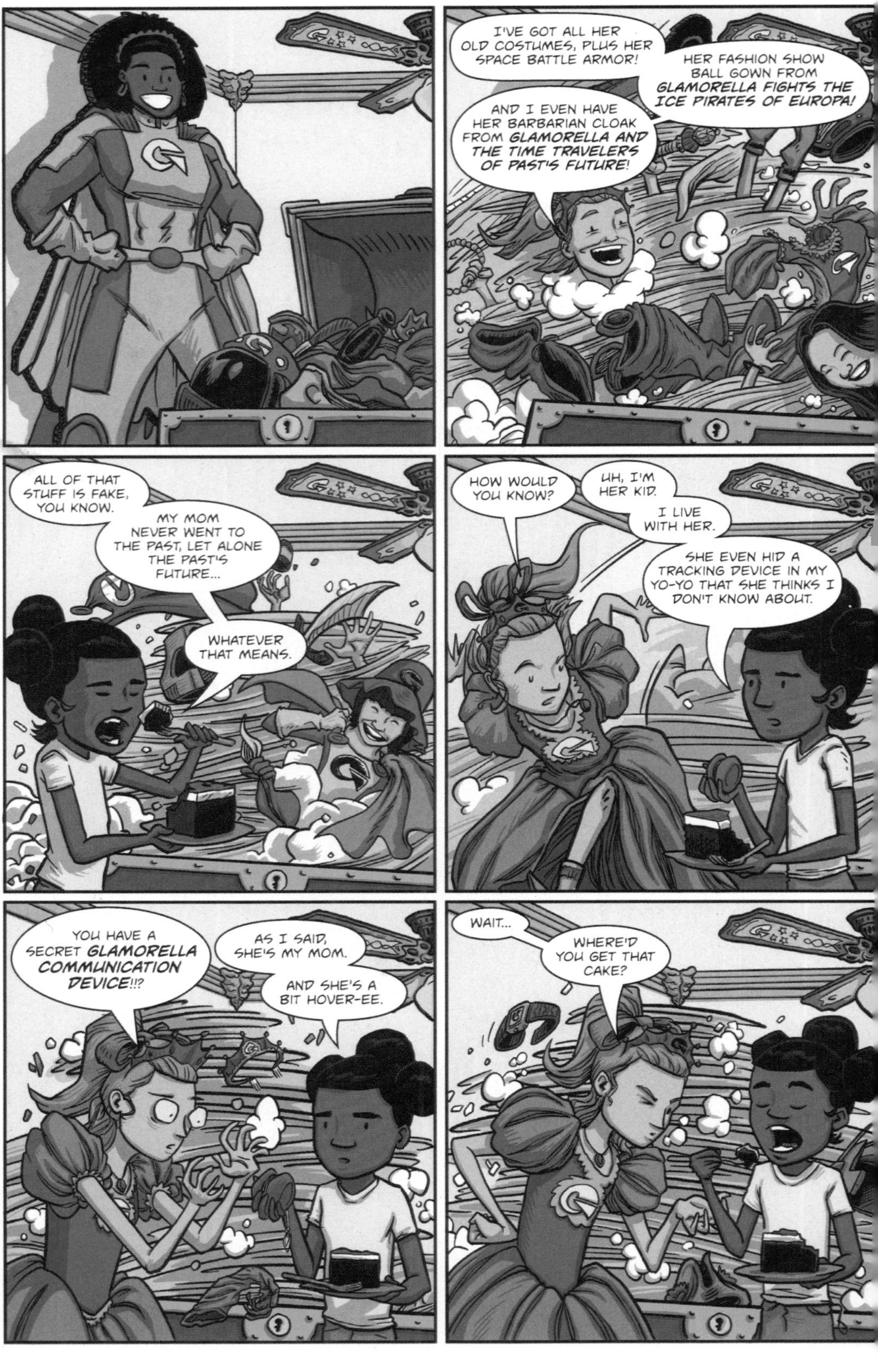
I'VE GOT ALL HER OLD COSTUMES, PLUS HER SPACE BATTLE ARMOR!
HER FASHION SHOW BALL GOWN FROM GLAMORELLA FIGHTS THE ICE PIRATES OF EUROPA!
AND I EVEN HAVE HER BARBARIAN CLOAK FROM GLAMORELLA AND THE TIME TRAVELERS OF PAST'S FUTURE!
ALL OF THAT STUFF IS FAKE, YOU KNOW.
MY MOM NEVER WENT TO THE PAST, LET ALONE THE PAST'S FUTURE...
WHATEVER THAT MEANS.
HOW WOULD YOU KNOW?
UH, I'M HER KID.
I LIVE WITH HER.
SHE EVEN HID A TRACKING DEVICE IN MY YO-YO THAT SHE THINKS I DON'T KNOW ABOUT.
YOU HAVE A SECRET GLAMORELLA COMMUNICATION DEVICE!!?
AS I SAID, SHE'S MY MOM.
AND SHE'S A BIT HOVER-EE.
WAIT...
WHERE'D YOU GET THAT CAKE?

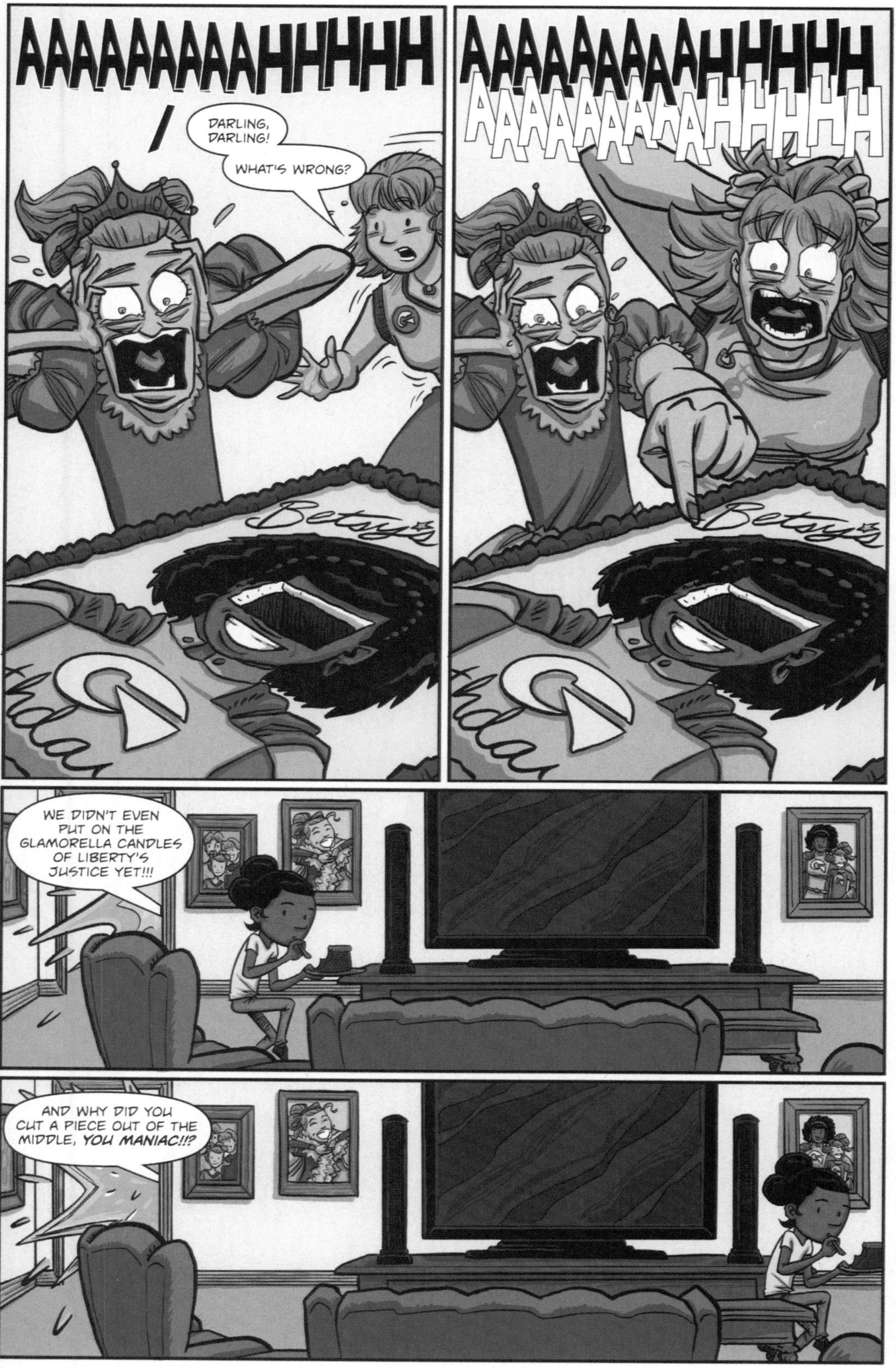
AAAAAAAAAHHHHH!
DARLING, DARLING!
WHAT'S WRONG?
AAAAAAAAAHHHHH
AAAAAAAAAHHHHHH
Betsy's
WE DIDN'T EVEN PUT ON THE GLAMORELLA CANDLES OF LIBERTY'S JUSTICE YET!!!
AND WHY DID YOU CUT A PIECE OUT OF THE MIDDLE, YOU MANIAC!!?

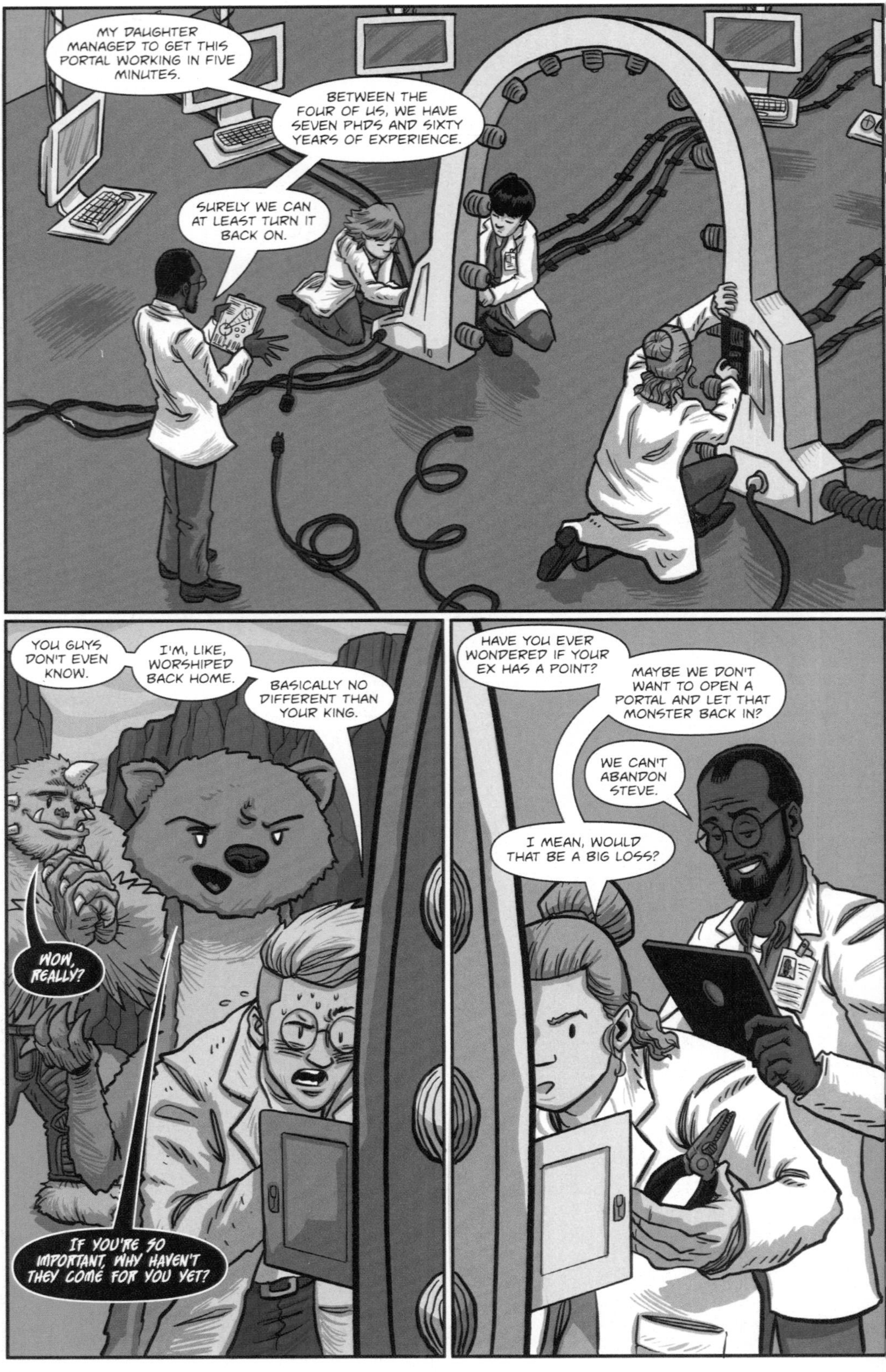
MY DAUGHTER MANAGED TO GET THIS PORTAL WORKING IN FIVE MINUTES.
BETWEEN THE FOUR OF US, WE HAVE SEVEN PHDS AND SIXTY YEARS OF EXPERIENCE.
SURELY WE CAN AT LEAST TURN IT BACK ON.
YOU GUYS DON'T EVEN KNOW.
I'M, LIKE, WORSHIPED BACK HOME.
BASICALLY NO DIFFERENT THAN YOUR KING.
WOW, REALLY?
IF YOU'RE SO IMPORTANT, WHY HAVEN'T THEY COME FOR YOU YET?
HAVE YOU EVER WONDERED IF YOUR EX HAS A POINT?
MAYBE WE DON'T WANT TO OPEN A PORTAL AND LET THAT MONSTER BACK IN?
WE CAN'T ABANDON STEVE.
I MEAN, WOULD THAT BE A BIG LOSS?

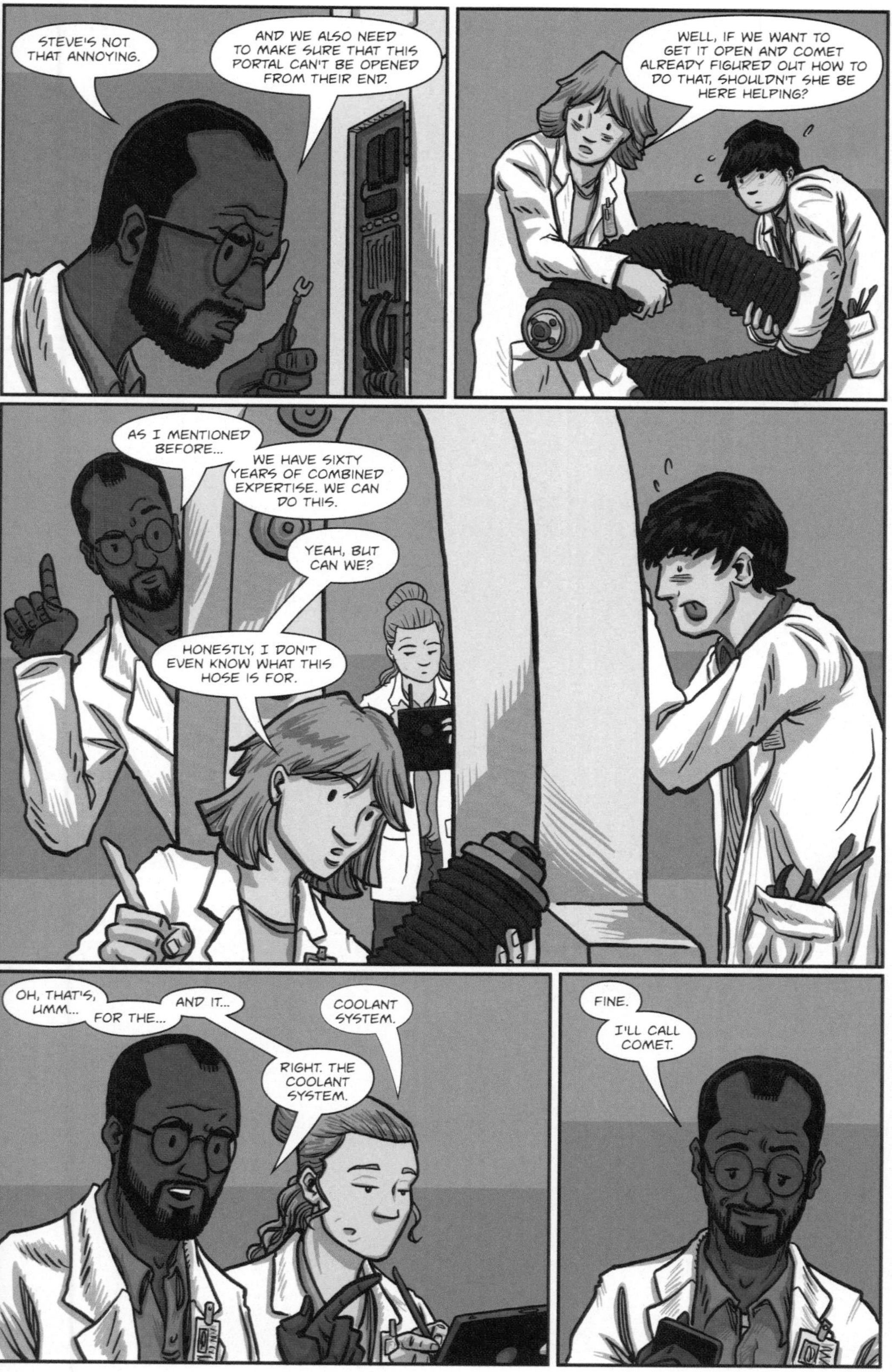
STEVE'S NOT THAT ANNOYING.
AND WE ALSO NEED TO MAKE SURE THAT THIS PORTAL CAN'T BE OPENED FROM THEIR END.
WELL, IF WE WANT TO GET IT OPEN AND COMET ALREADY FIGURED OUT HOW TO DO THAT, SHOULDN'T SHE BE HERE HELPING?
AS I MENTIONED BEFORE...
WE HAVE SIXTY YEARS OF COMBINED EXPERTISE. WE CAN DO THIS.
YEAH, BUT CAN WE?
HONESTLY, I DON'T EVEN KNOW WHAT THIS HOSE IS FOR.
OH, THAT'S, UMM...
FOR THE...
AND IT...
COOLANT SYSTEM.
RIGHT. THE COOLANT SYSTEM.
FINE.
I'LL CALL COMET.

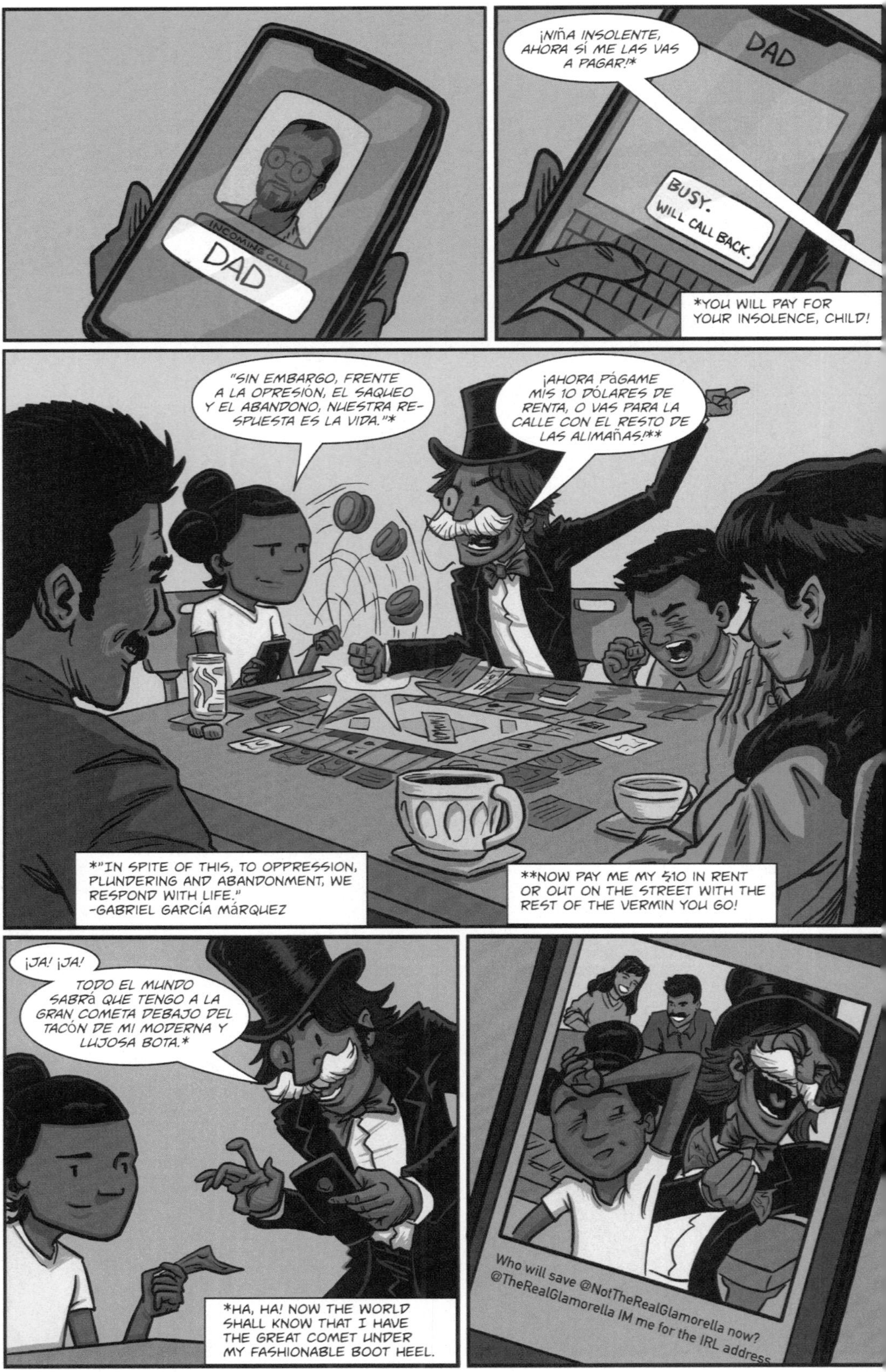
INCOMING CALL
DAD
DAD
¡NIñA INSOLENTE, AHORA SÍ ME LAS VAS A PAGAR!*
BUSY. WILL CALL BACK.
*YOU WILL PAY FOR YOUR INSOLENCE, CHILD!
"SIN EMBARGO, FRENTE A LA OPRESIÓN, EL SAQUEO Y EL ABANDONO, NUESTRA RESPUESTA ES LA VIDA."*
¡AHORA PáGAME MIS 10 DÓLARES DE RENTA, O VAS PARA LA CALLE CON EL RESTO DE LAS ALIMAñAS!**
*"IN SPITE OF THIS, TO OPPRESSION, PLUNDERING AND ABANDONMENT, WE RESPOND WITH LIFE." -GABRIEL GARCÍA MáRQUEZ
**NOW PAY ME MY $10 IN RENT OR OUT ON THE STREET WITH THE REST OF THE VERMIN YOU GO!
¡JA! ¡JA! TODO EL MUNDO SABRá QUE TENGO A LA GRAN COMETA DEBAJO DEL TACÓN DE MI MODERNA Y LUJOSA BOTA.*
*HA, HA! NOW THE WORLD SHALL KNOW THAT I HAVE THE GREAT COMET UNDER MY FASHIONABLE BOOT HEEL.
Who will save @NotTheRealGlamorella now? @TheRealGlamorella IM me for the IRL address

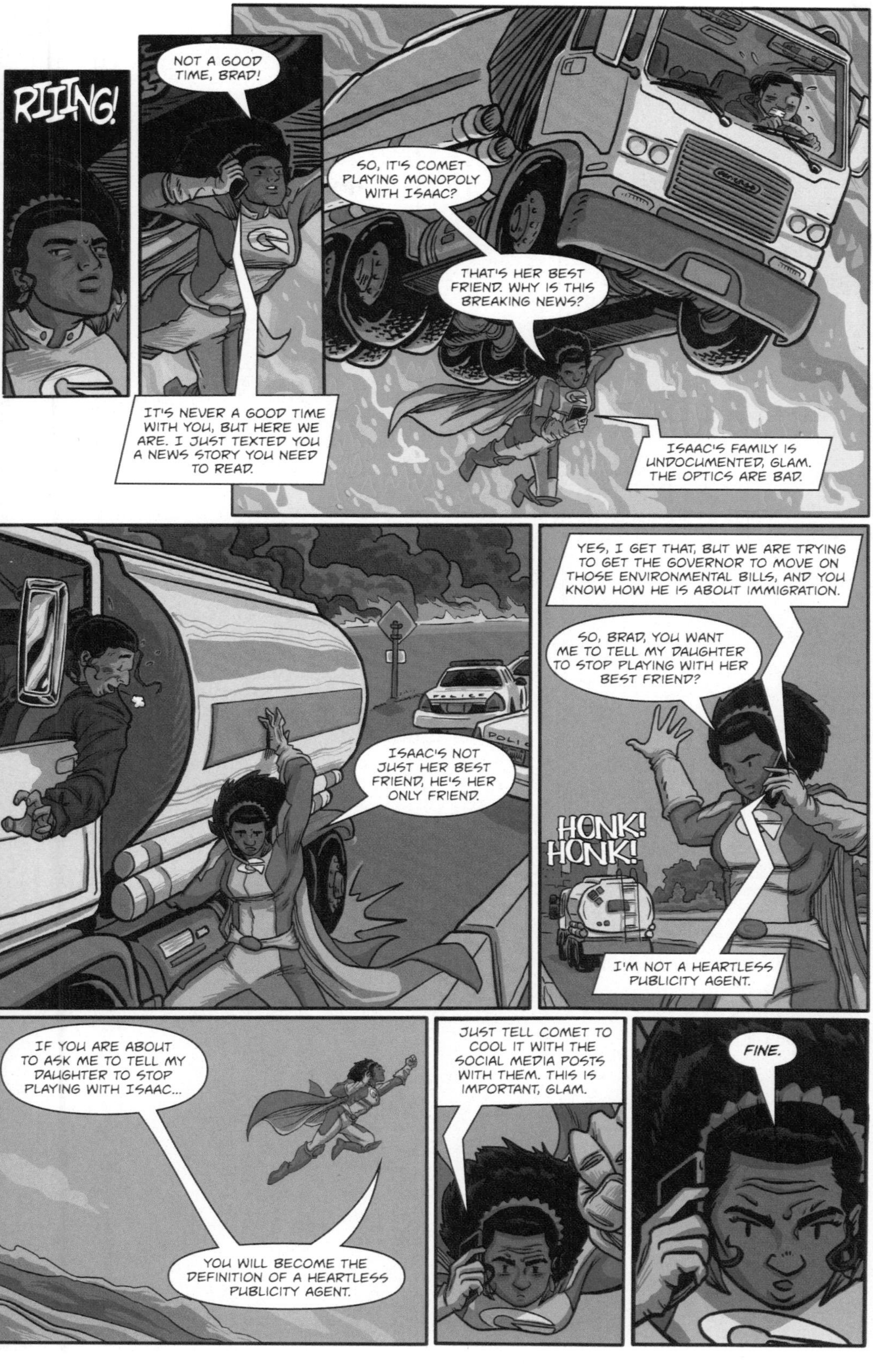
RIIING!
NOT A GOOD TIME, BRAD!
IT'S NEVER A GOOD TIME WITH YOU, BUT HERE WE ARE. I JUST TEXTED YOU A NEWS STORY YOU NEED TO READ.
SO, IT'S COMET PLAYING MONOPOLY WITH ISAAC?
THAT'S HER BEST FRIEND. WHY IS THIS BREAKING NEWS?
ISAAC'S FAMILY IS UNDOCUMENTED, GLAM. THE OPTICS ARE BAD.
ISAAC'S NOT JUST HER BEST FRIEND, HE'S HER ONLY FRIEND.
YES, I GET THAT, BUT WE ARE TRYING TO GET THE GOVERNOR TO MOVE ON THOSE ENVIRONMENTAL BILLS, AND YOU KNOW HOW HE IS ABOUT IMMIGRATION.
SO, BRAD, YOU WANT ME TO TELL MY DAUGHTER TO STOP PLAYING WITH HER BEST FRIEND?
HONK! HONK!
I'M NOT A HEARTLESS PUBLICITY AGENT.
IF YOU ARE ABOUT TO ASK ME TO TELL MY DAUGHTER TO STOP PLAYING WITH ISAAC...
YOU WILL BECOME THE DEFINITION OF A HEARTLESS PUBLICITY AGENT.
JUST TELL COMET TO COOL IT WITH THE SOCIAL MEDIA POSTS WITH THEM. THIS IS IMPORTANT, GLAM.
FINE.

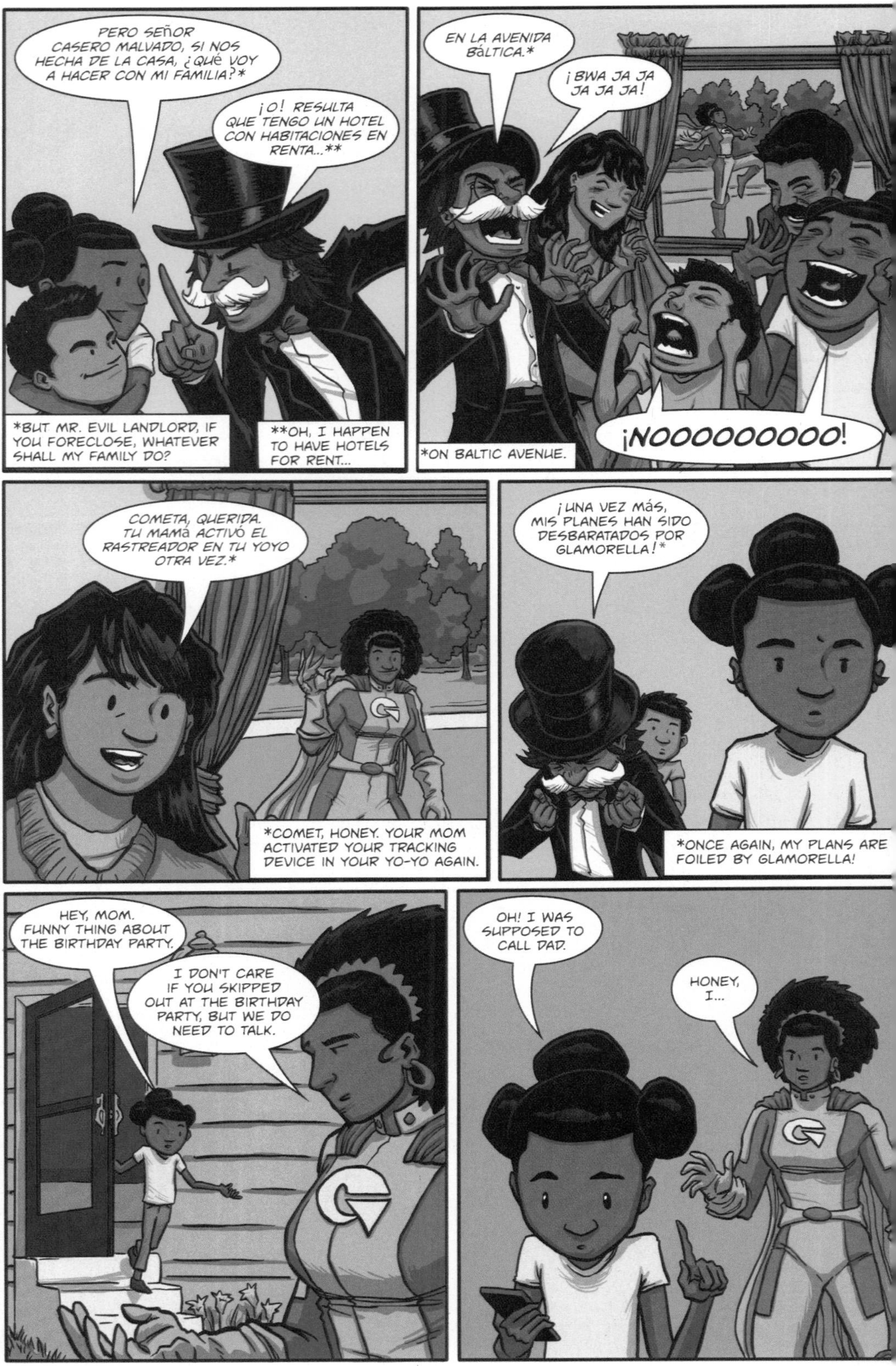
PERO SEÑOR CASERO MALVADO, SI NOS HECHA DE LA CASA, ¿QUÉ VOY A HACER CON MI FAMILIA?*
¡O! RESULTA QUE TENGO UN HOTEL CON HABITACIONES EN RENTA...**
*BUT MR. EVIL LANDLORD, IF YOU FORECLOSE, WHATEVER SHALL MY FAMILY DO?
**OH, I HAPPEN TO HAVE HOTELS FOR RENT...
EN LA AVENIDA BÁLTICA.*
¡BWA JA JA JA JA JA!
¡NOOOOOOOOO!
*ON BALTIC AVENUE.
COMETA, QUERIDA. TU MAMÁ ACTIVÓ EL RASTREADOR EN TU YOYO OTRA VEZ.*
*COMET, HONEY. YOUR MOM ACTIVATED YOUR TRACKING DEVICE IN YOUR YO-YO AGAIN.
¡UNA VEZ MÁS, MIS PLANES HAN SIDO DESBARATADOS POR GLAMORELLA!*
*ONCE AGAIN, MY PLANS ARE FOILED BY GLAMORELLA!
HEY, MOM. FUNNY THING ABOUT THE BIRTHDAY PARTY.
I DON'T CARE IF YOU SKIPPED OUT AT THE BIRTHDAY PARTY, BUT WE DO NEED TO TALK.
OH! I WAS SUPPOSED TO CALL DAD.
HONEY, I...

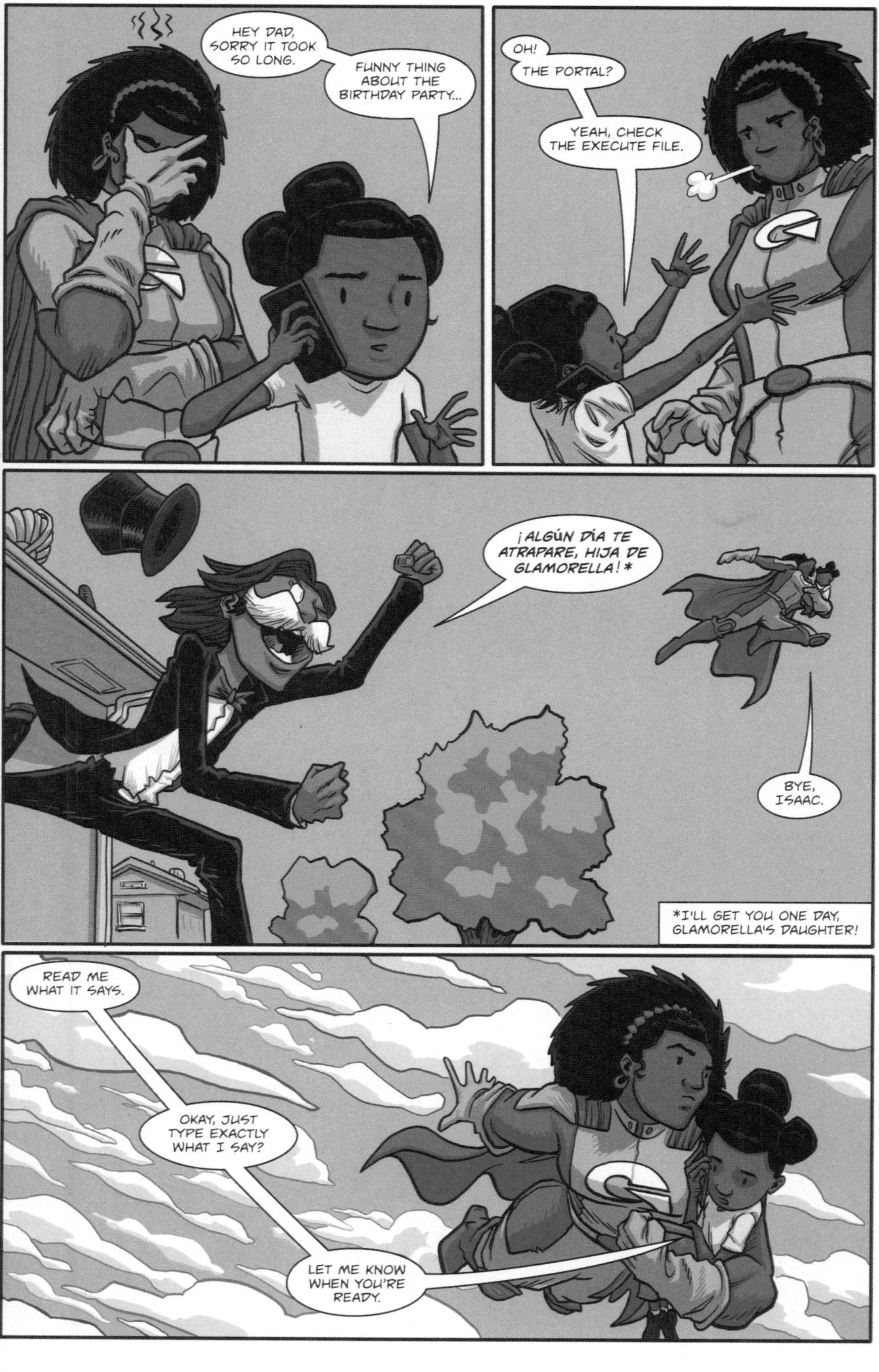
HEY DAD, SORRY IT TOOK SO LONG.
FUNNY THING ABOUT THE BIRTHDAY PARTY...
OH!
THE PORTAL?
YEAH, CHECK THE EXECUTE FILE.
¡ALGÚN DÍA TE ATRAPARE, HIJA DE GLAMORELLA! *
BYE, ISAAC.
*I'LL GET YOU ONE DAY, GLAMORELLA'S DAUGHTER!
READ ME WHAT IT SAYS.
OKAY, JUST TYPE EXACTLY WHAT I SAY?
LET ME KNOW WHEN YOU'RE READY.

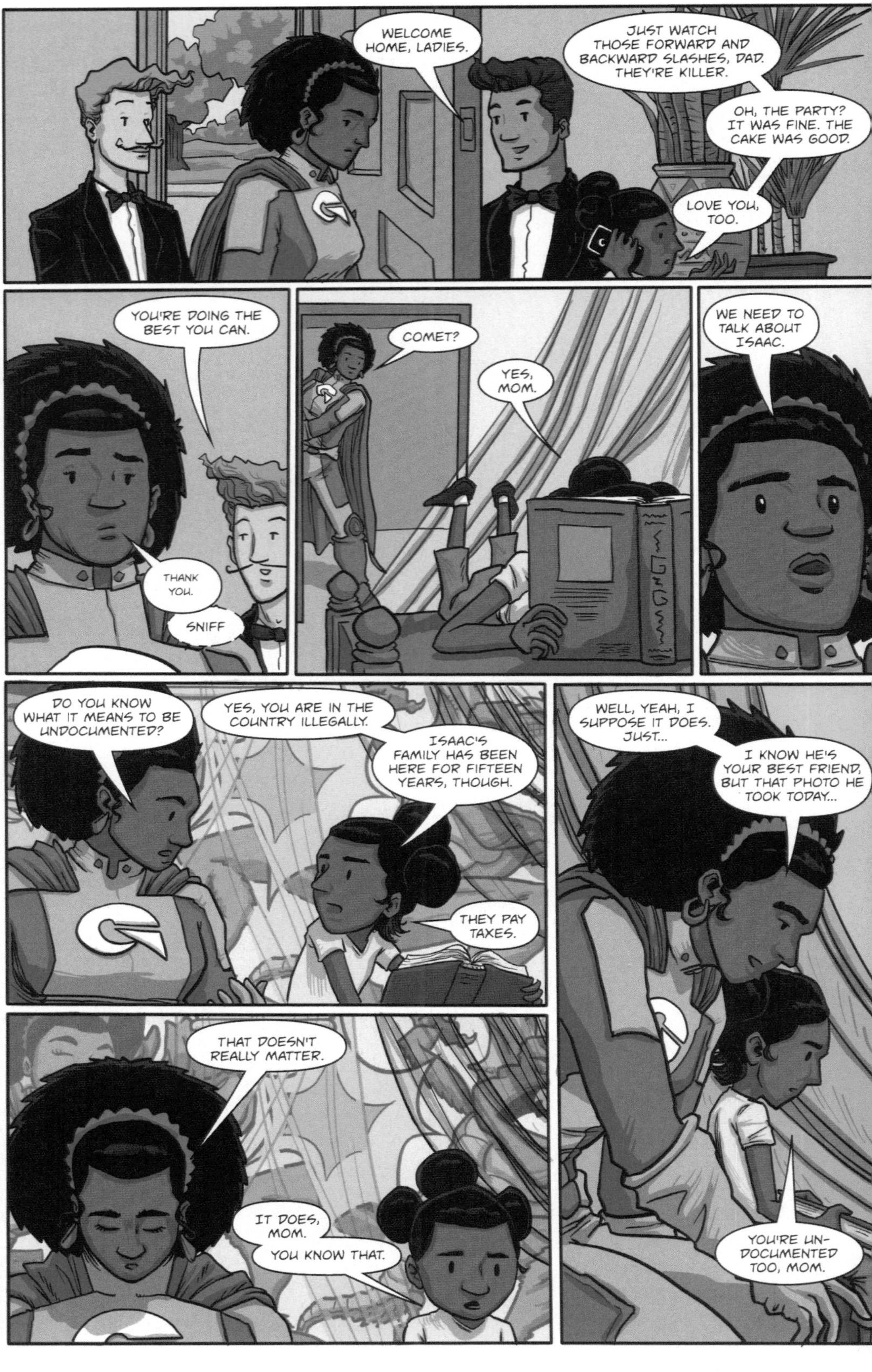
WELCOME HOME, LADIES.
JUST WATCH THOSE FORWARD AND BACKWARD SLASHES, DAD. THEY'RE KILLER.
OH, THE PARTY? IT WAS FINE. THE CAKE WAS GOOD.
LOVE YOU, TOO.
YOU'RE DOING THE BEST YOU CAN.
THANK YOU.
SNIFF
COMET?
YES, MOM.
WE NEED TO TALK ABOUT ISAAC.
DO YOU KNOW WHAT IT MEANS TO BE UNDOCUMENTED?
YES, YOU ARE IN THE COUNTRY ILLEGALLY.
ISAAC'S FAMILY HAS BEEN HERE FOR FIFTEEN YEARS, THOUGH.
THEY PAY TAXES.
WELL, YEAH, I SUPPOSE IT DOES. JUST...
I KNOW HE'S YOUR BEST FRIEND, BUT THAT PHOTO HE TOOK TODAY...
THAT DOESN'T REALLY MATTER.
IT DOES, MOM.
YOU KNOW THAT.
YOU'RE UN-DOCUMENTED TOO, MOM.

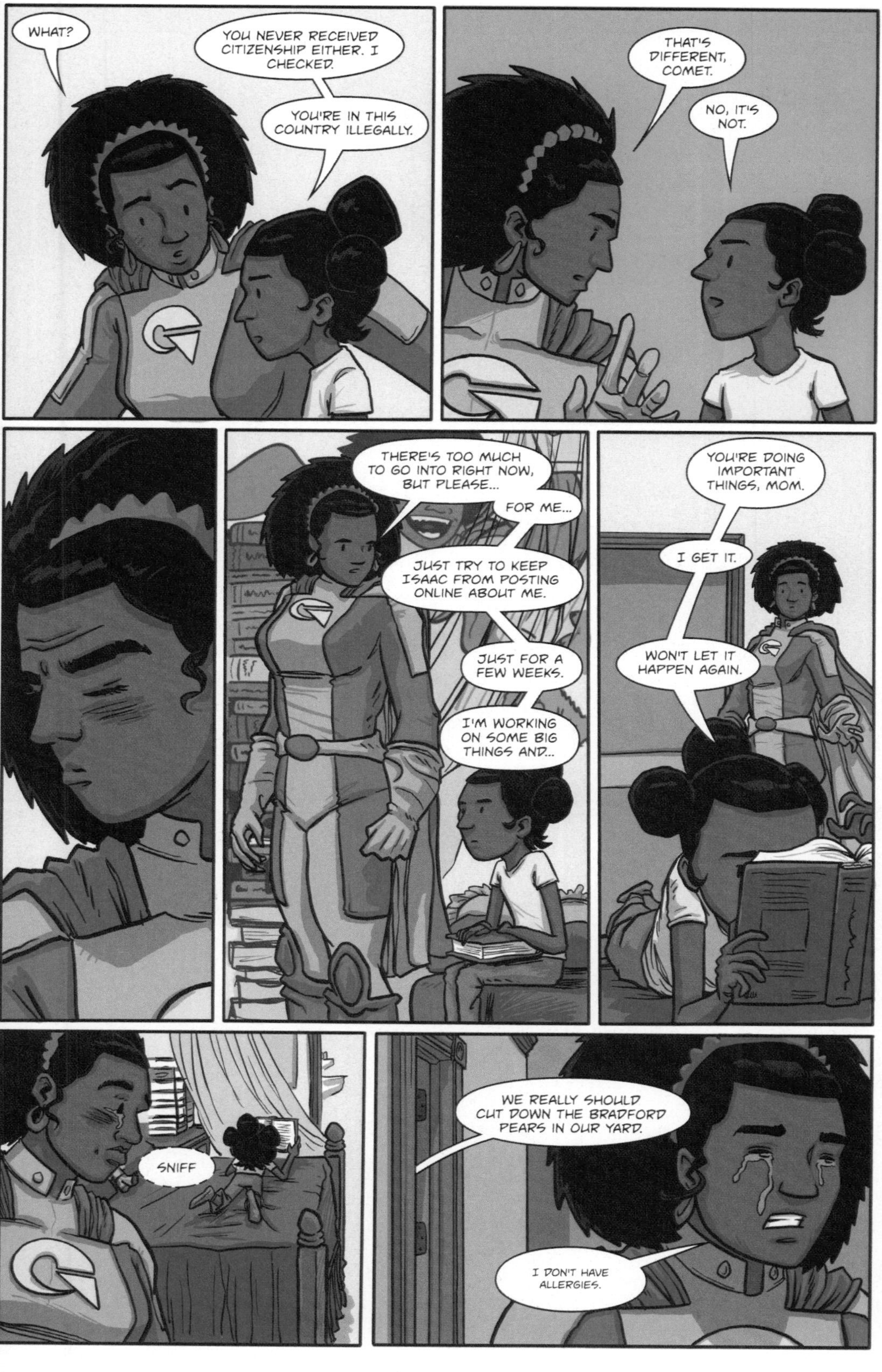
WHAT?
YOU NEVER RECEIVED CITIZENSHIP EITHER. I CHECKED.
YOU'RE IN THIS COUNTRY ILLEGALLY.
THAT'S DIFFERENT, COMET.
NO, IT'S NOT.
THERE'S TOO MUCH TO GO INTO RIGHT NOW, BUT PLEASE...
FOR ME...
JUST TRY TO KEEP ISAAC FROM POSTING ONLINE ABOUT ME.
JUST FOR A FEW WEEKS.
I'M WORKING ON SOME BIG THINGS AND...
YOU'RE DOING IMPORTANT THINGS, MOM.
I GET IT.
WON'T LET IT HAPPEN AGAIN.
SNIFF
WE REALLY SHOULD CUT DOWN THE BRADFORD PEARS IN OUR YARD.
I DON'T HAVE ALLERGIES.

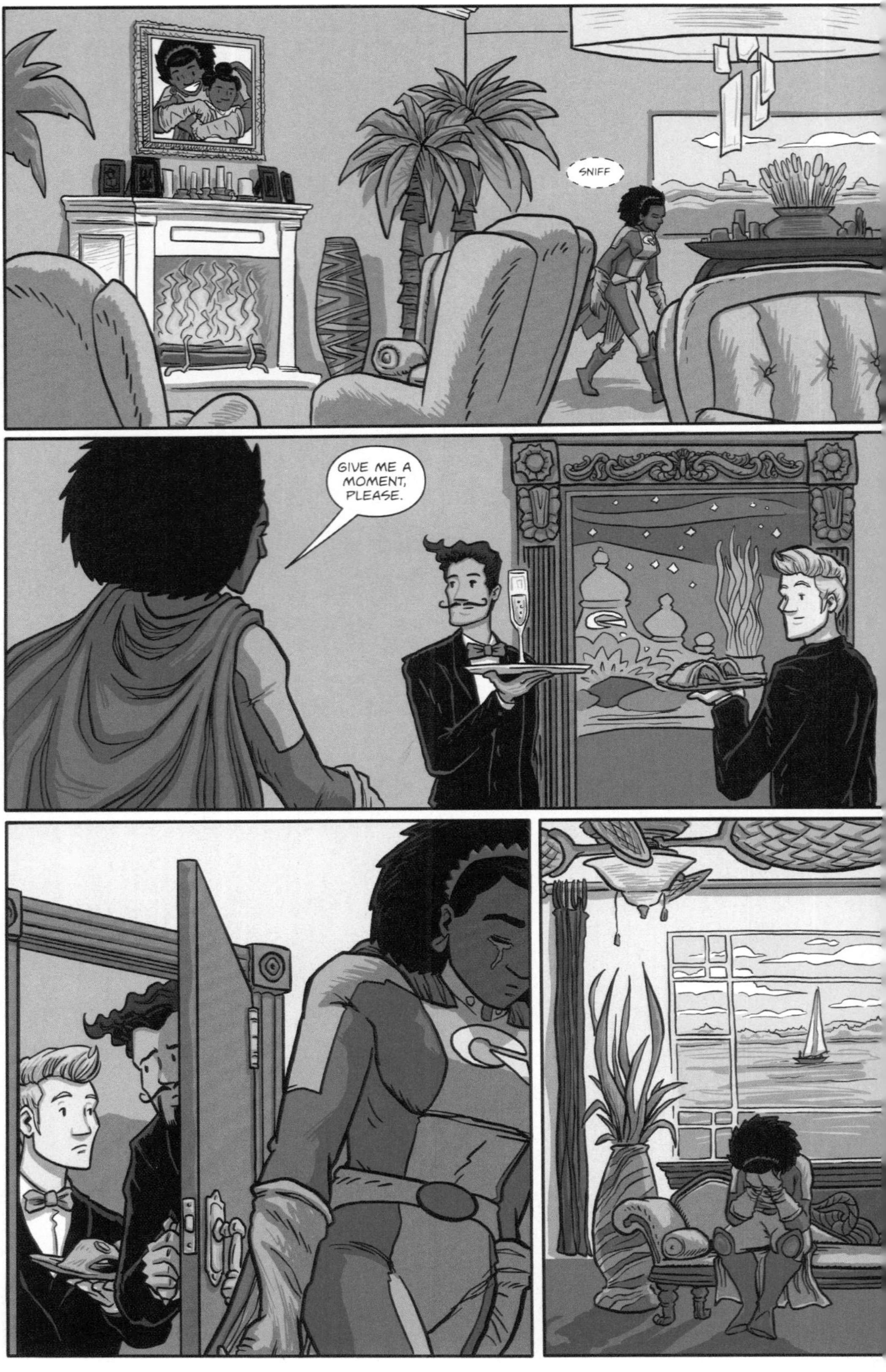
SNIFF
GIVE ME A MOMENT, PLEASE.

LET'S JUST SEE WHAT THERE IS TO SEE ON THE OTHER SIDE.

IF WE SEE DEAD STEVE AND CAN'T DRAG HIM BACK, WE BLOW UP THE PORTAL FROM THEIR SIDE. RIGHT?

RIGHT. DEAD STEVE EQUALS EXPLOSION.

IT'S KIND OF SURPRISING THAT YOU KEEP TELLING US ABOUT YOUR SUPER INTELLECT AND YET SOMEHOW THE PORTAL WON'T WORK.

IT'S NOT MY FAULT!

IT'S THIS STUPID TECH!

AND I DON'T HAVE MY TOOLS!

AND WHY DID WE USE A NON-STANDARD PLUG-IN PORT?

WHO EVEN HAS A 30-PIN ADAPTER THESE DAYS?

IT'S NOT 2007, YOU JERKS!

TINK

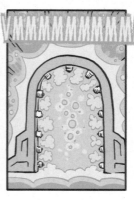

VMMMMMMMMM

I DID IT!

I AM A GENIUS!

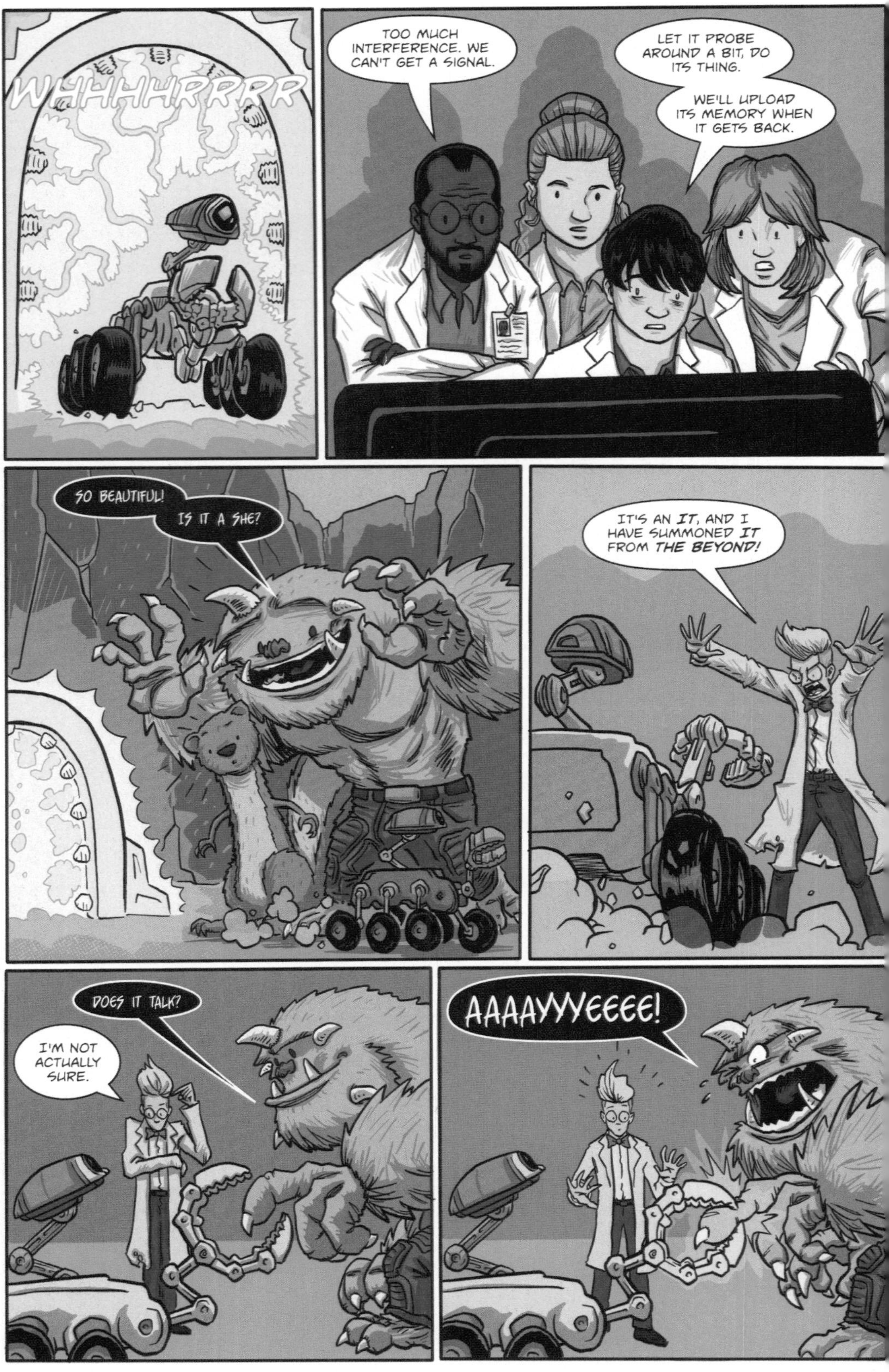
WHHHHRRRR
TOO MUCH INTERFERENCE. WE CAN'T GET A SIGNAL.
LET IT PROBE AROUND A BIT, DO ITS THING.
WE'LL UPLOAD ITS MEMORY WHEN IT GETS BACK.
SO BEAUTIFUL!
IS IT A SHE?
IT'S AN IT, AND I HAVE SUMMONED IT FROM THE BEYOND!
DOES IT TALK?
I'M NOT ACTUALLY SURE.
AAAAYYYEEEE!

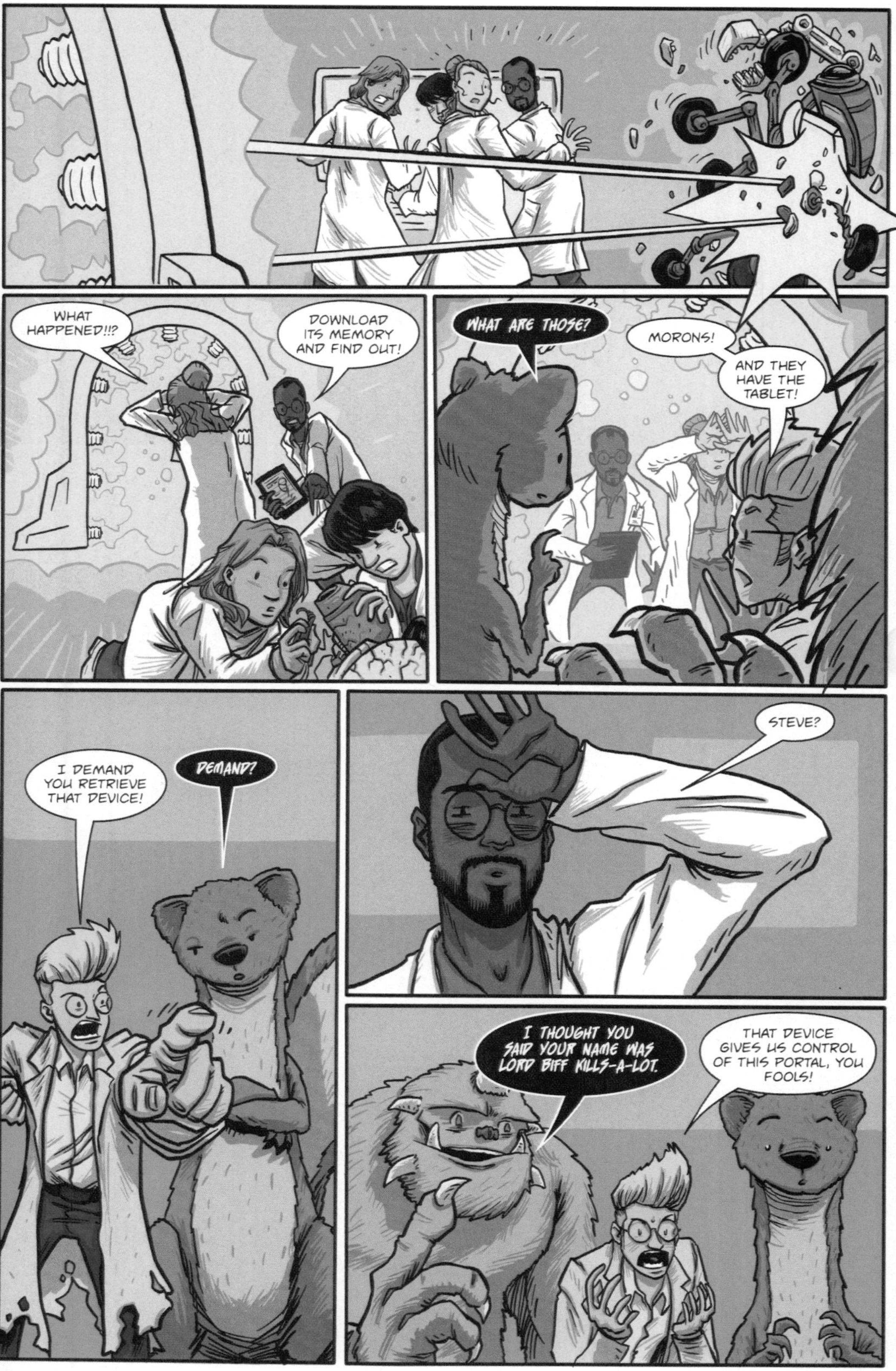
WHAT HAPPENED!!?
DOWNLOAD ITS MEMORY AND FIND OUT!
WHAT ARE THOSE?
MORONS!
AND THEY HAVE THE TABLET!
I DEMAND YOU RETRIEVE THAT DEVICE!
DEMAND?
STEVE?
I THOUGHT YOU SAID YOUR NAME WAS LORD BIFF KILLS-A-LOT.
THAT DEVICE GIVES US CONTROL OF THIS PORTAL, YOU FOOLS!

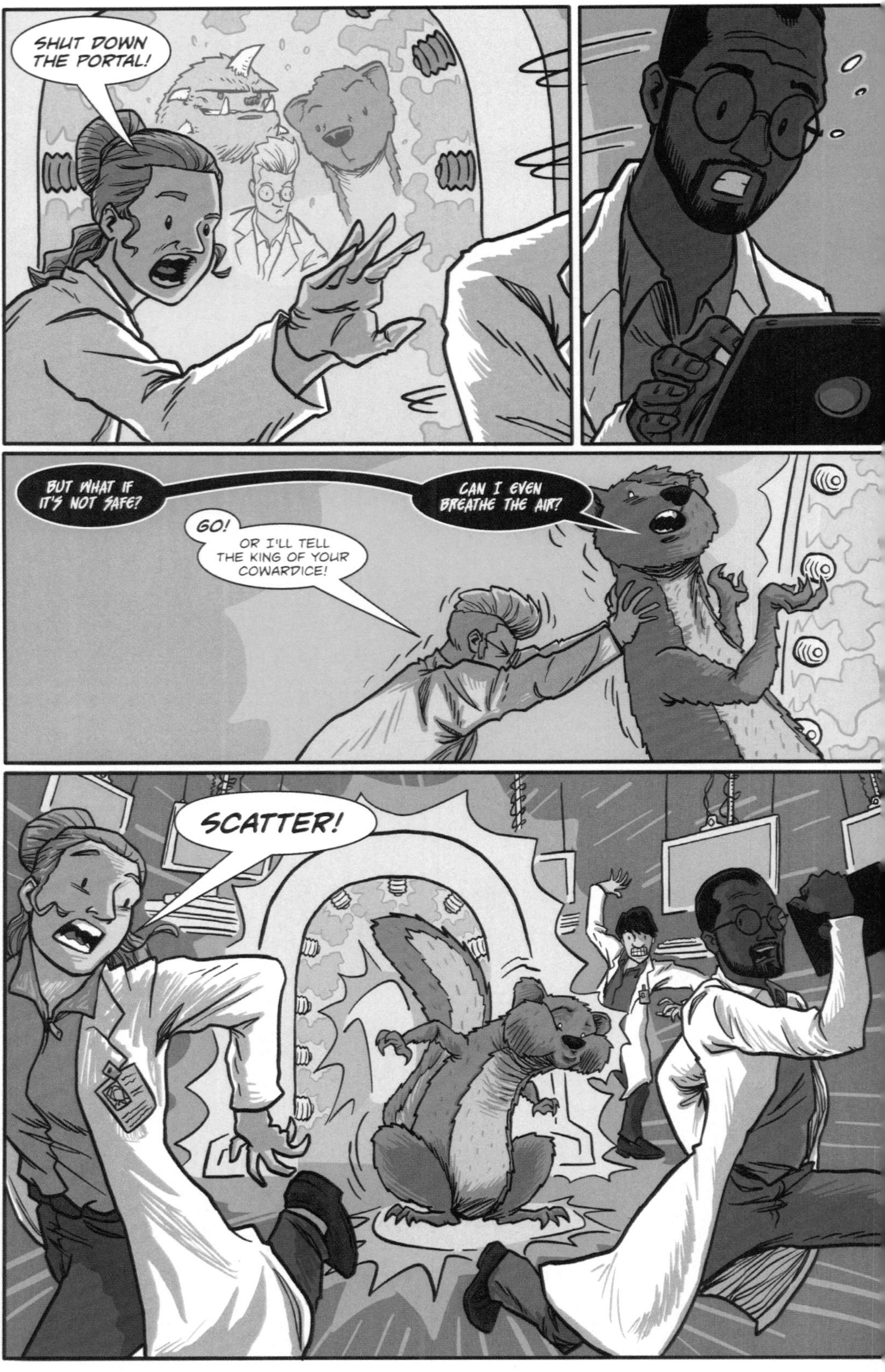
SHUT DOWN THE PORTAL!
BUT WHAT IF IT'S NOT SAFE?
CAN I EVEN BREATHE THE AIR?
GO!
OR I'LL TELL THE KING OF YOUR COWARDICE!
SCATTER!

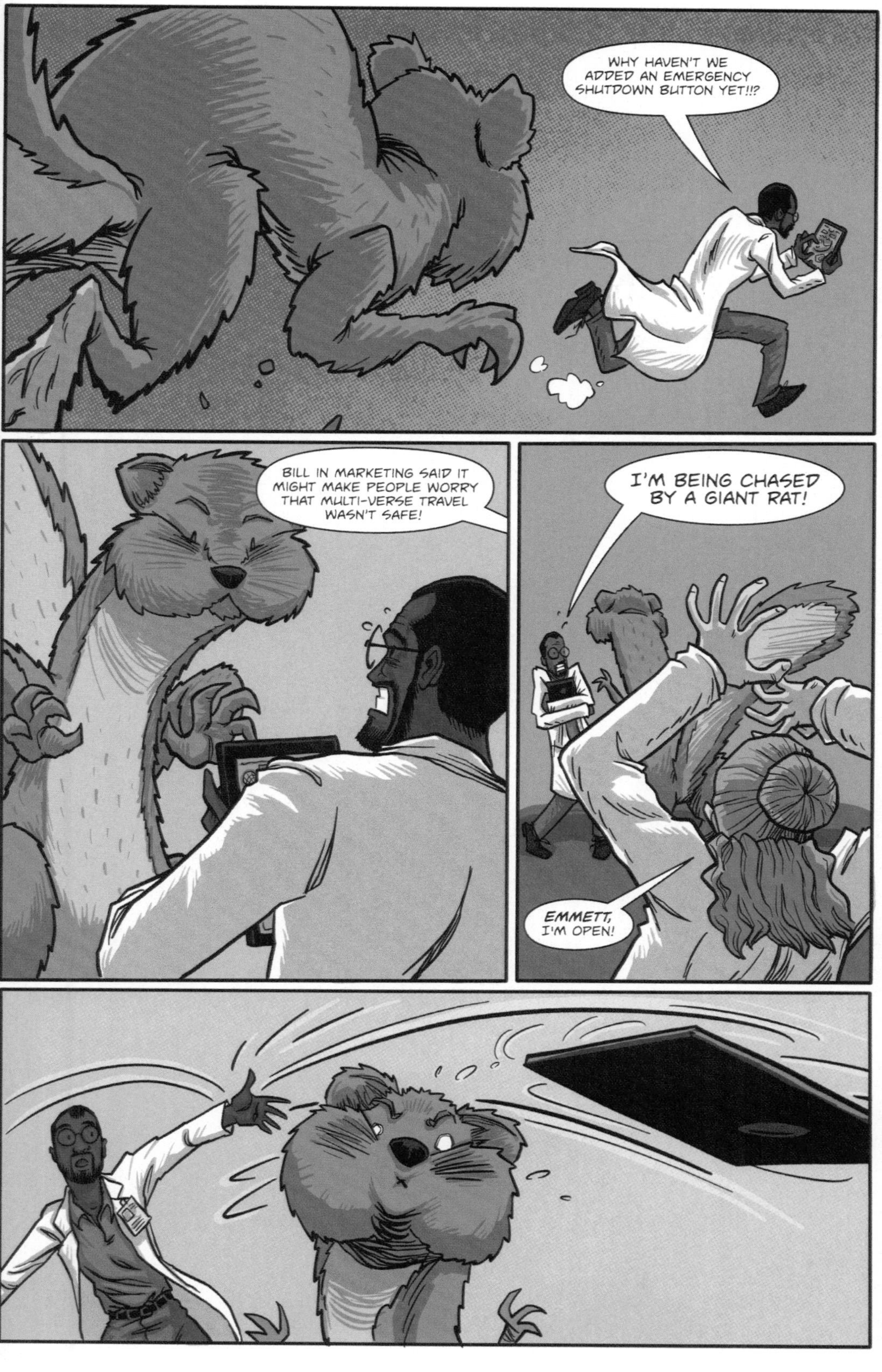
WHY HAVEN'T WE ADDED AN EMERGENCY SHUTDOWN BUTTON YET!!?
BILL IN MARKETING SAID IT MIGHT MAKE PEOPLE WORRY THAT MULTI-VERSE TRAVEL WASN'T SAFE!
I'M BEING CHASED BY A GIANT RAT!
EMMETT, I'M OPEN!

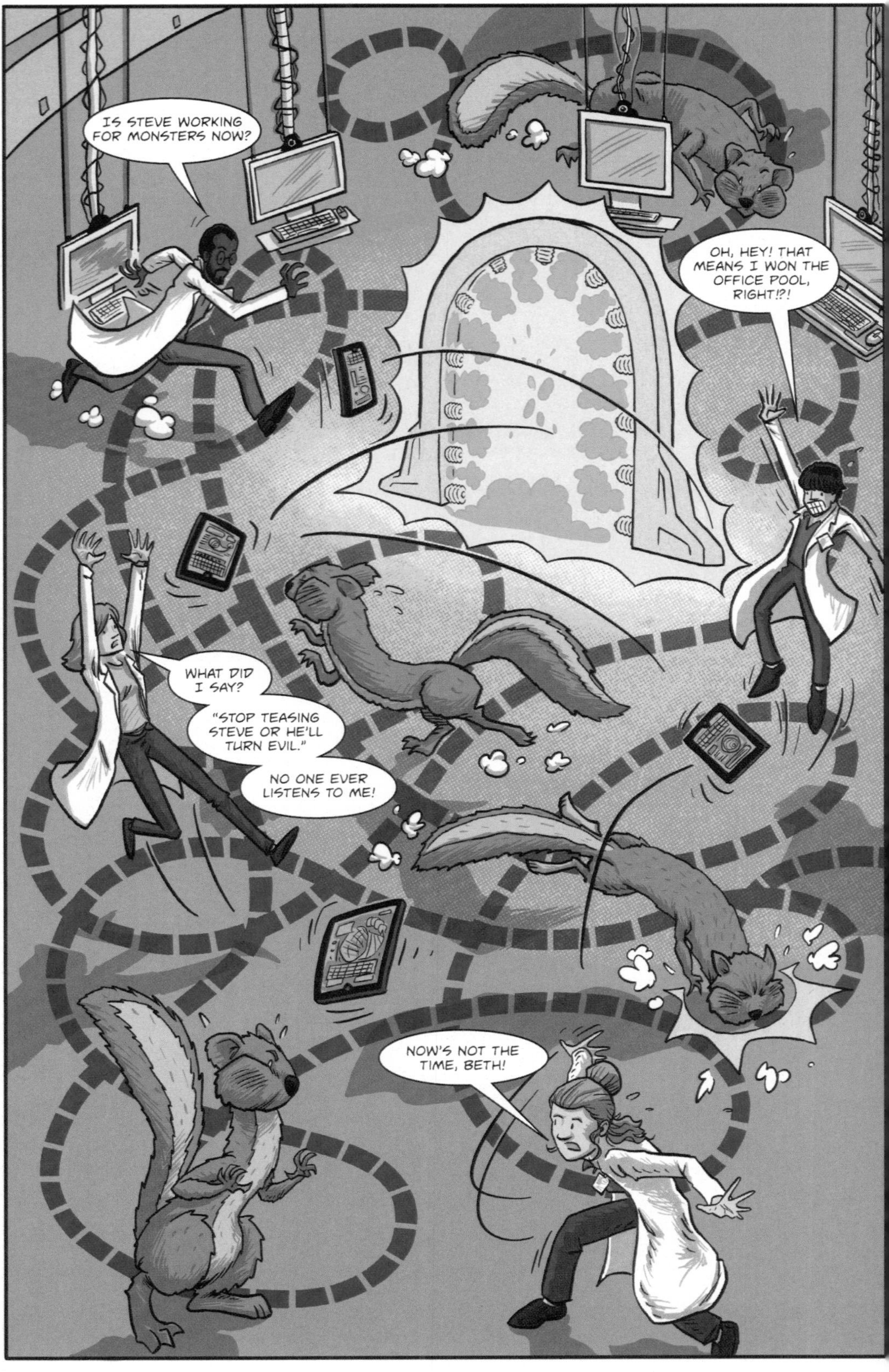
IS STEVE WORKING FOR MONSTERS NOW?
OH, HEY! THAT MEANS I WON THE OFFICE POOL, RIGHT!?!
WHAT DID I SAY?
"STOP TEASING STEVE OR HE'LL TURN EVIL."
NO ONE EVER LISTENS TO ME!
NOW'S NOT THE TIME, BETH!

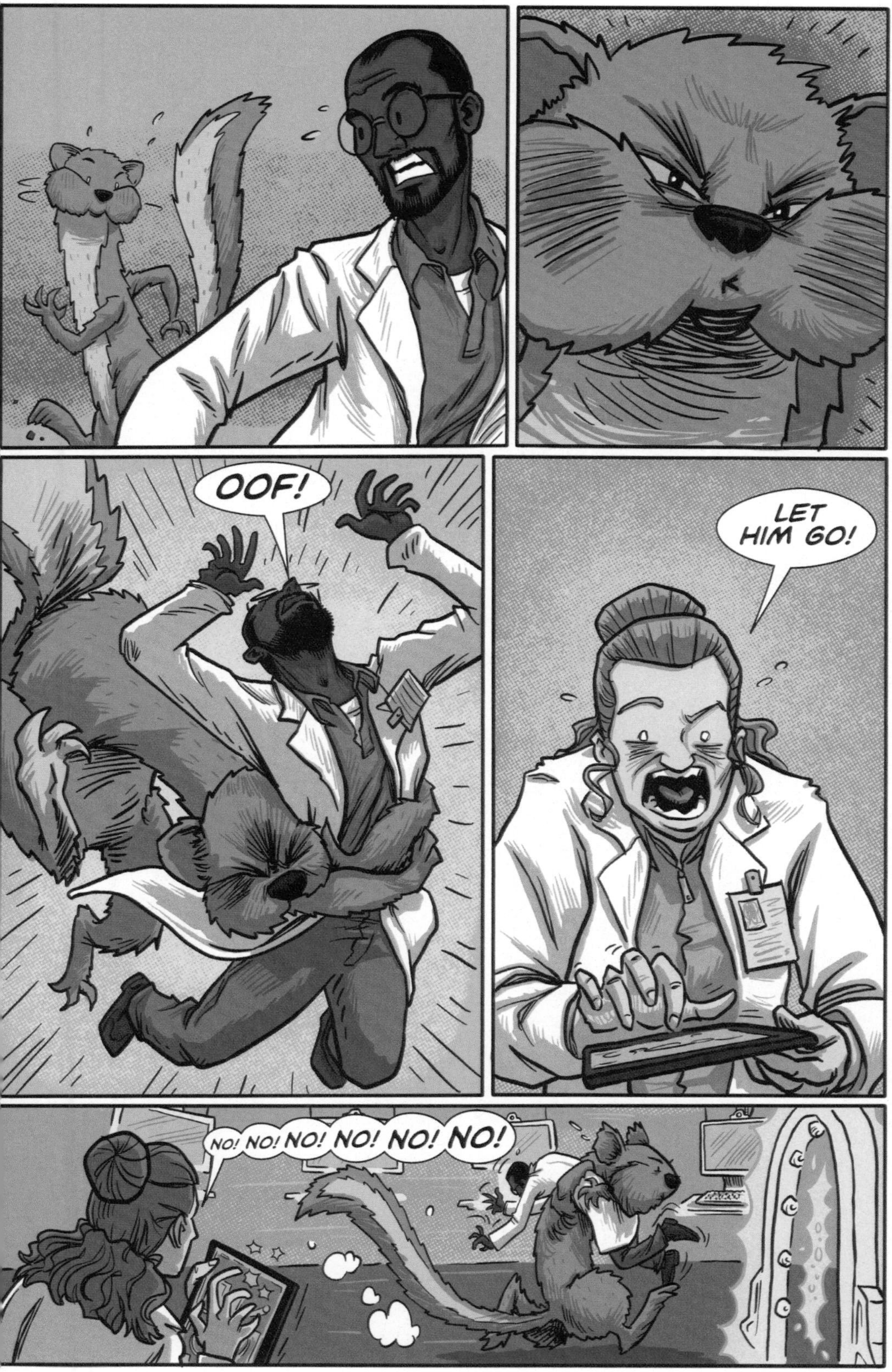

OOF!
LET HIM GO!
NO! NO! NO! NO! NO! NO!

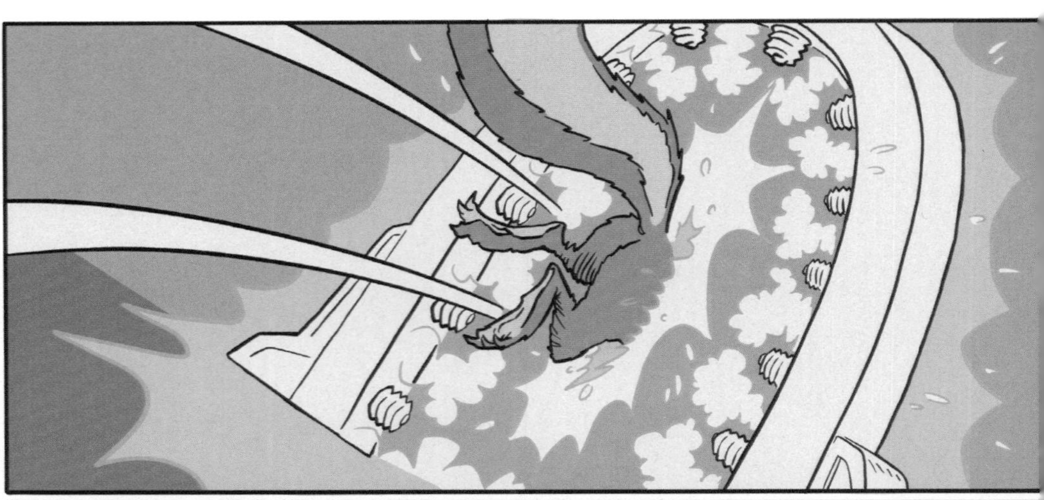

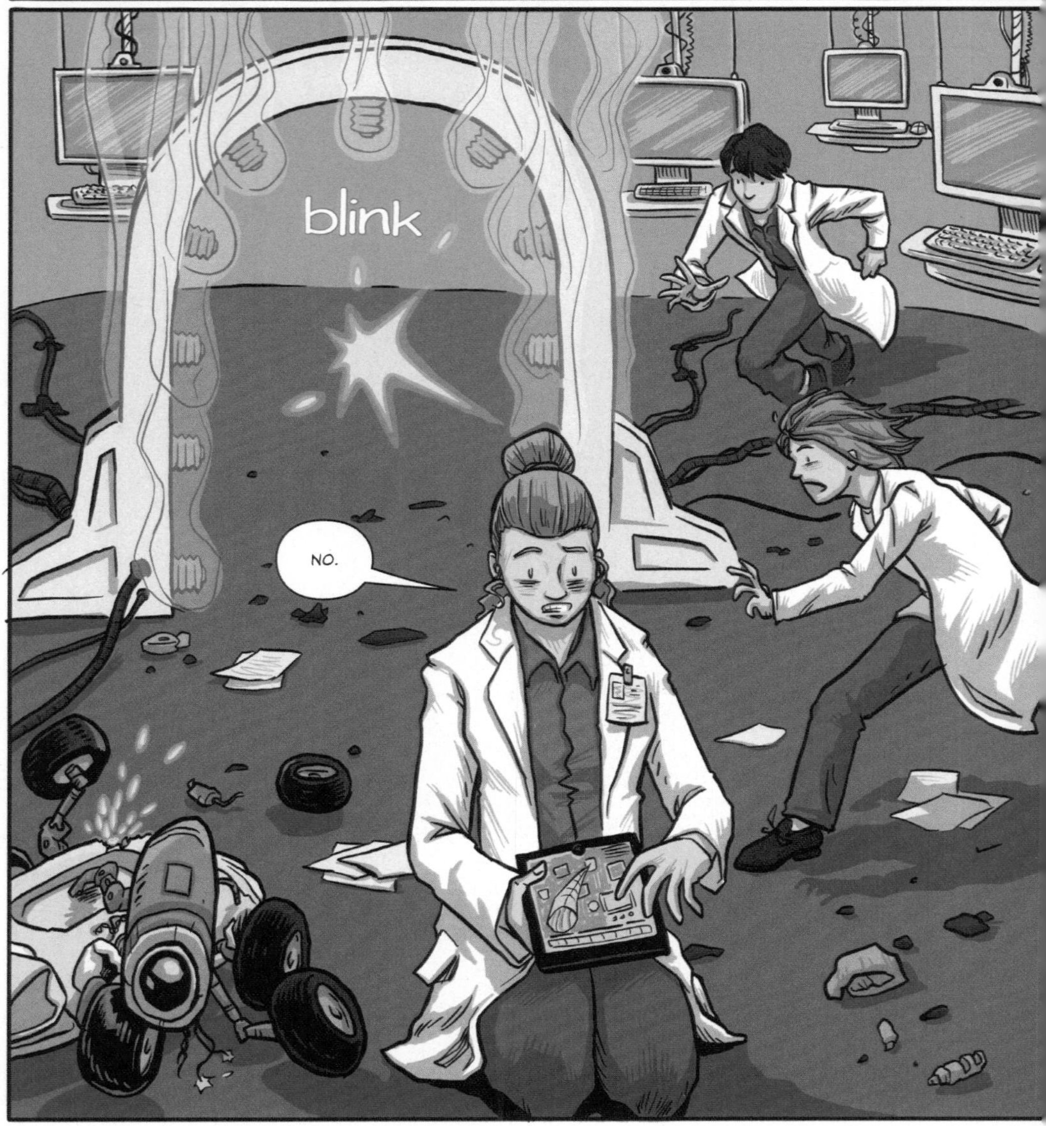
blink
NO.

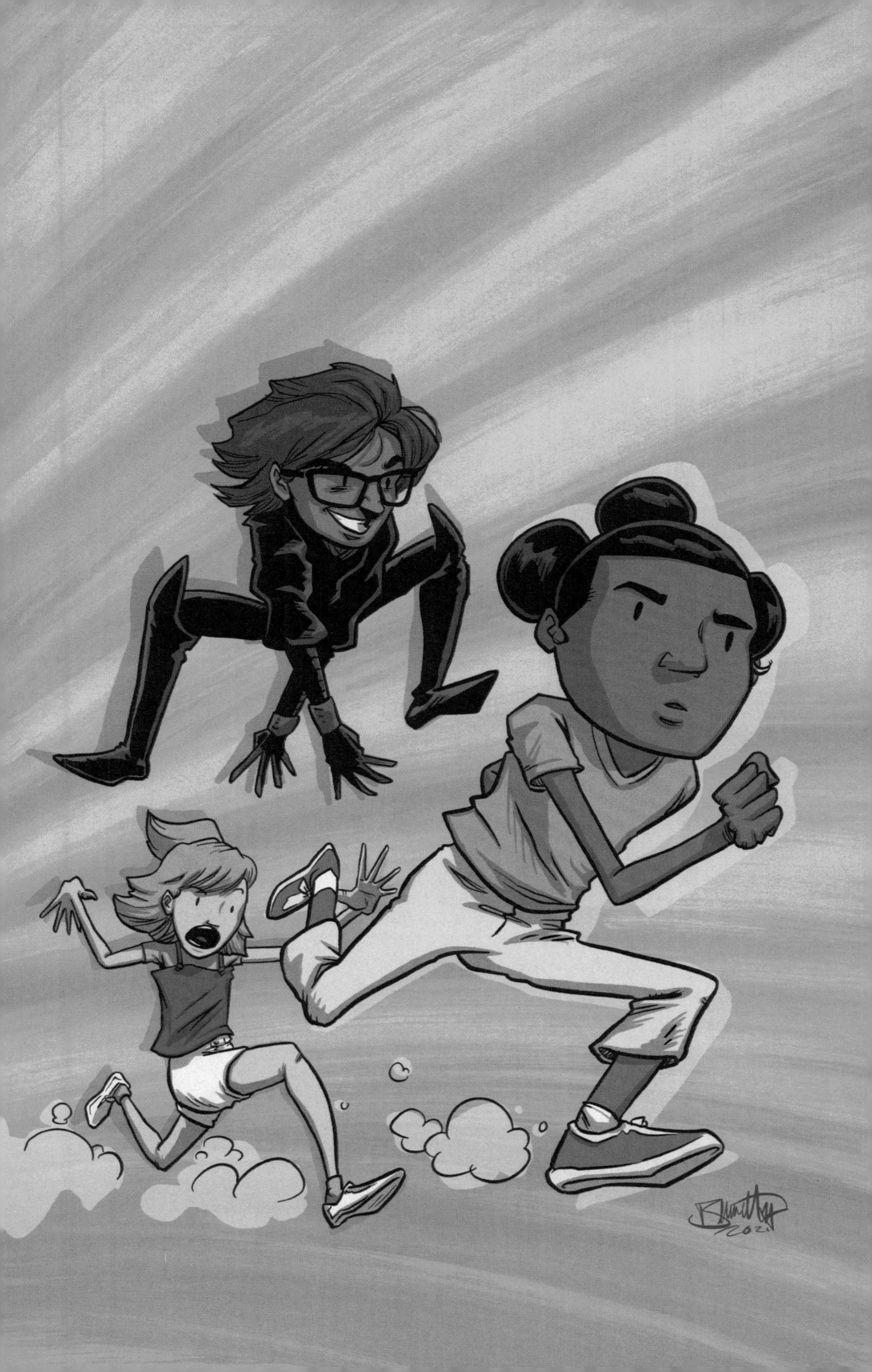

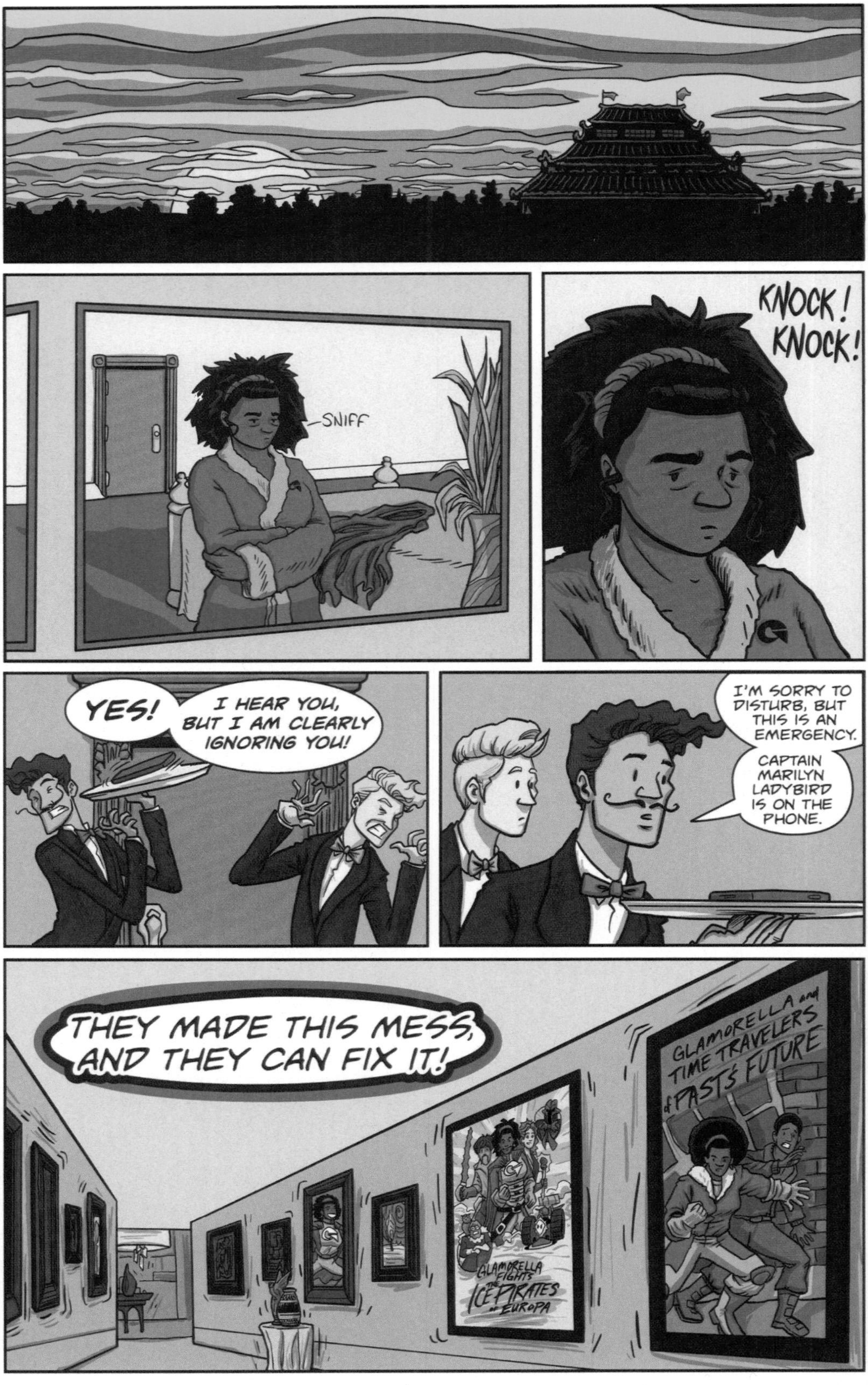

SNIFF
KNOCK! KNOCK!
YES!
I HEAR YOU, BUT I AM CLEARLY IGNORING YOU!
I'M SORRY TO DISTURB, BUT THIS IS AN EMERGENCY.
CAPTAIN MARILYN LADYBIRD IS ON THE PHONE.
THEY MADE THIS MESS, AND THEY CAN FIX IT!
GLAMORELLA FIGHTS THE ICE PIRATES OF EUROPA
GLAMORELLA and TIME TRAVELERS of PAST'S FUTURE

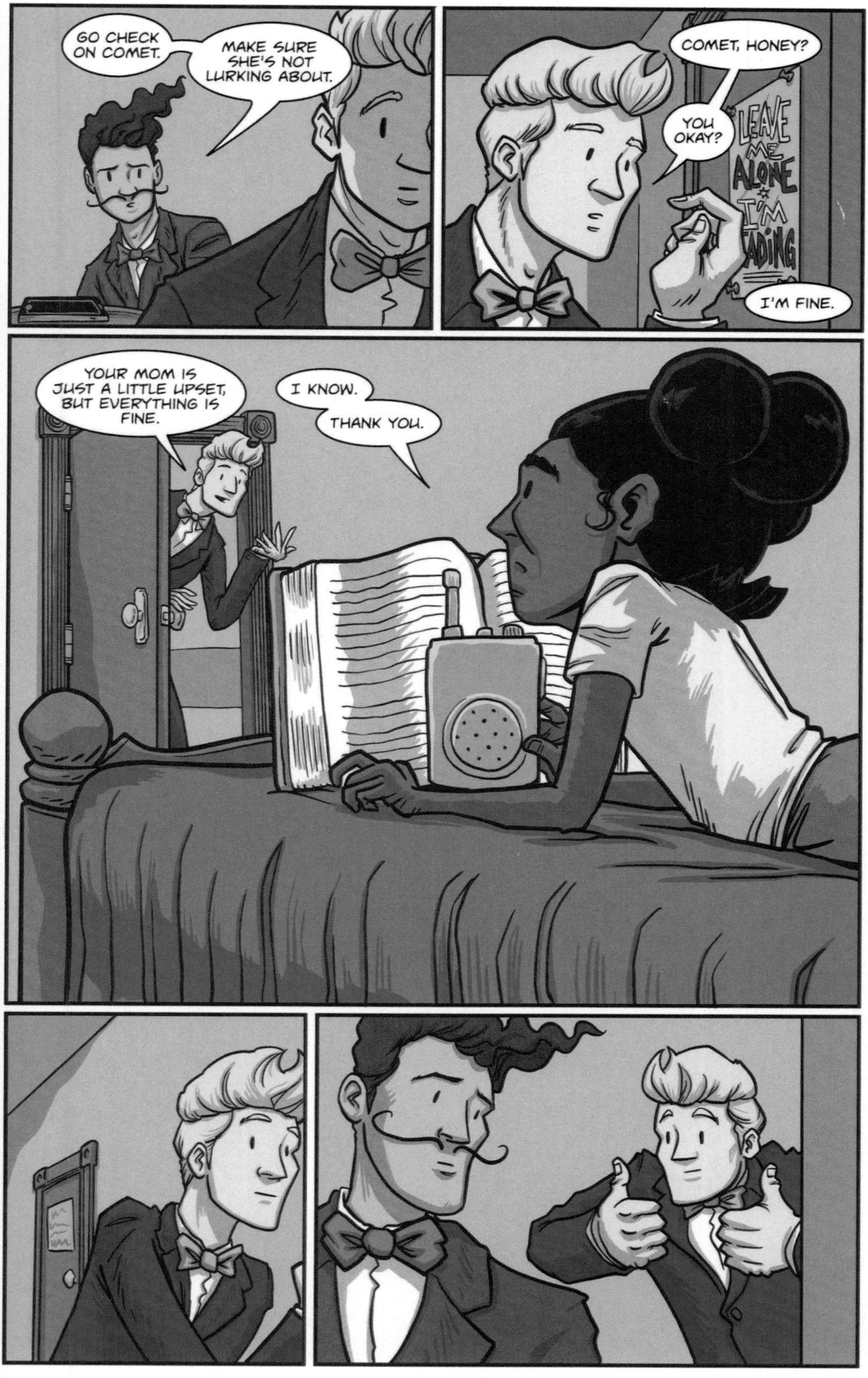
GO CHECK ON COMET.
MAKE SURE SHE'S NOT LURKING ABOUT.
COMET, HONEY?
YOU OKAY?
LEAVE ME ALONE I'M READING
I'M FINE.
YOUR MOM IS JUST A LITTLE UPSET, BUT EVERYTHING IS FINE.
I KNOW.
THANK YOU.

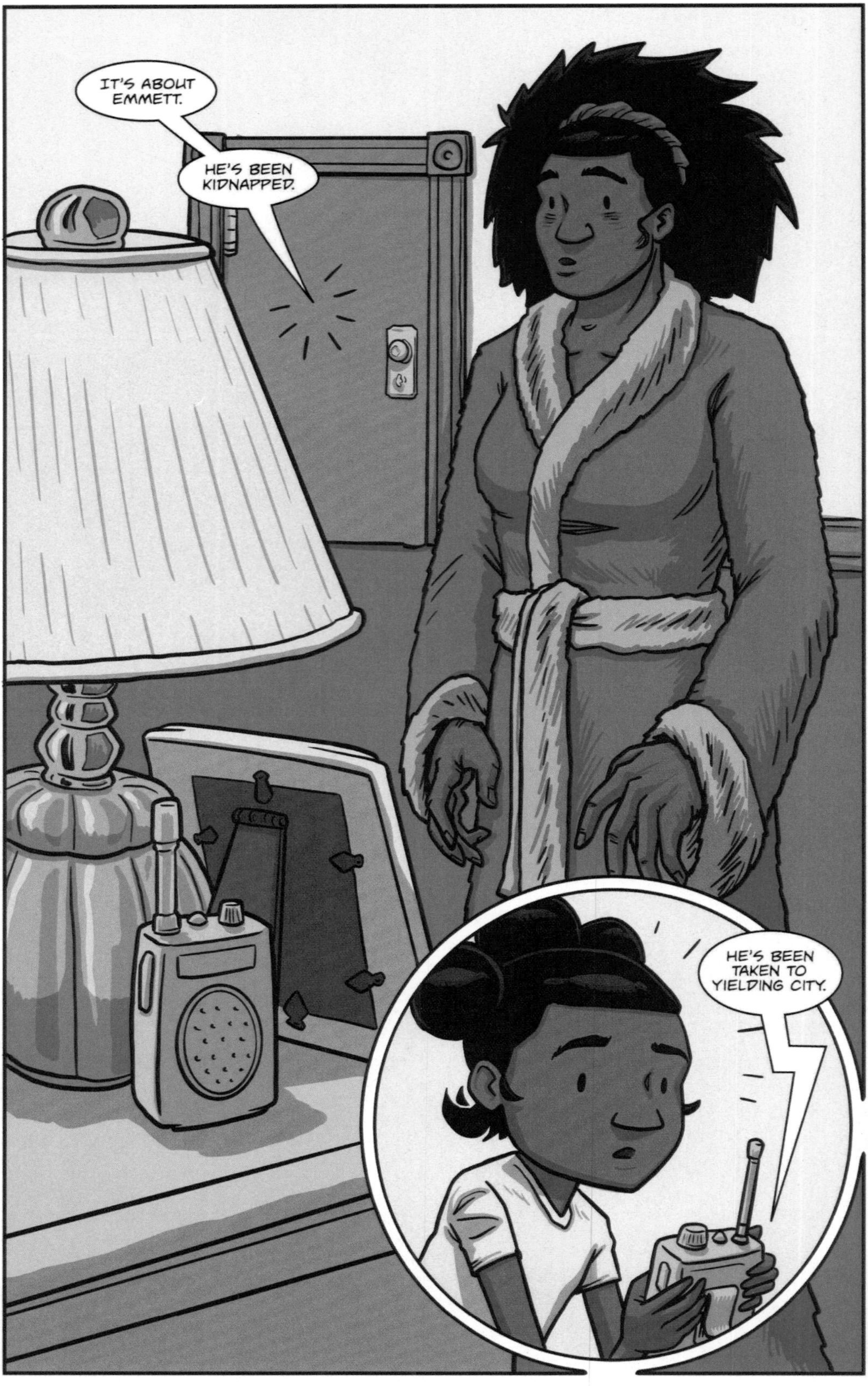
IT'S ABOUT EMMETT.
HE'S BEEN KIDNAPPED.
HE'S BEEN TAKEN TO YIELDING CITY.

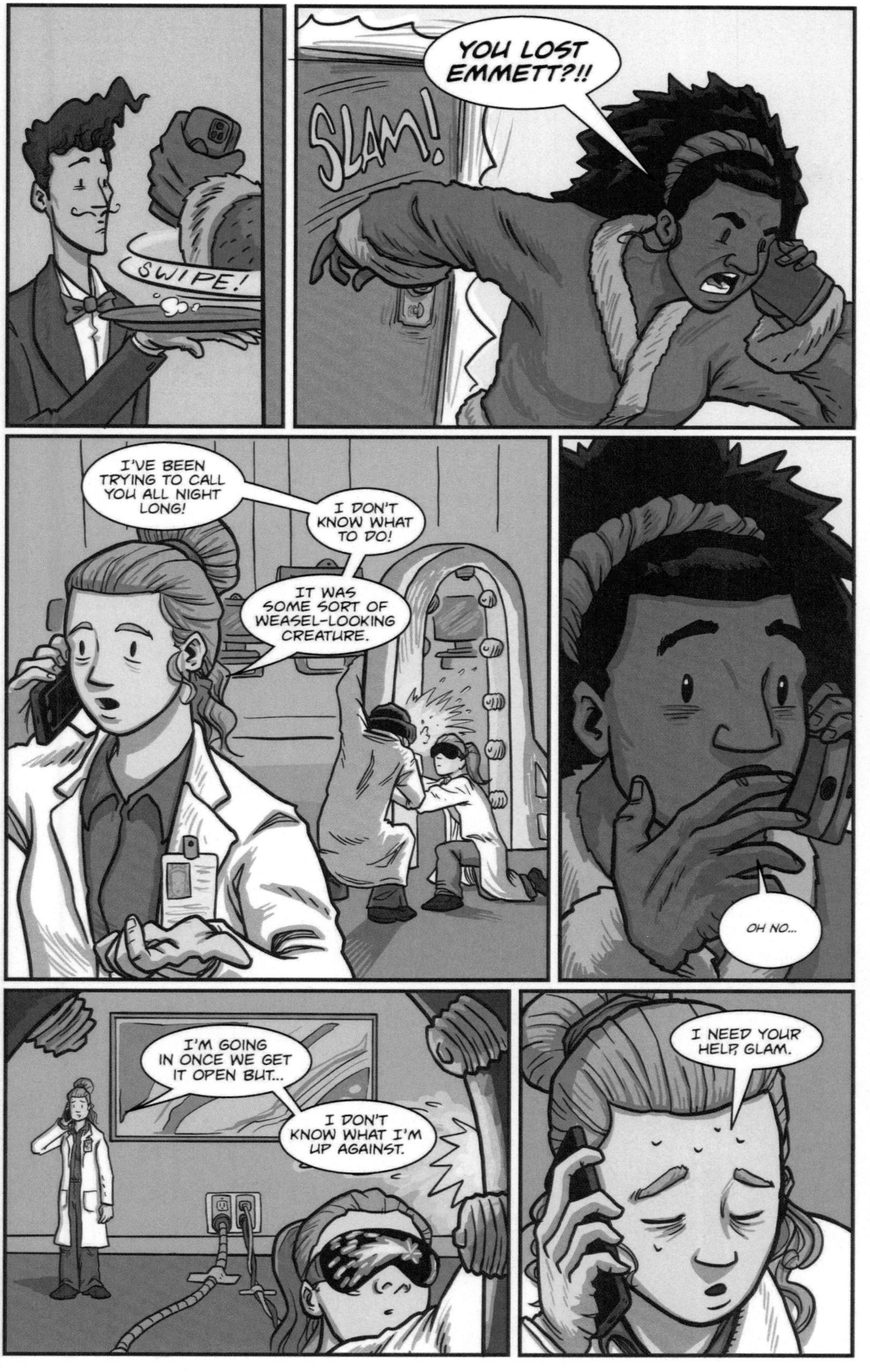
SWIPE!
SLAM!
YOU LOST EMMETT?!!
I'VE BEEN TRYING TO CALL YOU ALL NIGHT LONG!
I DON'T KNOW WHAT TO DO!
IT WAS SOME SORT OF WEASEL-LOOKING CREATURE.
OH NO...
I'M GOING IN ONCE WE GET IT OPEN BUT...
I DON'T KNOW WHAT I'M UP AGAINST.
I NEED YOUR HELP, GLAM.

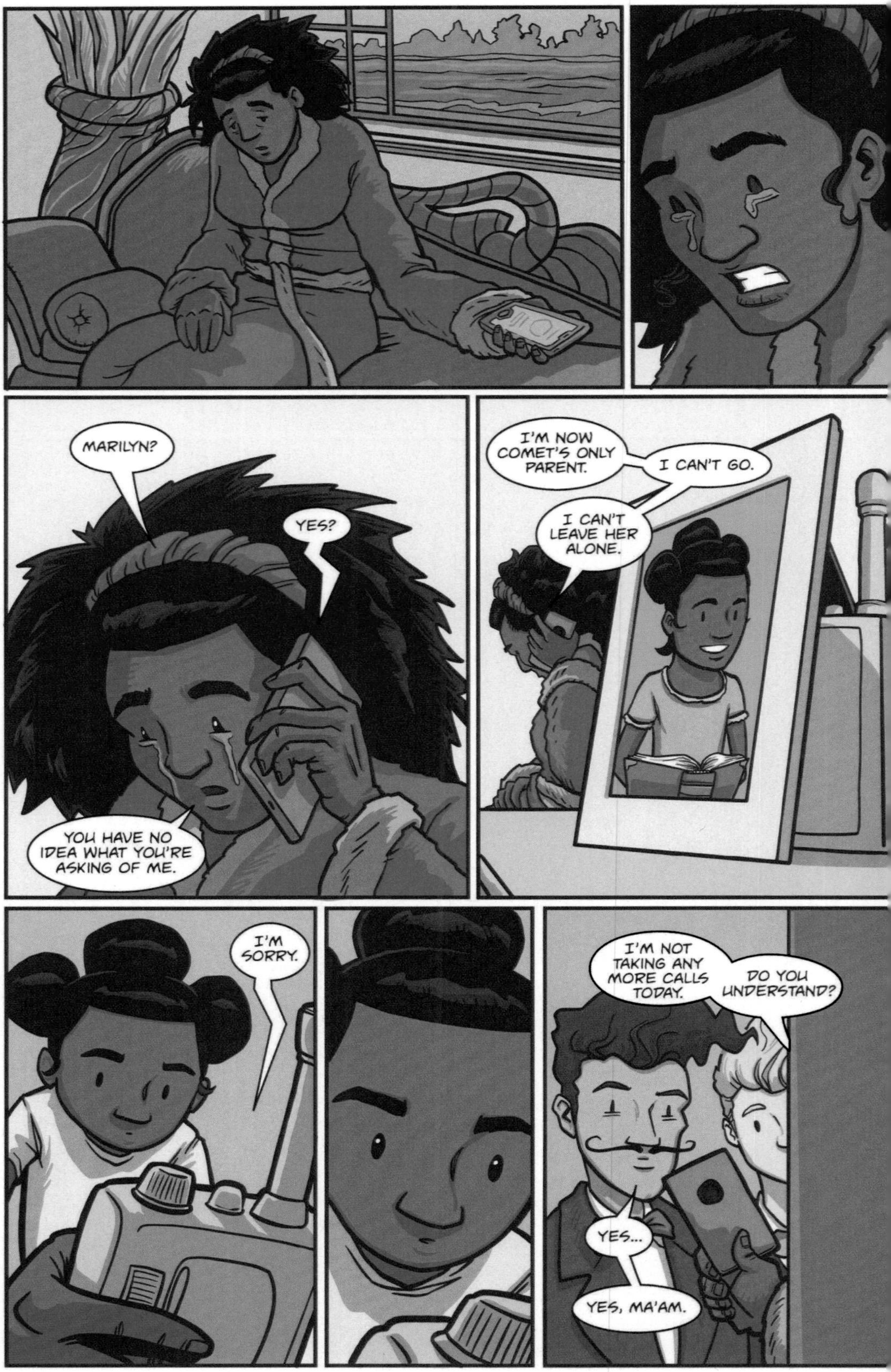
MARILYN?
YES?
YOU HAVE NO IDEA WHAT YOU'RE ASKING OF ME.
I'M NOW COMET'S ONLY PARENT.
I CAN'T GO.
I CAN'T LEAVE HER ALONE.
I'M SORRY.
I'M NOT TAKING ANY MORE CALLS TODAY.
DO YOU UNDERSTAND?
YES...
YES, MA'AM.

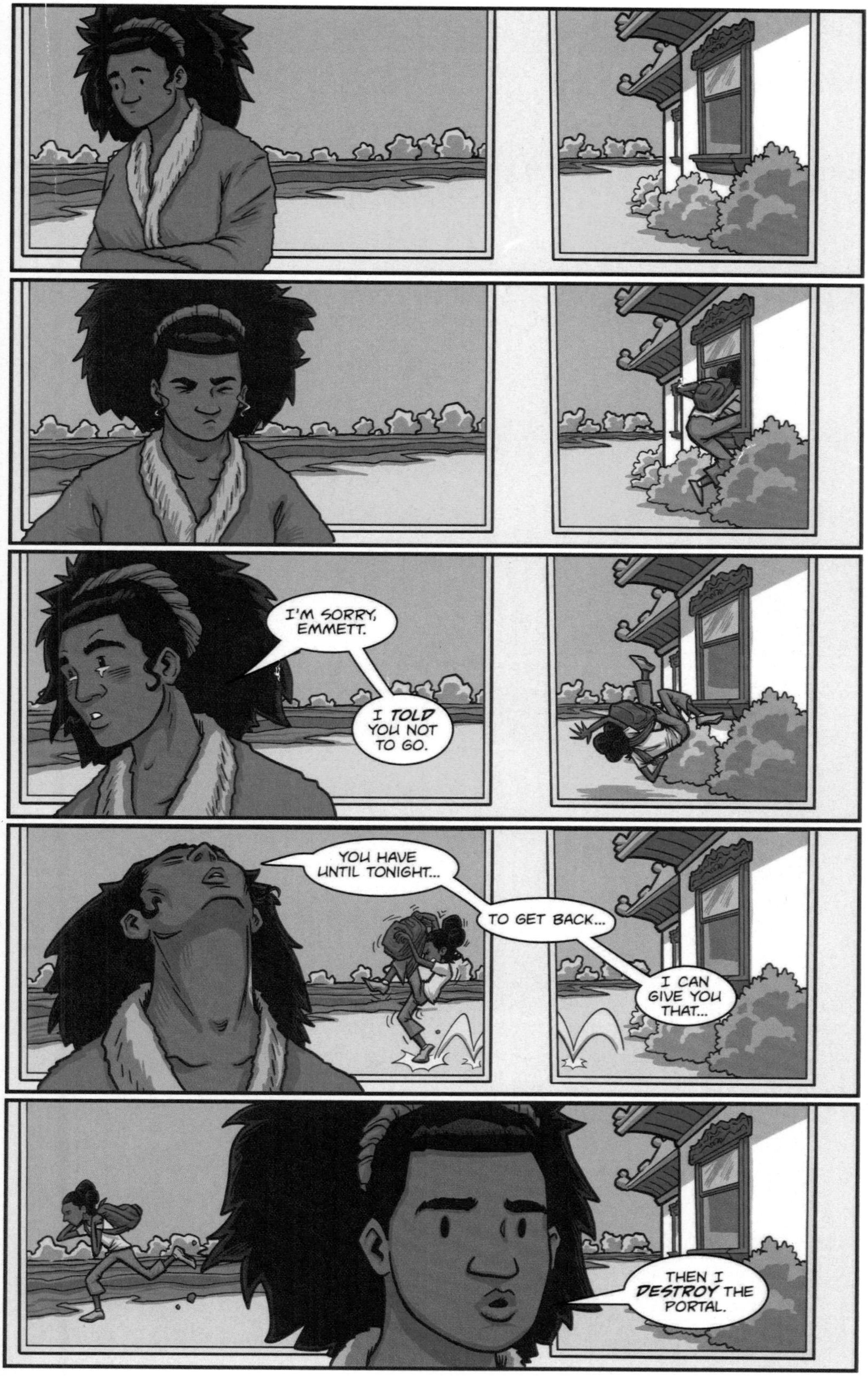
I'M SORRY, EMMETT.
I *TOLD* YOU NOT TO GO.
YOU HAVE UNTIL TONIGHT...
TO GET BACK...
I CAN GIVE YOU THAT...
THEN I *DESTROY* THE PORTAL.

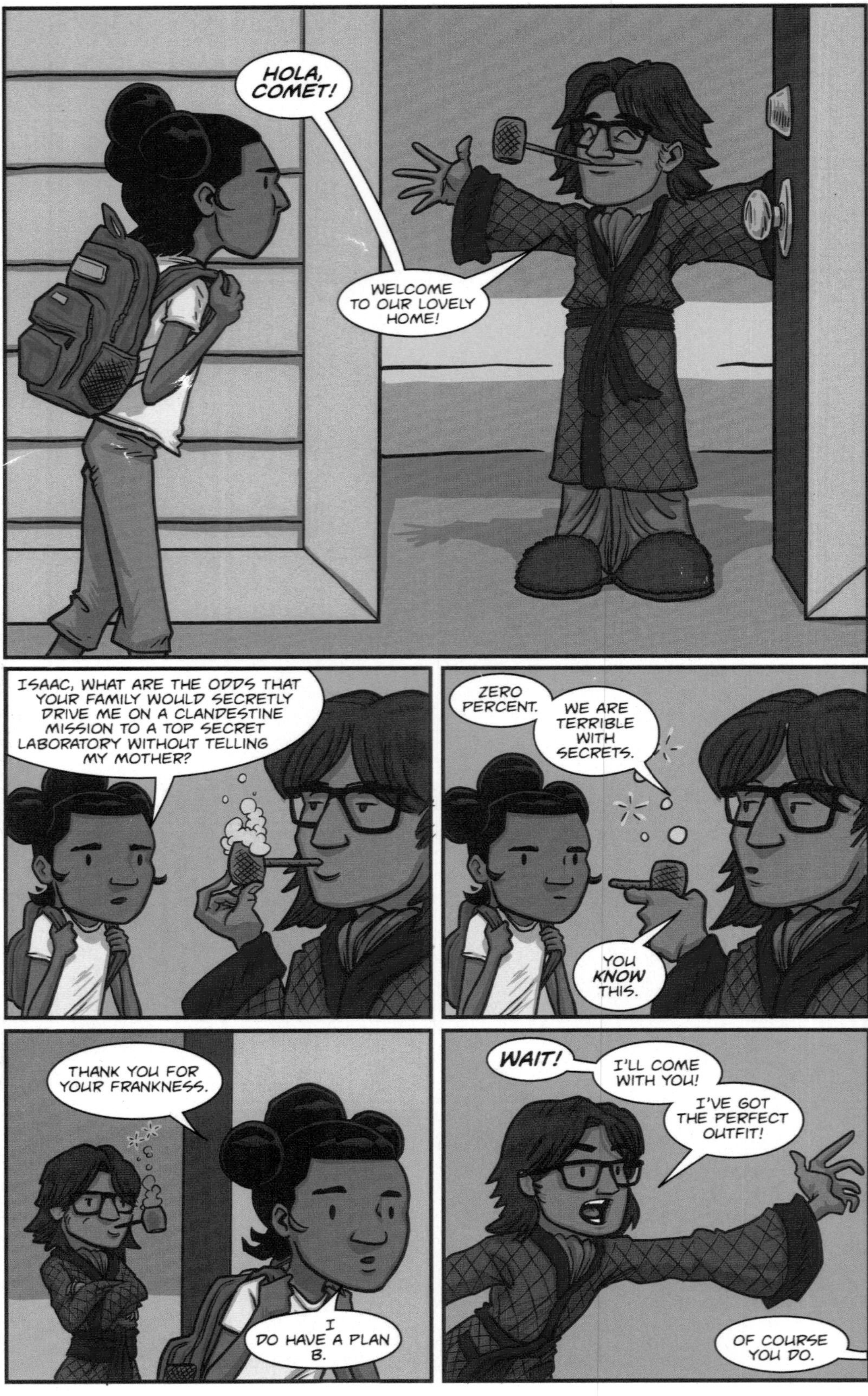
HOLA, COMET!
WELCOME TO OUR LOVELY HOME!
ISAAC, WHAT ARE THE ODDS THAT YOUR FAMILY WOULD SECRETLY DRIVE ME ON A CLANDESTINE MISSION TO A TOP SECRET LABORATORY WITHOUT TELLING MY MOTHER?
ZERO PERCENT.
WE ARE TERRIBLE WITH SECRETS.
YOU *KNOW* THIS.
THANK YOU FOR YOUR FRANKNESS.
I DO HAVE A PLAN B.
WAIT!
I'LL COME WITH YOU!
I'VE GOT THE PERFECT OUTFIT!
OF COURSE YOU DO.

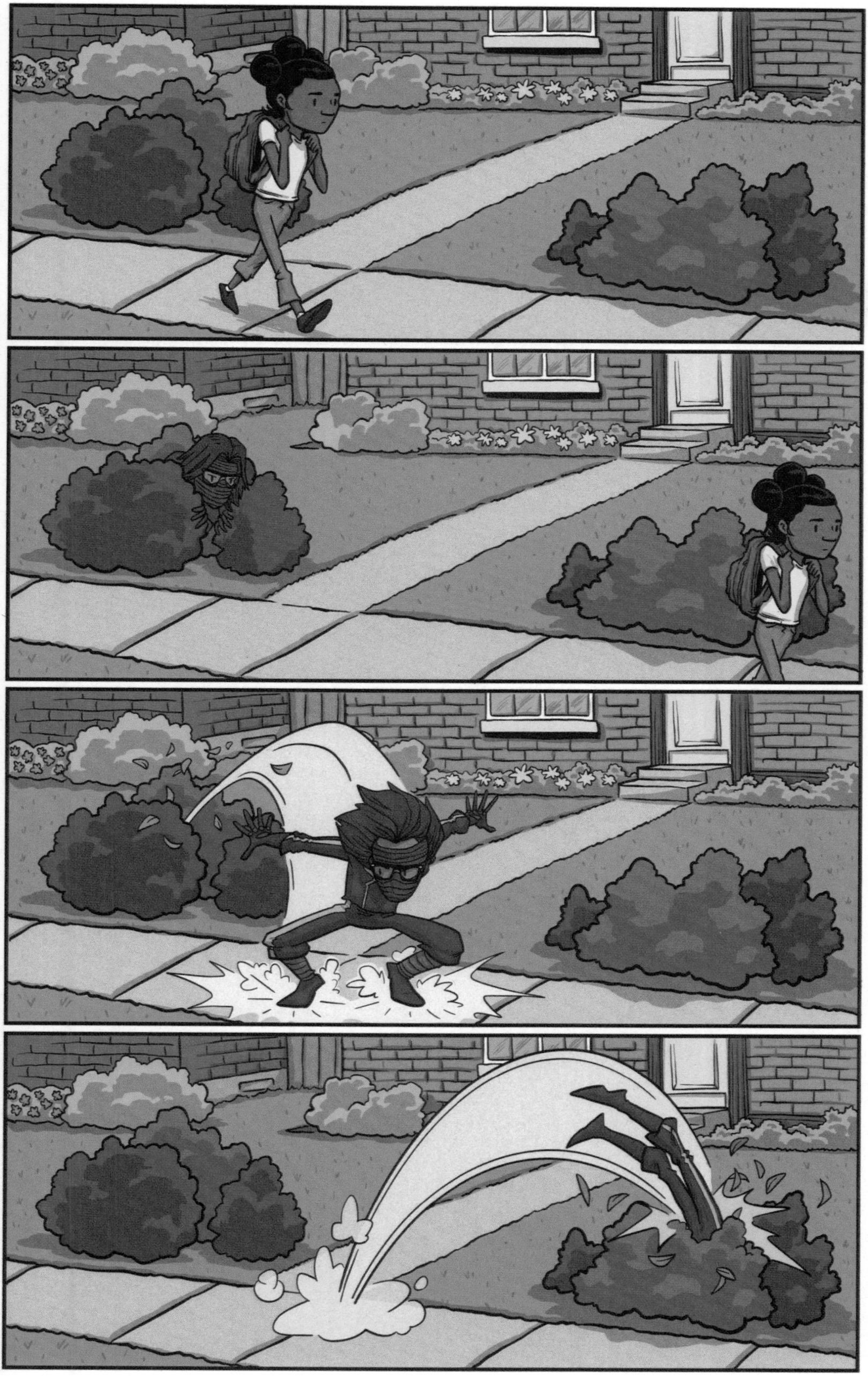

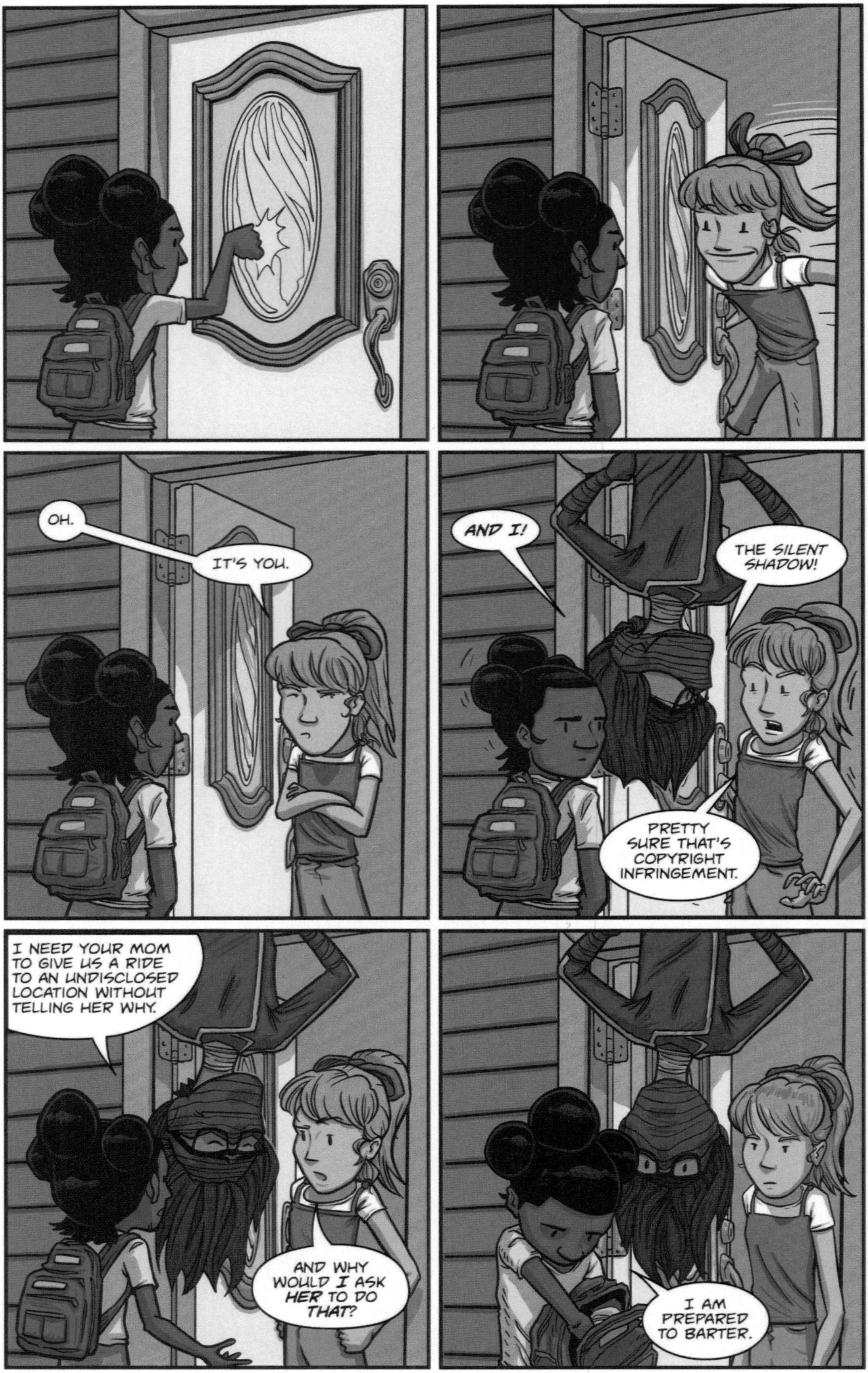
OH.
IT'S YOU.
AND I!
THE SILENT SHADOW!
PRETTY SURE THAT'S COPYRIGHT INFRINGEMENT.
I NEED YOUR MOM TO GIVE US A RIDE TO AN UNDISCLOSED LOCATION WITHOUT TELLING HER WHY.
AND WHY WOULD *I* ASK *HER* TO DO *THAT*?
I AM PREPARED TO BARTER.

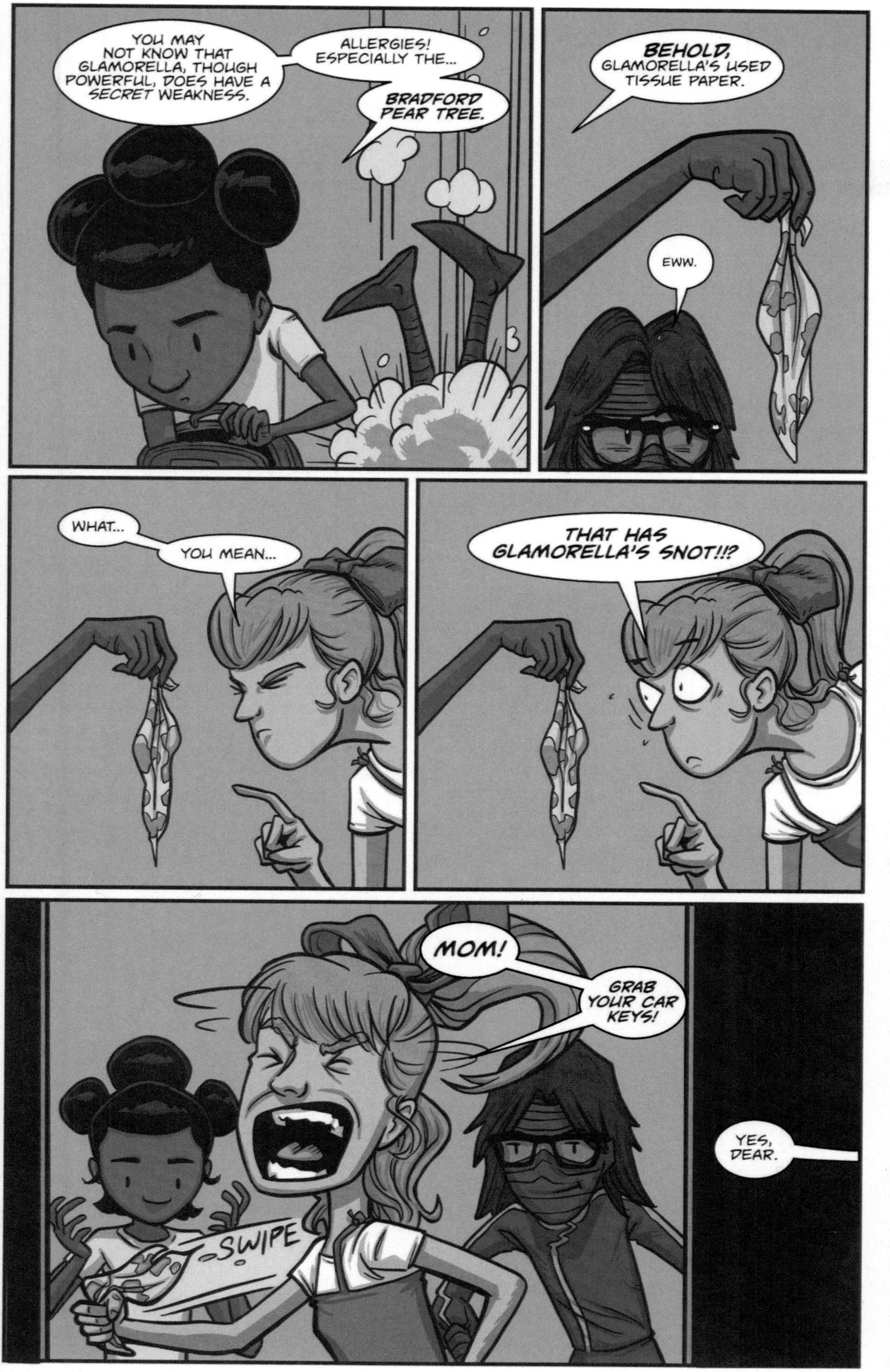
YOU MAY NOT KNOW THAT GLAMORELLA, THOUGH POWERFUL, DOES HAVE A SECRET WEAKNESS.
ALLERGIES! ESPECIALLY THE...
BRADFORD PEAR TREE.
BEHOLD, GLAMORELLA'S USED TISSUE PAPER.
EWW.
WHAT...
YOU MEAN...
THAT HAS GLAMORELLA'S SNOT!!?
MOM!
GRAB YOUR CAR KEYS!
YES, DEAR.
SWIPE

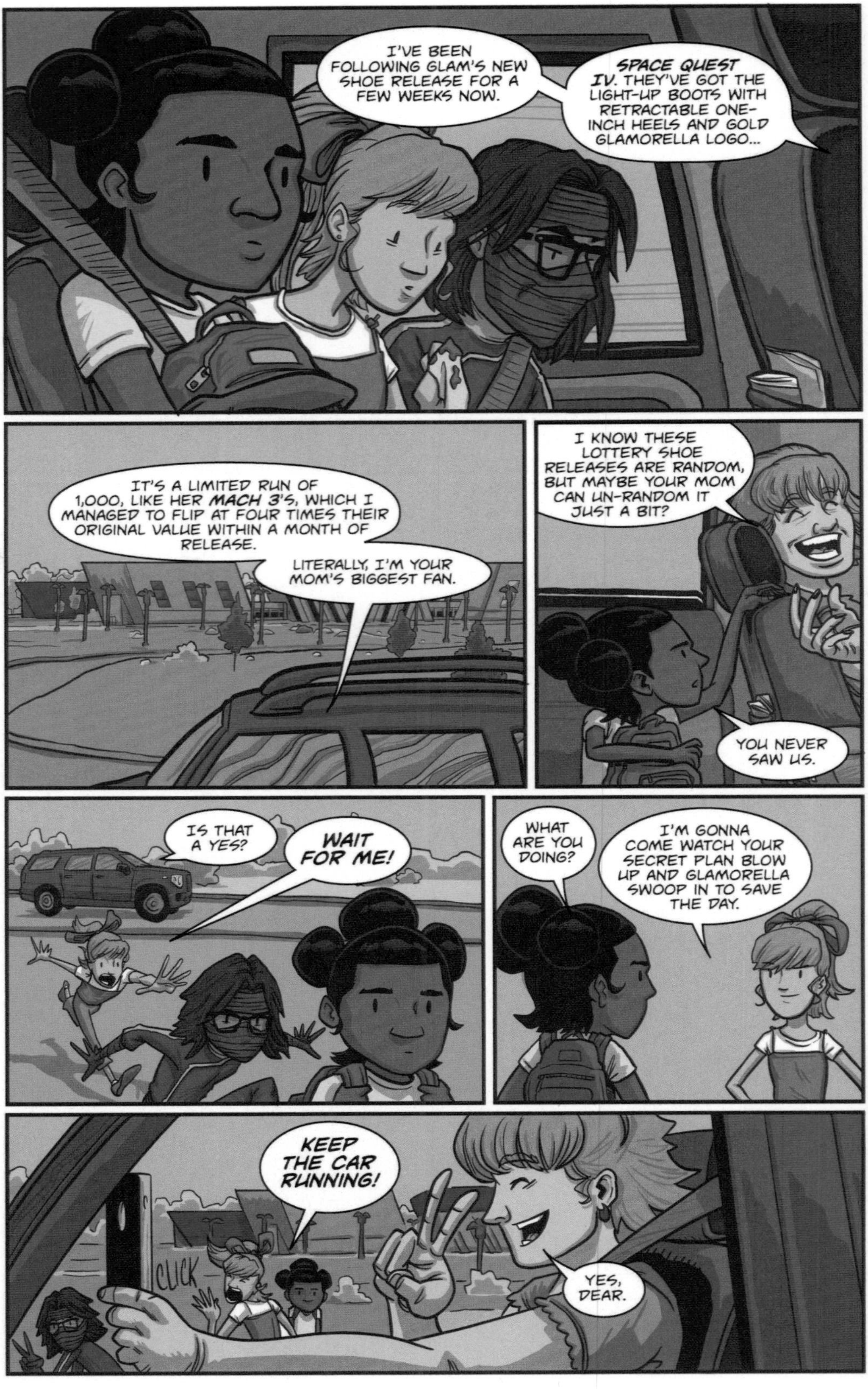
I'VE BEEN FOLLOWING GLAM'S NEW SHOE RELEASE FOR A FEW WEEKS NOW.
SPACE QUEST IV. THEY'VE GOT THE LIGHT-UP BOOTS WITH RETRACTABLE ONE-INCH HEELS AND GOLD GLAMORELLA LOGO...
IT'S A LIMITED RUN OF 1,000, LIKE HER *MACH 3*'S, WHICH I MANAGED TO FLIP AT FOUR TIMES THEIR ORIGINAL VALUE WITHIN A MONTH OF RELEASE.
LITERALLY, I'M YOUR MOM'S BIGGEST FAN.
I KNOW THESE LOTTERY SHOE RELEASES ARE RANDOM, BUT MAYBE YOUR MOM CAN UN-RANDOM IT JUST A BIT?
YOU NEVER SAW US.
IS THAT A YES?
WAIT FOR ME!
WHAT ARE YOU DOING?
I'M GONNA COME WATCH YOUR SECRET PLAN BLOW UP AND GLAMORELLA SWOOP IN TO SAVE THE DAY.
KEEP THE CAR RUNNING!
CLICK
YES, DEAR.

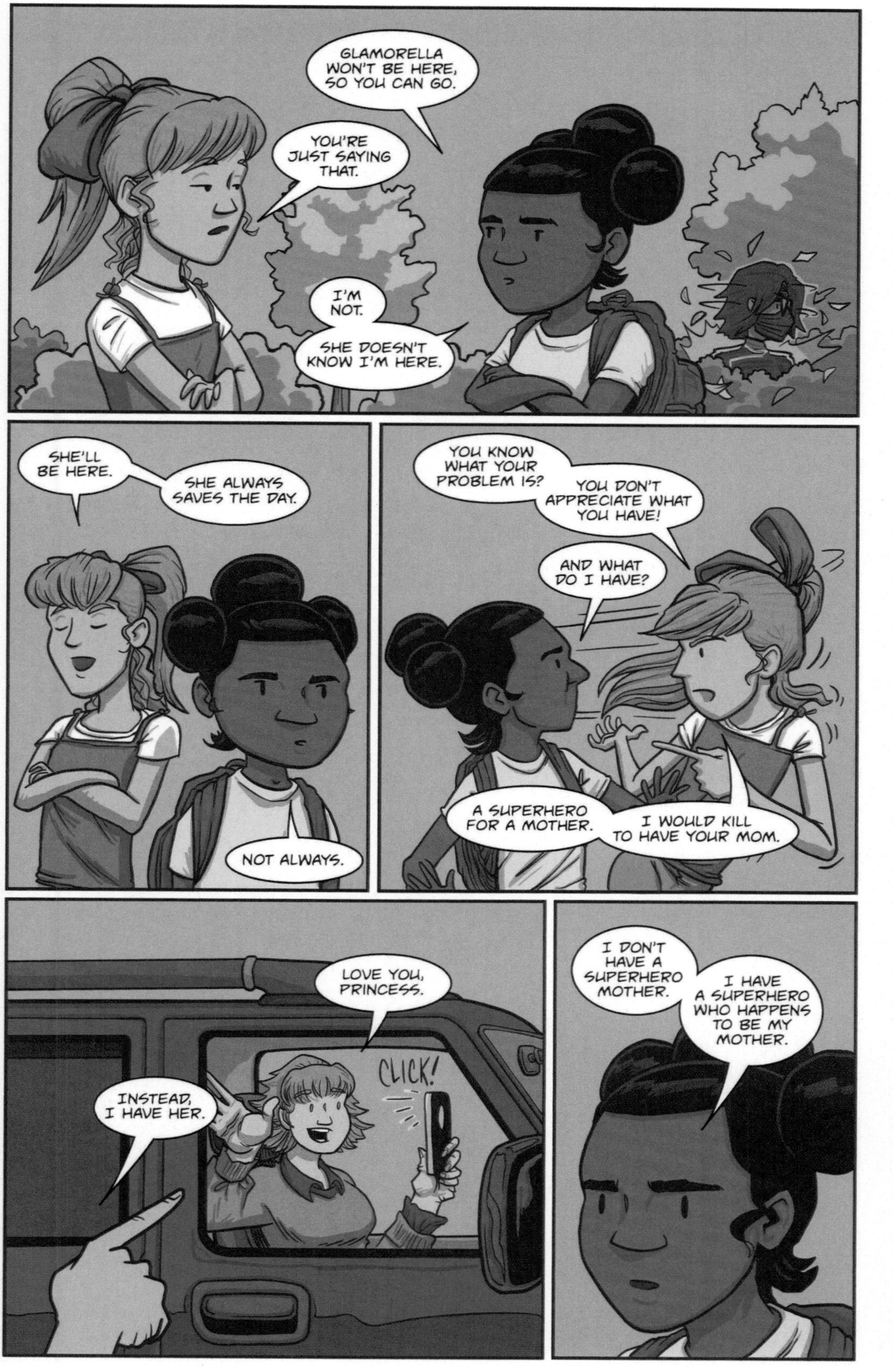
GLAMORELLA WON'T BE HERE, SO YOU CAN GO.
YOU'RE JUST SAYING THAT.
I'M NOT.
SHE DOESN'T KNOW I'M HERE.
SHE'LL BE HERE.
SHE ALWAYS SAVES THE DAY.
NOT ALWAYS.
YOU KNOW WHAT YOUR PROBLEM IS?
YOU DON'T APPRECIATE WHAT YOU HAVE!
AND WHAT DO I HAVE?
A SUPERHERO FOR A MOTHER.
I WOULD KILL TO HAVE YOUR MOM.
LOVE YOU, PRINCESS.
CLICK!
INSTEAD, I HAVE HER.
I DON'T HAVE A SUPERHERO MOTHER.
I HAVE A SUPERHERO WHO HAPPENS TO BE MY MOTHER.

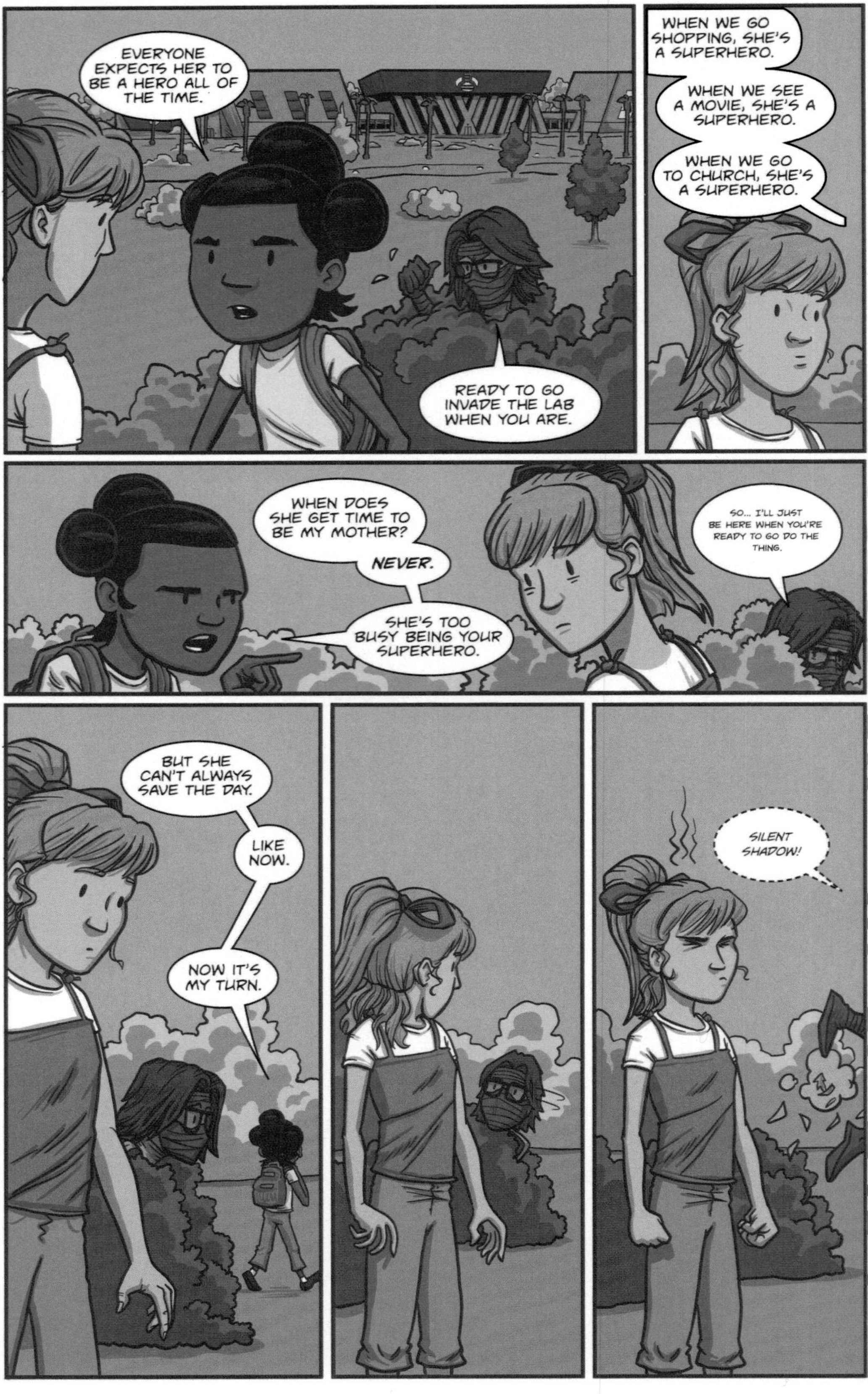
EVERYONE EXPECTS HER TO BE A HERO ALL OF THE TIME.
READY TO GO INVADE THE LAB WHEN YOU ARE.
WHEN WE GO SHOPPING, SHE'S A SUPERHERO.
WHEN WE SEE A MOVIE, SHE'S A SUPERHERO.
WHEN WE GO TO CHURCH, SHE'S A SUPERHERO.
WHEN DOES SHE GET TIME TO BE MY MOTHER?
NEVER.
SHE'S TOO BUSY BEING YOUR SUPERHERO.
SO... I'LL JUST BE HERE WHEN YOU'RE READY TO GO DO THE THING.
BUT SHE CAN'T ALWAYS SAVE THE DAY.
LIKE NOW.
NOW IT'S MY TURN.
SILENT SHADOW!

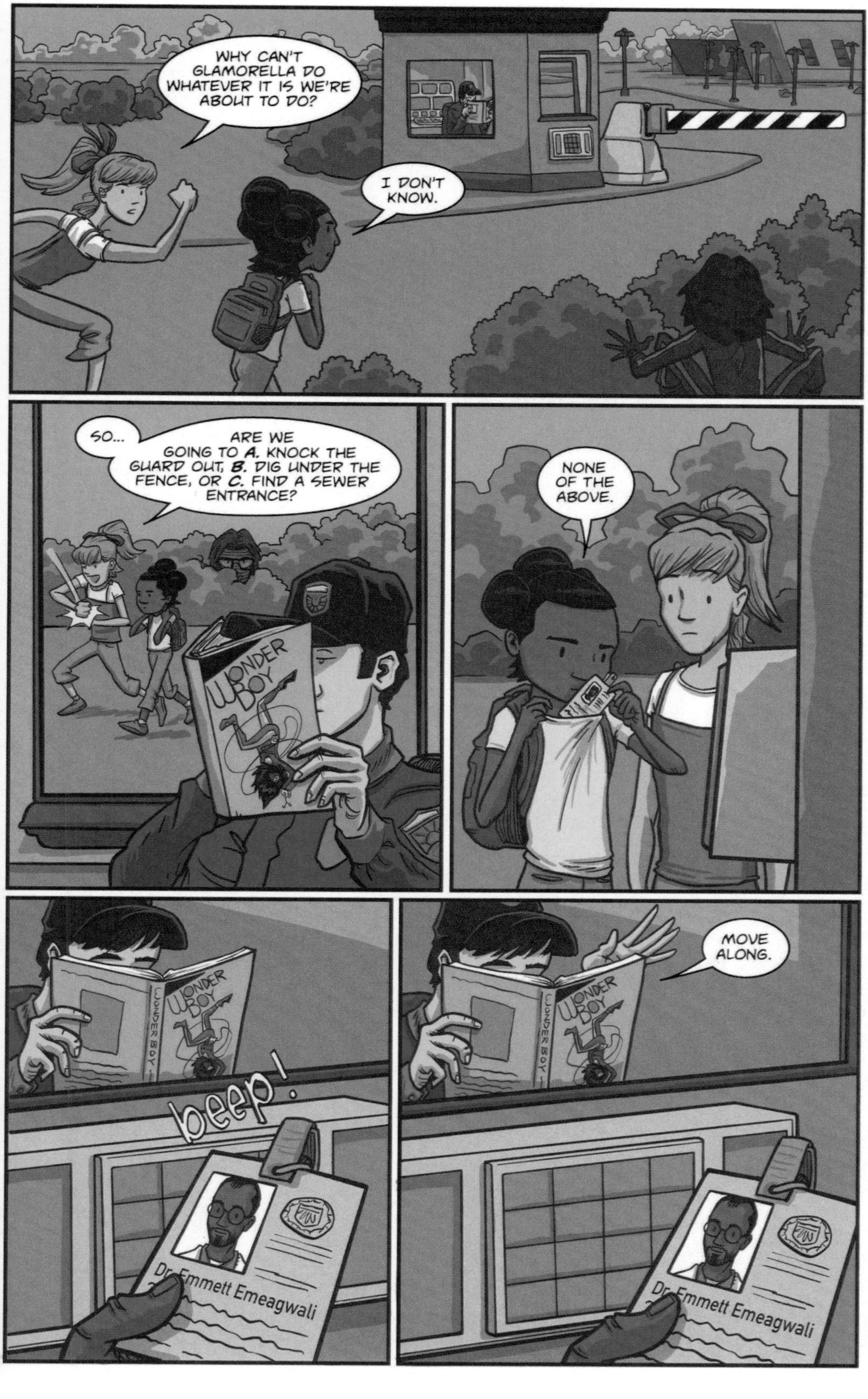
WHY CAN'T GLAMORELLA DO WHATEVER IT IS WE'RE ABOUT TO DO?
I DON'T KNOW.
SO...
ARE WE GOING TO A. KNOCK THE GUARD OUT, B. DIG UNDER THE FENCE, OR C. FIND A SEWER ENTRANCE?
WONDER BOY
NONE OF THE ABOVE.
WONDER BOY
WONDER BOY
beep!
Dr. Emmett Emeagwali
MOVE ALONG.
WONDER BOY
WONDER BOY
Dr. Emmett Emeagwali

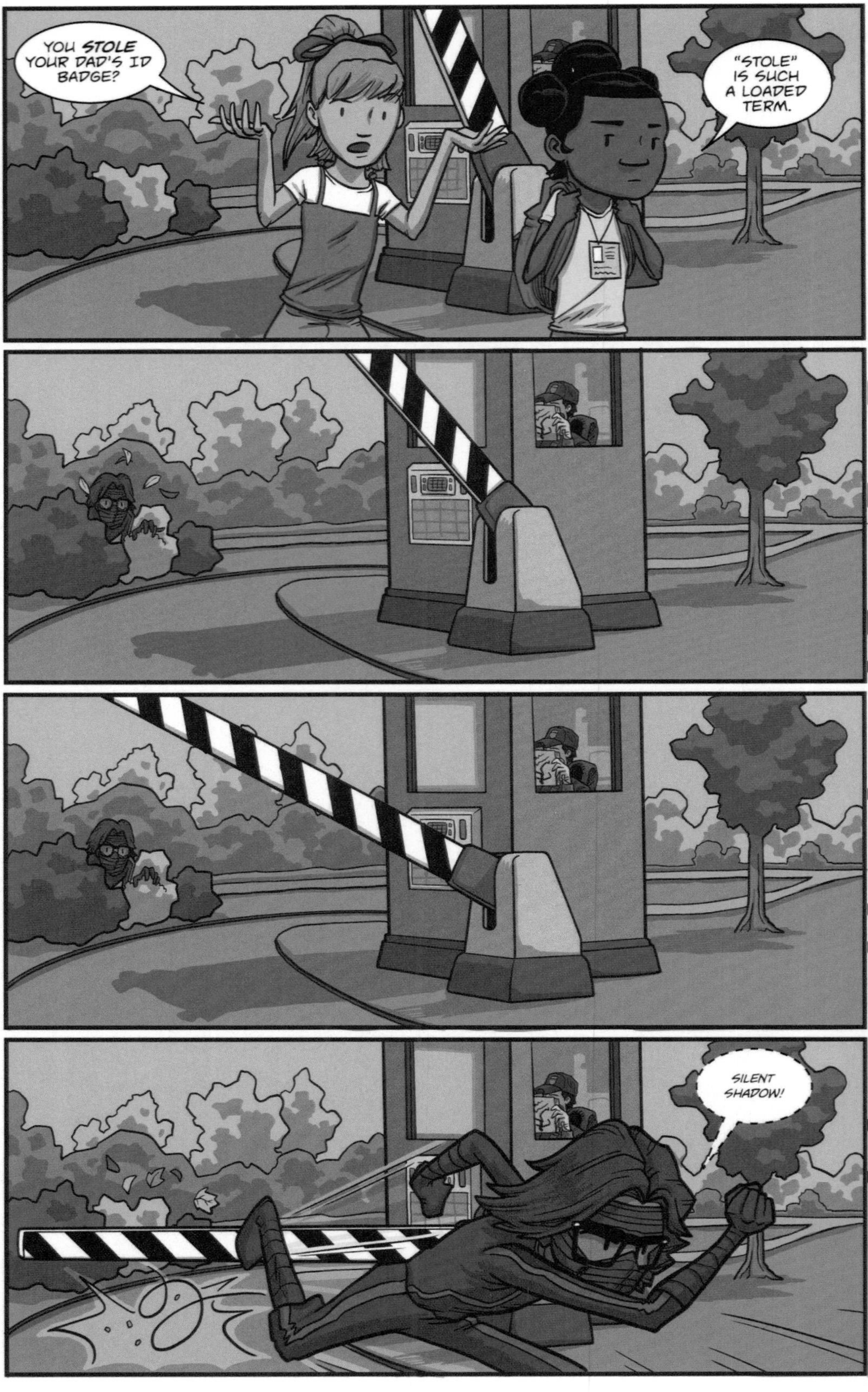
YOU STOLE YOUR DAD'S ID BADGE?
"STOLE" IS SUCH A LOADED TERM.
SILENT SHADOW!

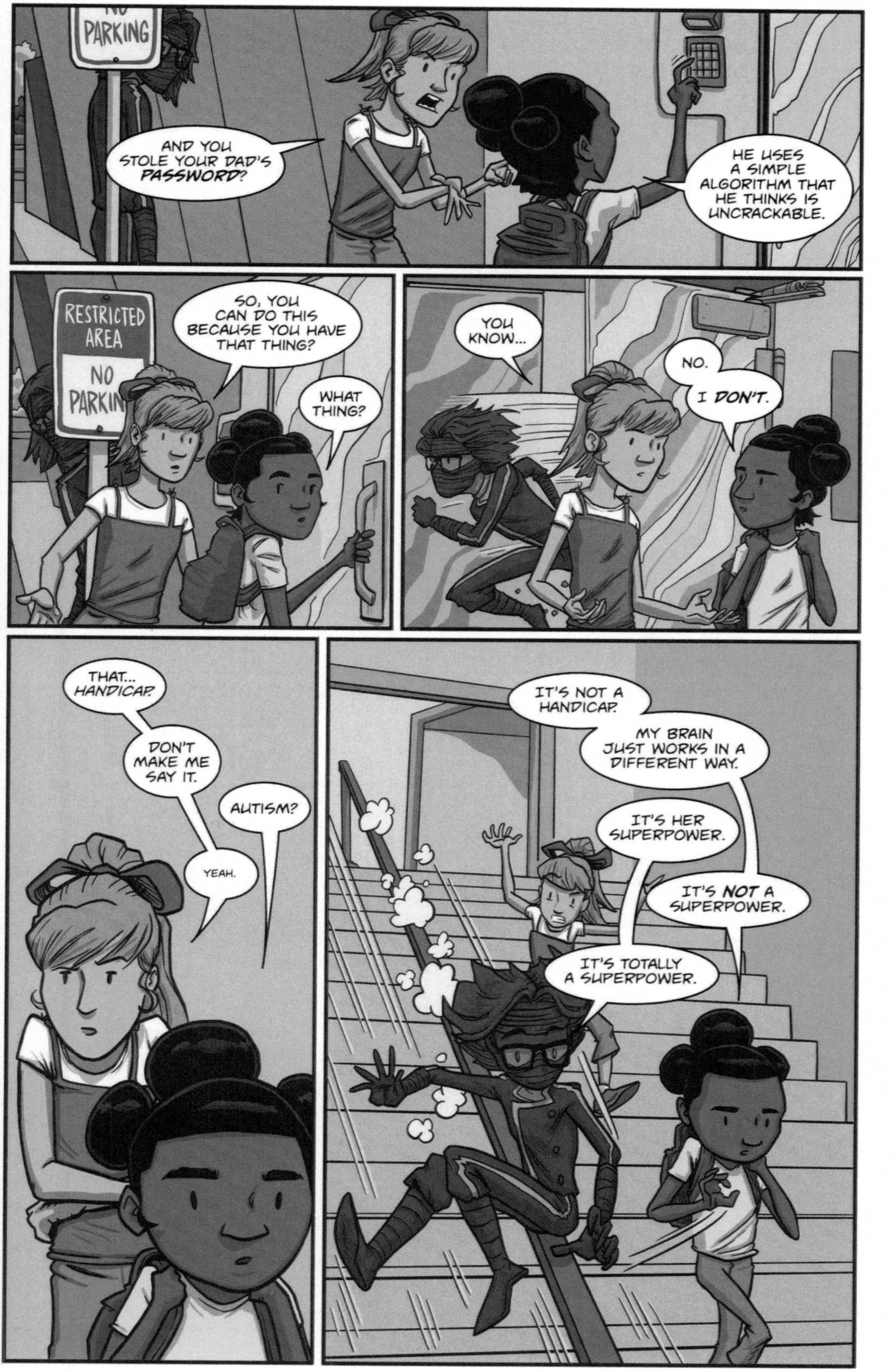
NO PARKING
AND YOU STOLE YOUR DAD'S PASSWORD?
HE USES A SIMPLE ALGORITHM THAT HE THINKS IS UNCRACKABLE.
RESTRICTED AREA NO PARKIN
SO, YOU CAN DO THIS BECAUSE YOU HAVE THAT THING?
WHAT THING?
YOU KNOW...
NO.
I DON'T.
THAT... HANDICAP.
DON'T MAKE ME SAY IT.
AUTISM?
YEAH.
IT'S NOT A HANDICAP.
MY BRAIN JUST WORKS IN A DIFFERENT WAY.
IT'S HER SUPERPOWER.
IT'S NOT A SUPERPOWER.
IT'S TOTALLY A SUPERPOWER.

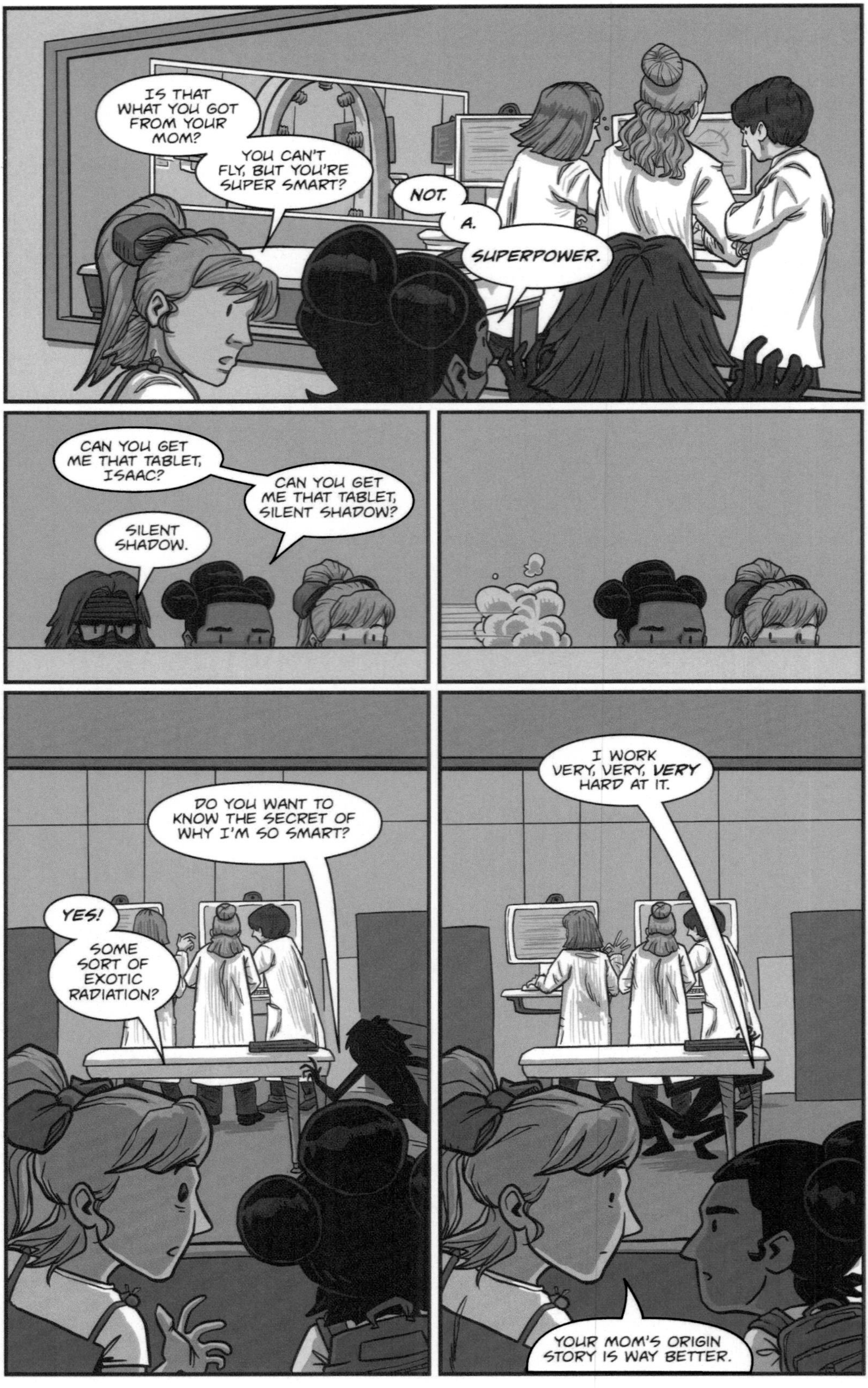
IS THAT WHAT YOU GOT FROM YOUR MOM?
YOU CAN'T FLY, BUT YOU'RE SUPER SMART?
NOT.
A.
SUPERPOWER.
CAN YOU GET ME THAT TABLET, ISAAC?
CAN YOU GET ME THAT TABLET, SILENT SHADOW?
SILENT SHADOW.
DO YOU WANT TO KNOW THE SECRET OF WHY I'M SO SMART?
YES!
SOME SORT OF EXOTIC RADIATION?
I WORK VERY, VERY, VERY HARD AT IT.
YOUR MOM'S ORIGIN STORY IS WAY BETTER.

PRINCESS PARTIES, SCHOOL DANCES, AND SUPERPOWERS ARE BORING TO ME.

BUT THIS...

THIS IS THE EXCITING STUFF.

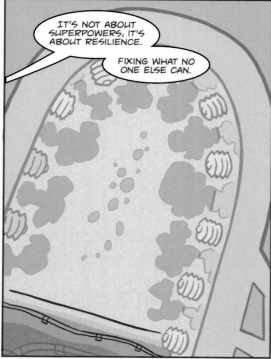

IT'S NOT ABOUT SUPERPOWERS, IT'S ABOUT RESILIENCE.

FIXING WHAT NO ONE ELSE CAN.

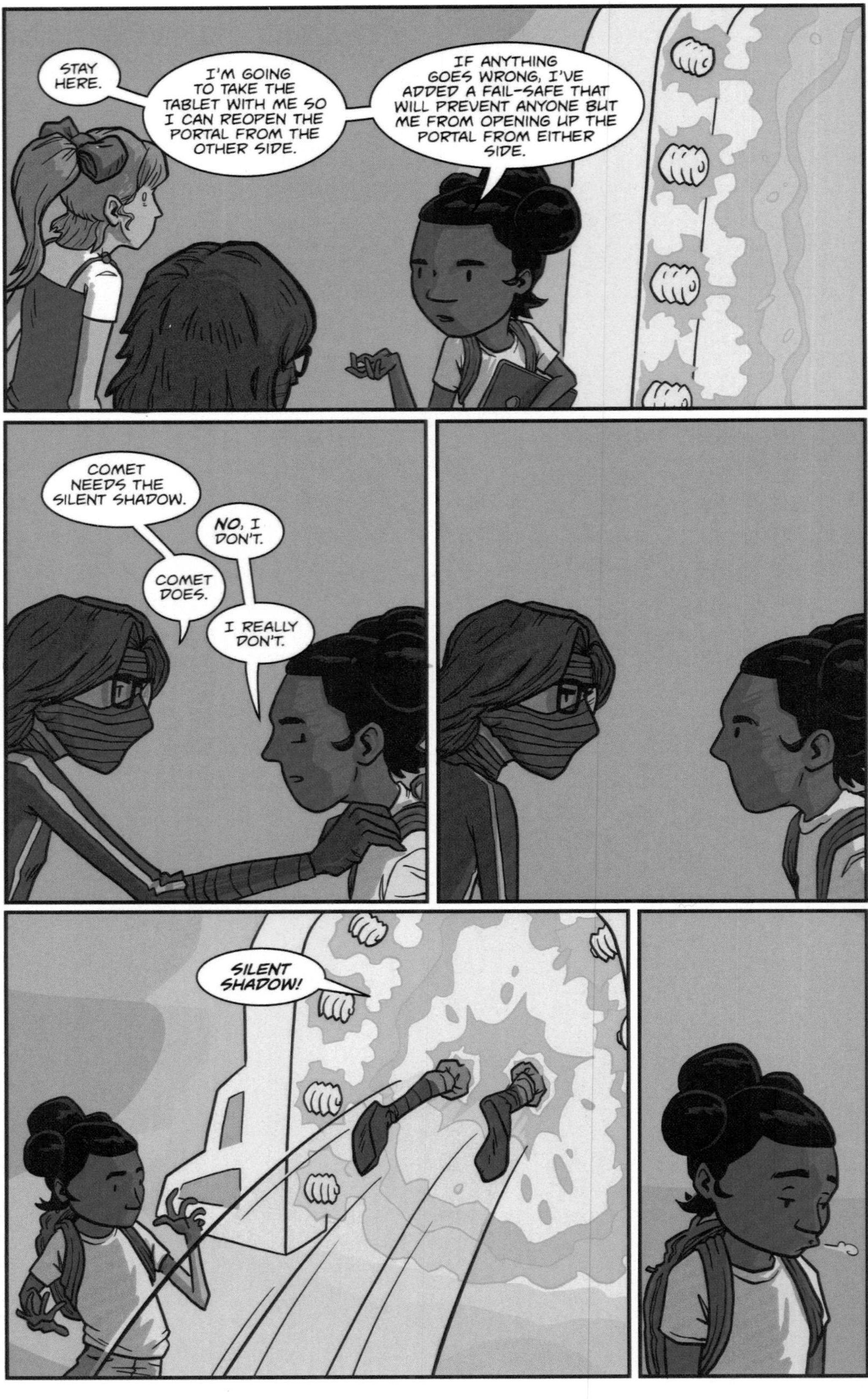
STAY HERE.
I'M GOING TO TAKE THE TABLET WITH ME SO I CAN REOPEN THE PORTAL FROM THE OTHER SIDE.
IF ANYTHING GOES WRONG, I'VE ADDED A FAIL-SAFE THAT WILL PREVENT ANYONE BUT ME FROM OPENING UP THE PORTAL FROM EITHER SIDE.
COMET NEEDS THE SILENT SHADOW.
NO, I DON'T.
COMET DOES.
I REALLY DON'T.
SILENT SHADOW!

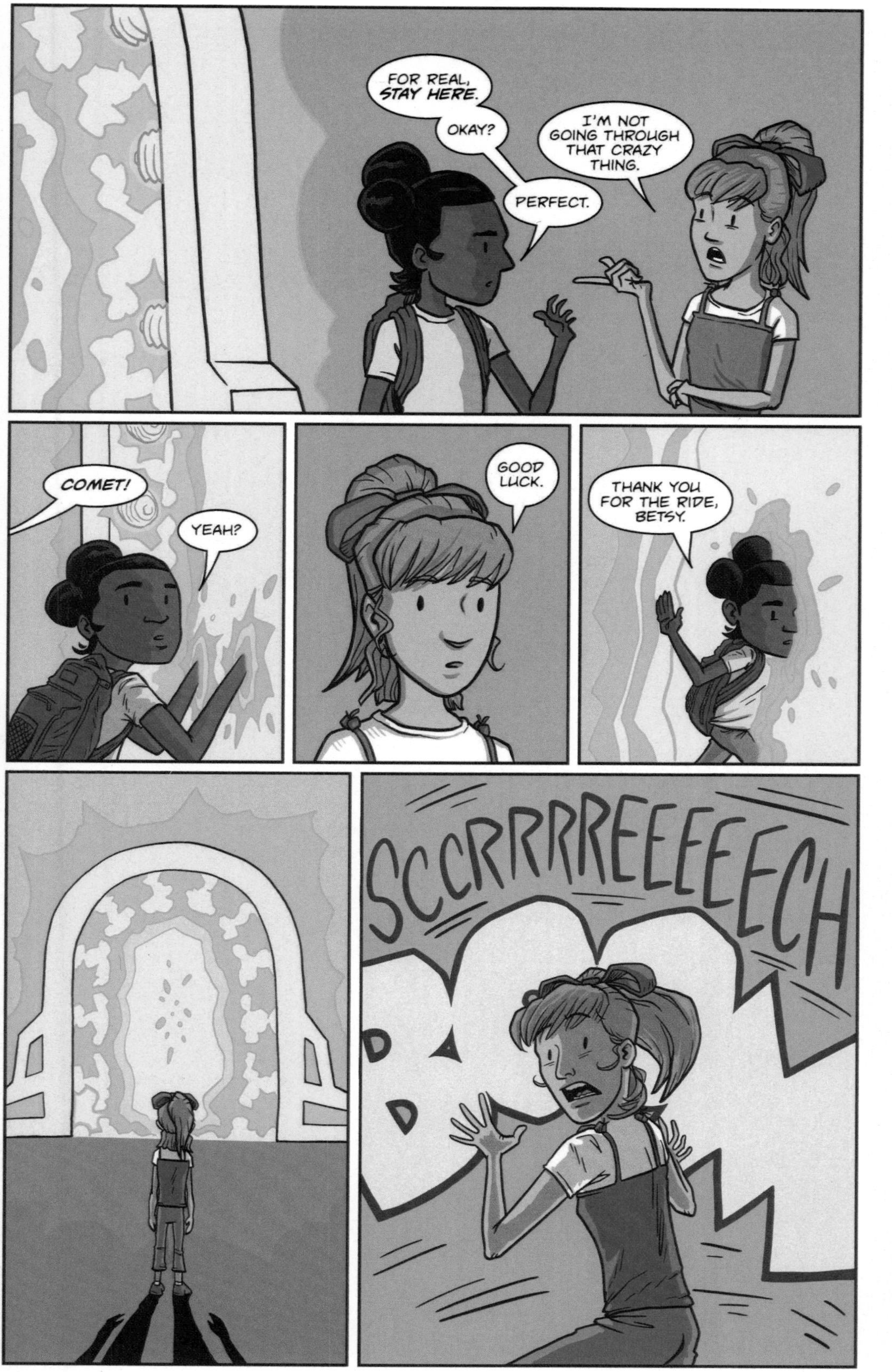
FOR REAL, *STAY HERE.*
OKAY?
I'M NOT GOING THROUGH THAT CRAZY THING.
PERFECT.
COMET!
YEAH?
GOOD LUCK.
THANK YOU FOR THE RIDE, BETSY.
SCCRRRRREEEEECH

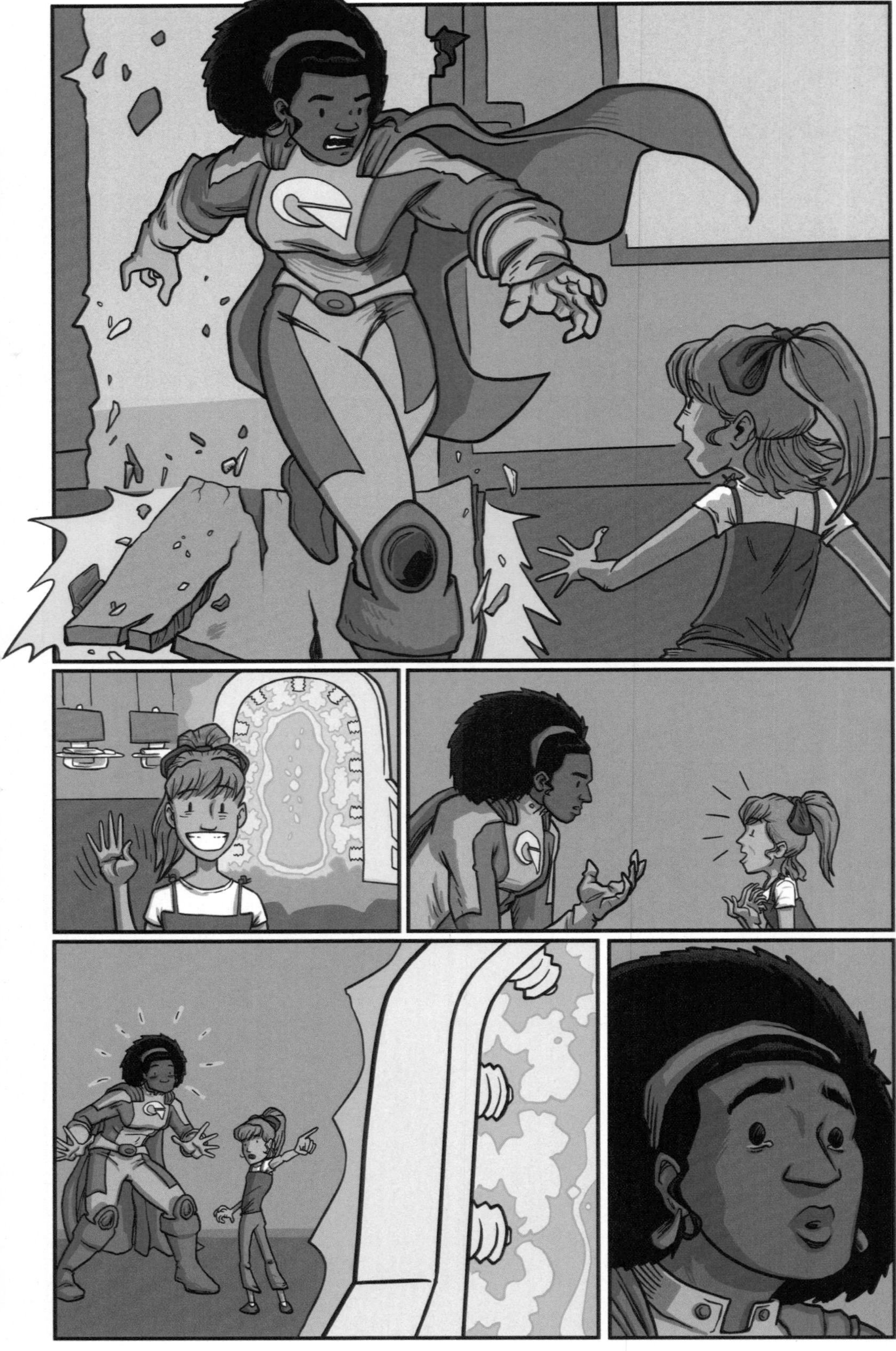

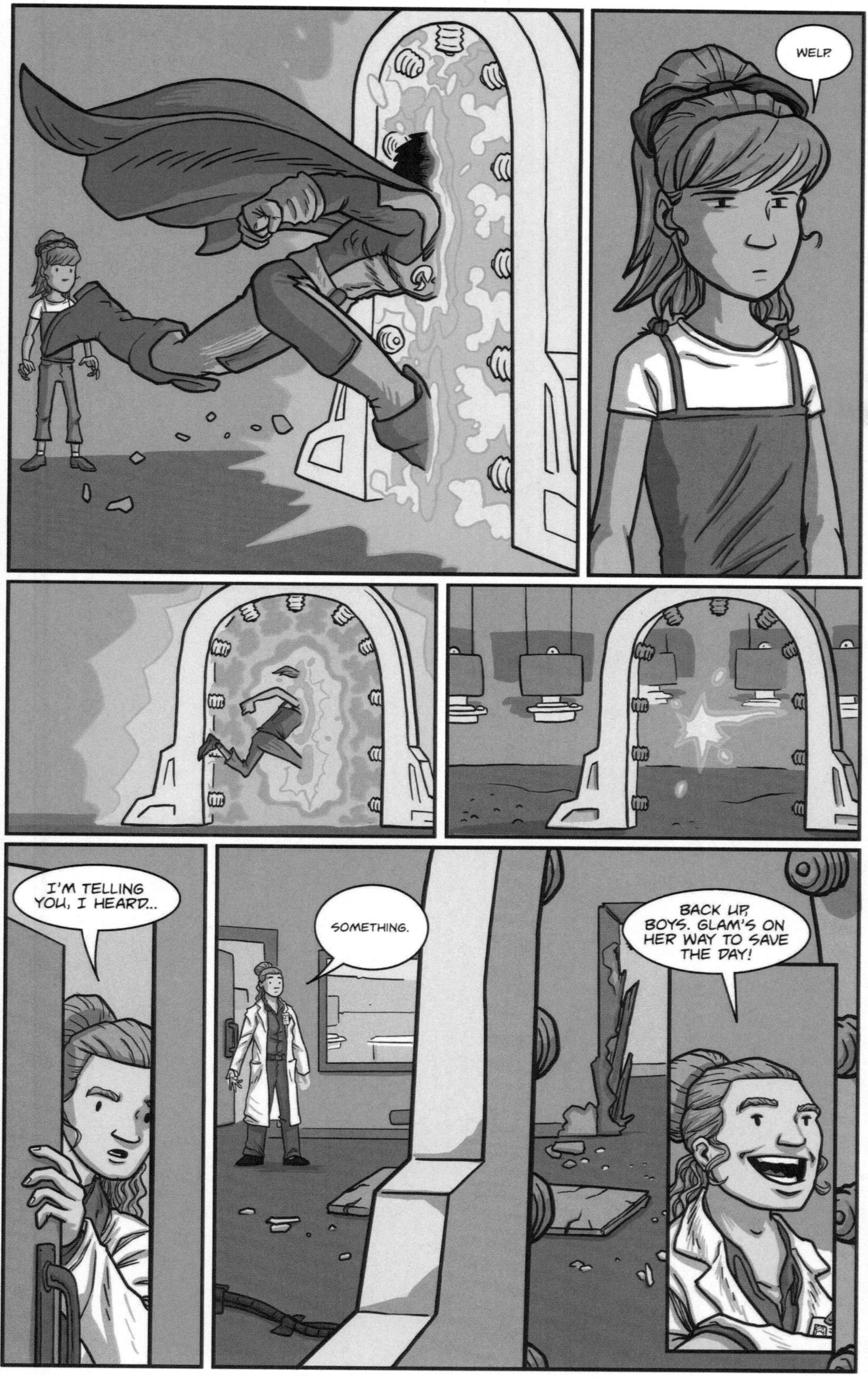
WELP.
I'M TELLING YOU, I HEARD...
SOMETHING.
BACK UP, BOYS. GLAM'S ON HER WAY TO SAVE THE DAY!

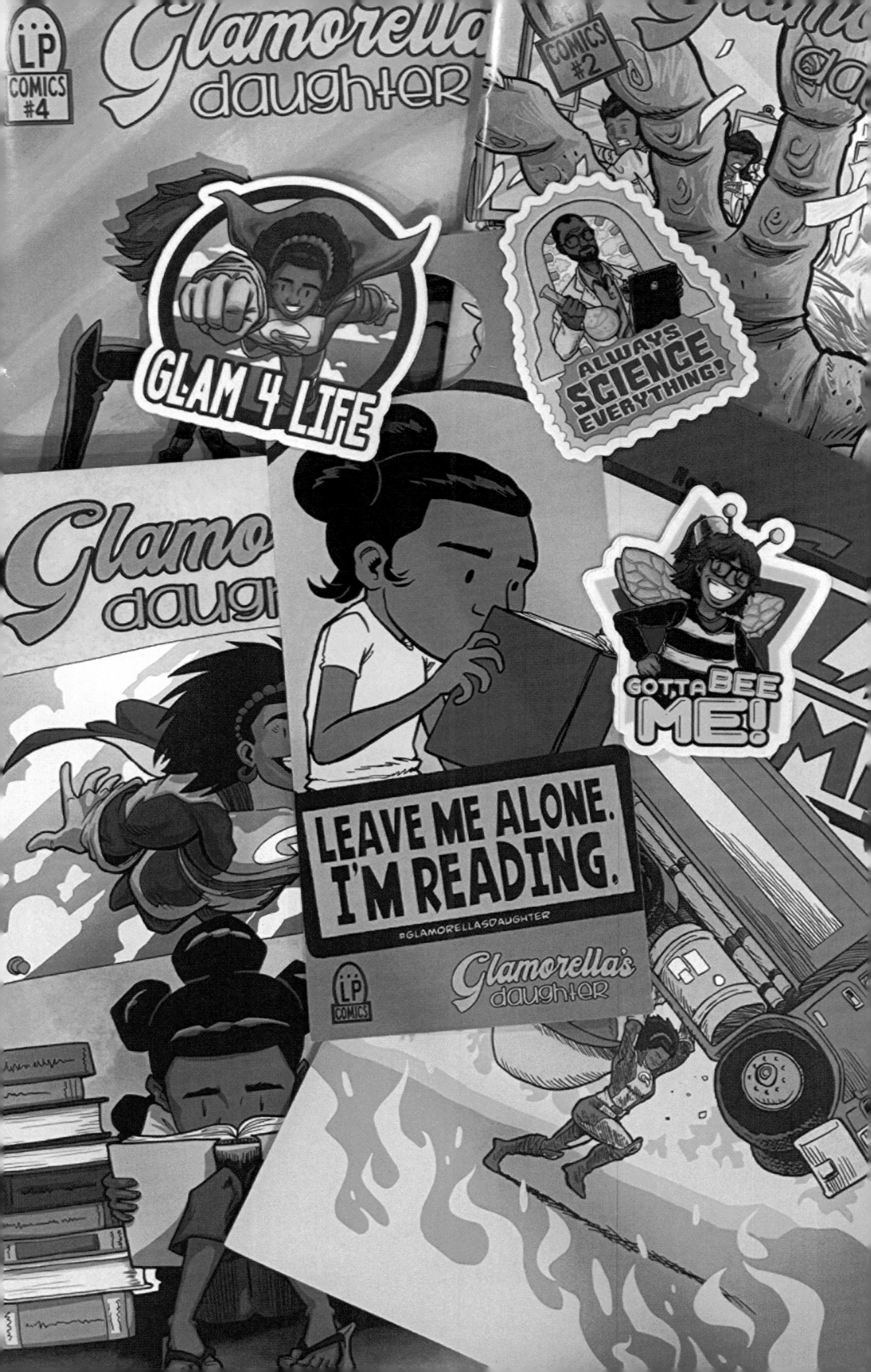

LP
COMICS #4
Glamorella
daughter
COMICS #2
GLAM 4 LIFE
ALWAYS SCIENCE EVERYTHING!
GOTTA BEE ME!
LEAVE ME ALONE. I'M READING.
#GLAMORELLASDAUGHTER
LP COMICS
Glamorella's daughter

Glamorella's daughter

Presents

"Not Particularly"

Starring . . . ISAAC!

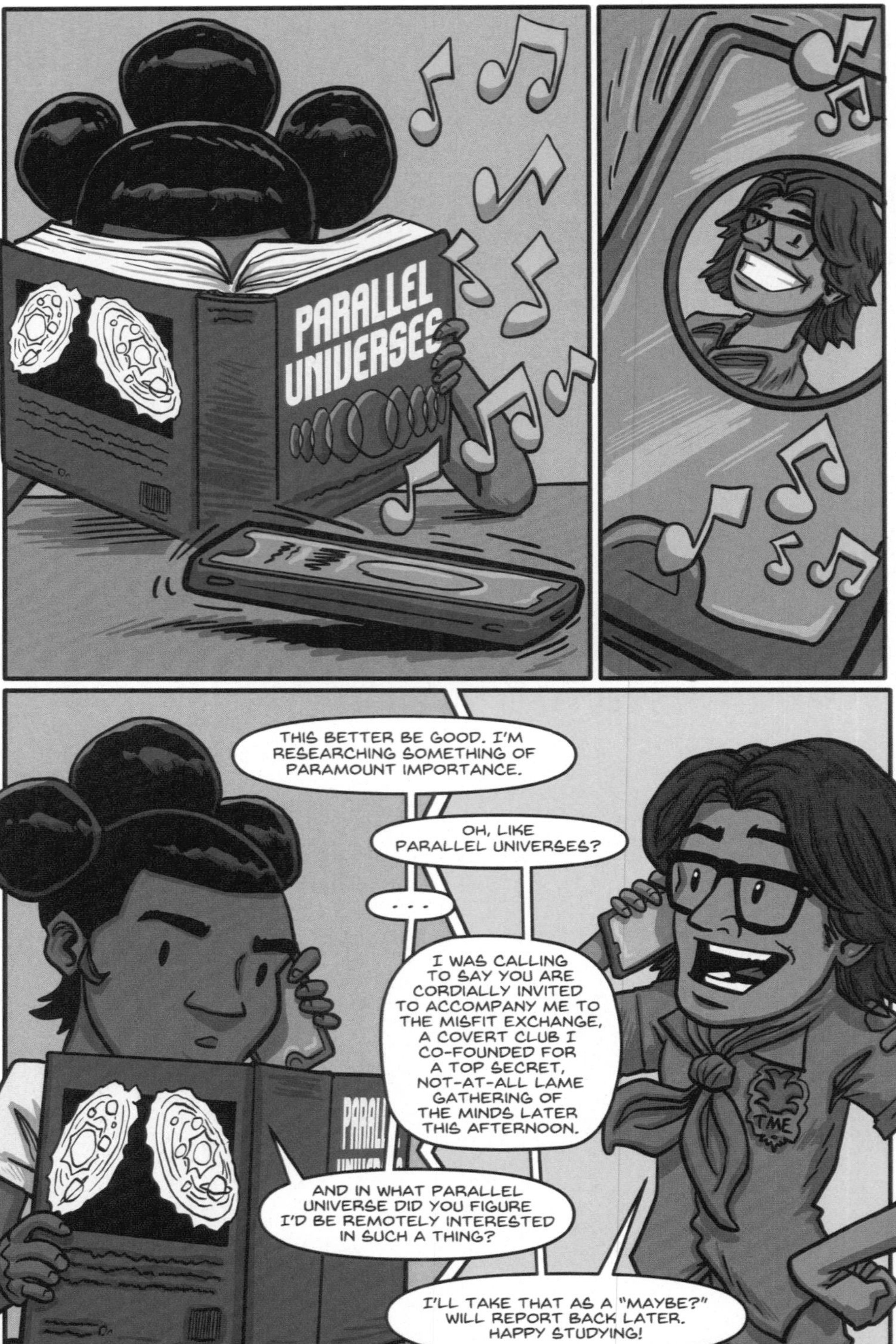
PARALLEL UNIVERSES
THIS BETTER BE GOOD. I'M RESEARCHING SOMETHING OF PARAMOUNT IMPORTANCE.
OH, LIKE PARALLEL UNIVERSES?
. . .
I WAS CALLING TO SAY YOU ARE CORDIALLY INVITED TO ACCOMPANY ME TO THE MISFIT EXCHANGE, A COVERT CLUB I CO-FOUNDED FOR A TOP SECRET, NOT-AT-ALL LAME GATHERING OF THE MINDS LATER THIS AFTERNOON.
AND IN WHAT PARALLEL UNIVERSE DID YOU FIGURE I'D BE REMOTELY INTERESTED IN SUCH A THING?
I'LL TAKE THAT AS A "MAYBE?" WILL REPORT BACK LATER. HAPPY STUDYING!

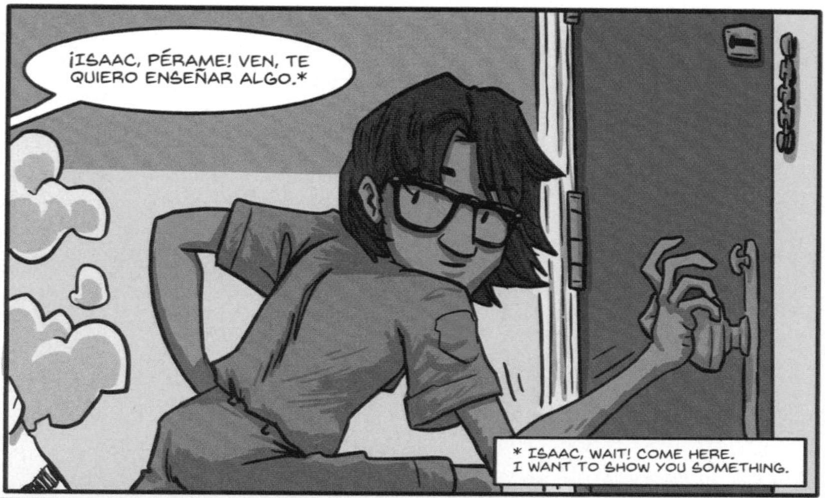
¡ISAAC, PÉRAME! VEN, TE QUIERO ENSEÑAR ALGO.*
* ISAAC, WAIT! COME HERE. I WANT TO SHOW YOU SOMETHING.

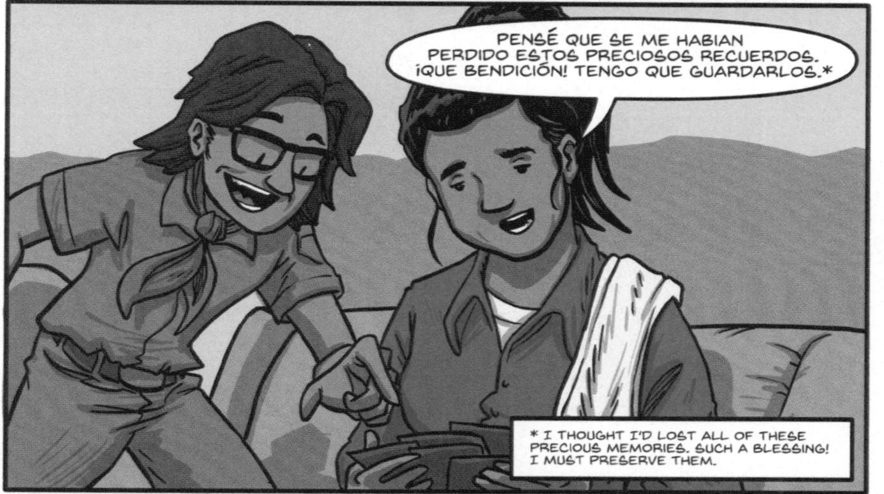
PENSÉ QUE SE ME HABIAN PERDIDO ESTOS PRECIOSOS RECUERDOS. ¡QUE BENDICIÓN! TENGO QUE GUARDARLOS.*
* I THOUGHT I'D LOST ALL OF THESE PRECIOUS MEMORIES. SUCH A BLESSING! I MUST PRESERVE THEM.

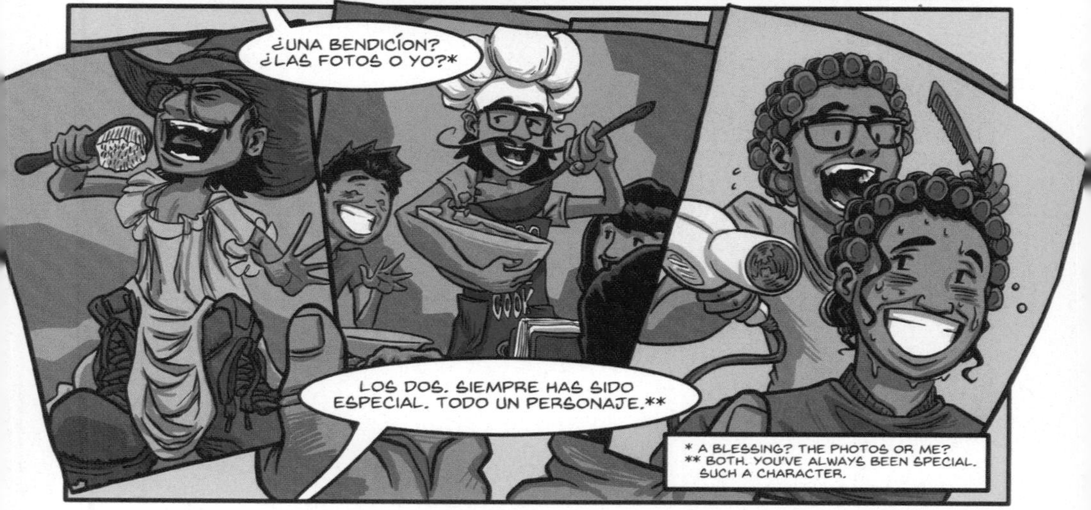
¿UNA BENDICÍON? ¿LAS FOTOS O YO?*
LOS DOS. SIEMPRE HAS SIDO ESPECIAL. TODO UN PERSONAJE.**
* A BLESSING? THE PHOTOS OR ME?
** BOTH. YOU'VE ALWAYS BEEN SPECIAL. SUCH A CHARACTER.

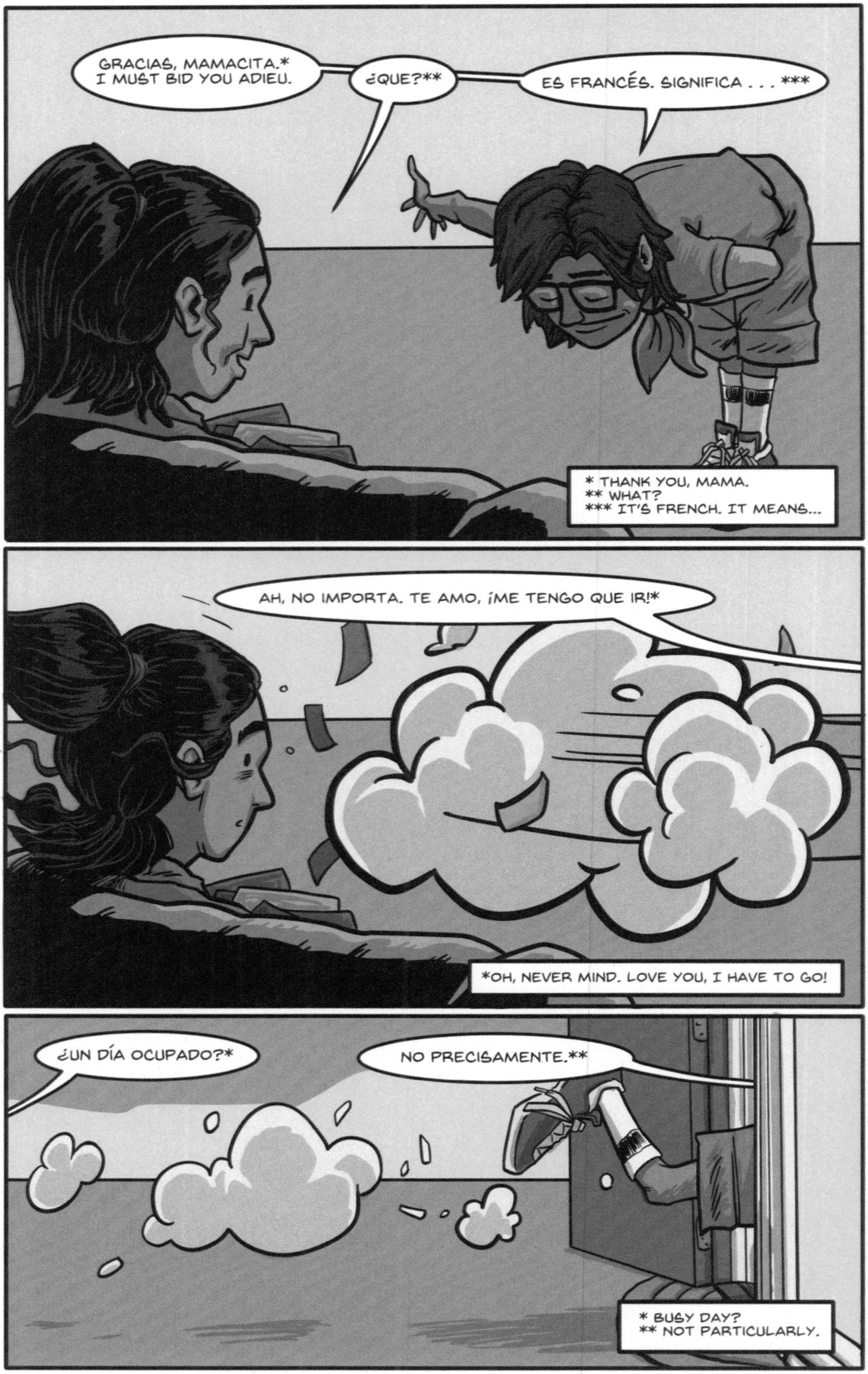

GRACIAS, MAMACITA.* I MUST BID YOU ADIEU.
¿QUE?**
ES FRANCÉS. SIGNIFICA . . . ***
* THANK YOU, MAMA.
** WHAT?
*** IT'S FRENCH. IT MEANS...
AH, NO IMPORTA. TE AMO, ¡ME TENGO QUE IR!*
*OH, NEVER MIND. LOVE YOU, I HAVE TO GO!
¿UN DÍA OCUPADO?*
NO PRECISAMENTE.**
* BUSY DAY?
** NOT PARTICULARLY.

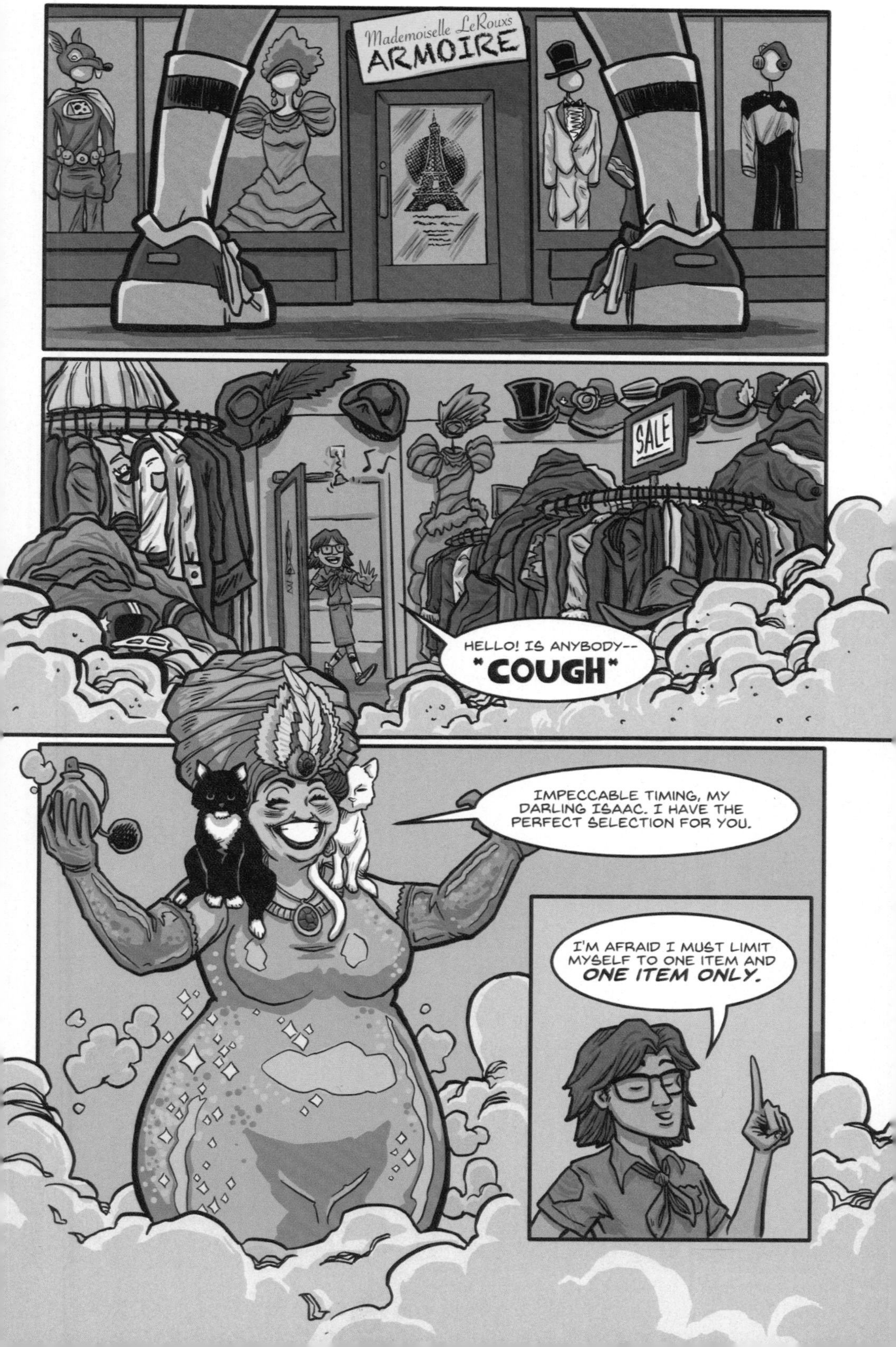

Mademoiselle LeRoux's
ARMOIRE
SALE
HELLO! IS ANYBODY--
COUGH
IMPECCABLE TIMING, MY DARLING ISAAC. I HAVE THE PERFECT SELECTION FOR YOU.
I'M AFRAID I MUST LIMIT MYSELF TO ONE ITEM AND ONE ITEM ONLY.

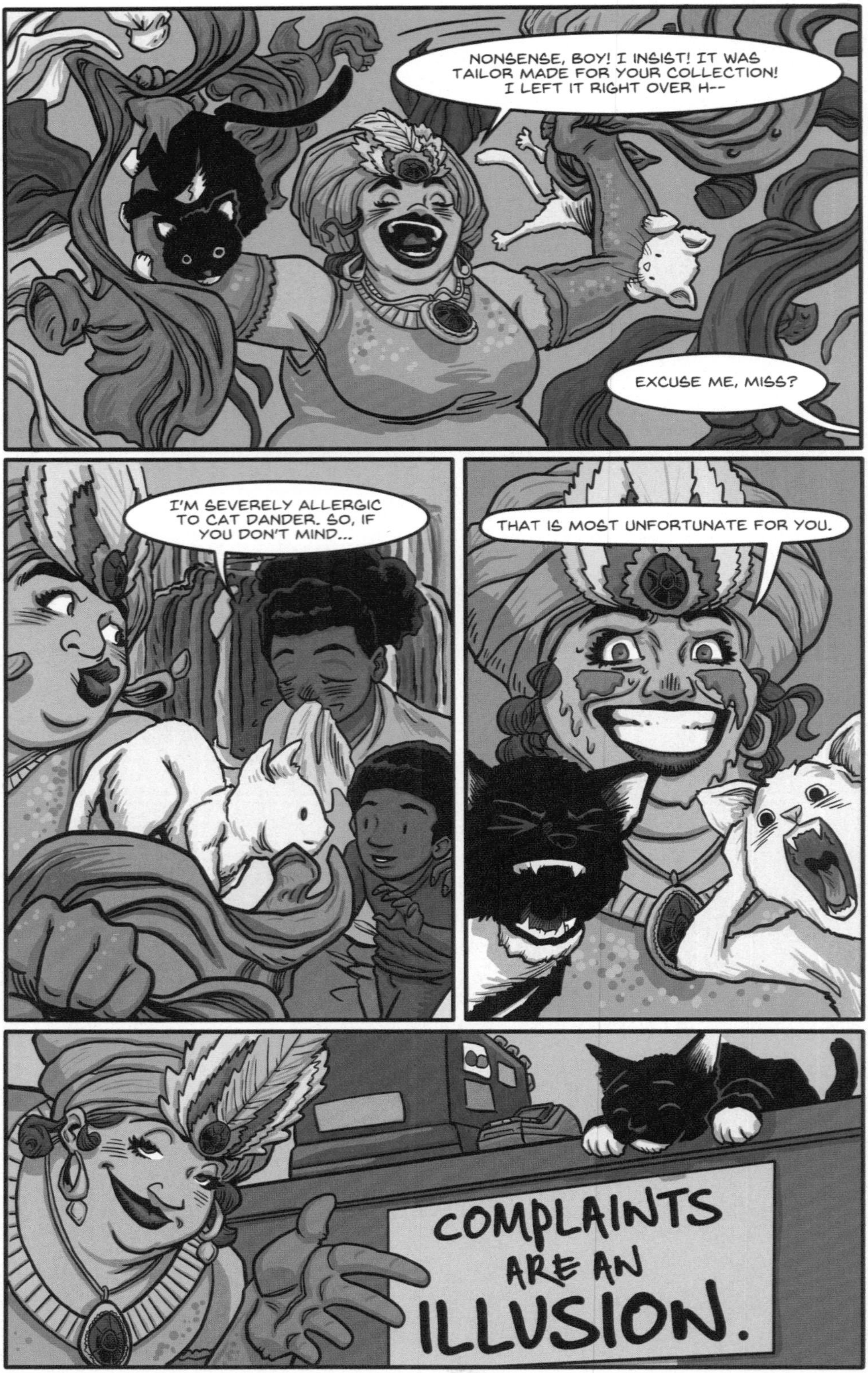
NONSENSE, BOY! I INSIST! IT WAS TAILOR MADE FOR YOUR COLLECTION! I LEFT IT RIGHT OVER H--
EXCUSE ME, MISS?
I'M SEVERELY ALLERGIC TO CAT DANDER. SO, IF YOU DON'T MIND...
THAT IS MOST UNFORTUNATE FOR YOU.
COMPLAINTS ARE AN ILLUSION.

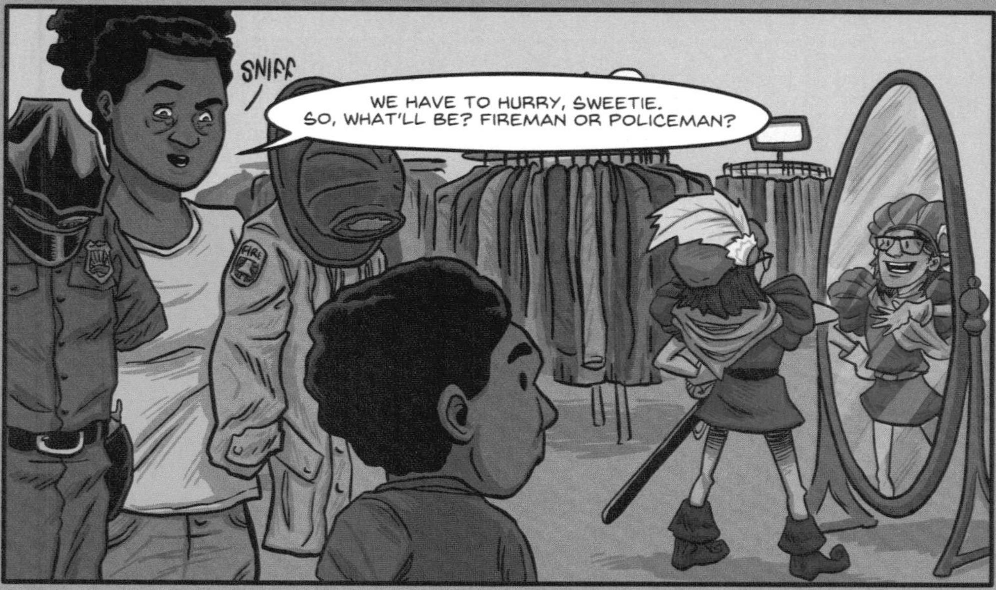
SNIFF
WE HAVE TO HURRY, SWEETIE. SO, WHAT'LL BE? FIREMAN OR POLICEMAN?

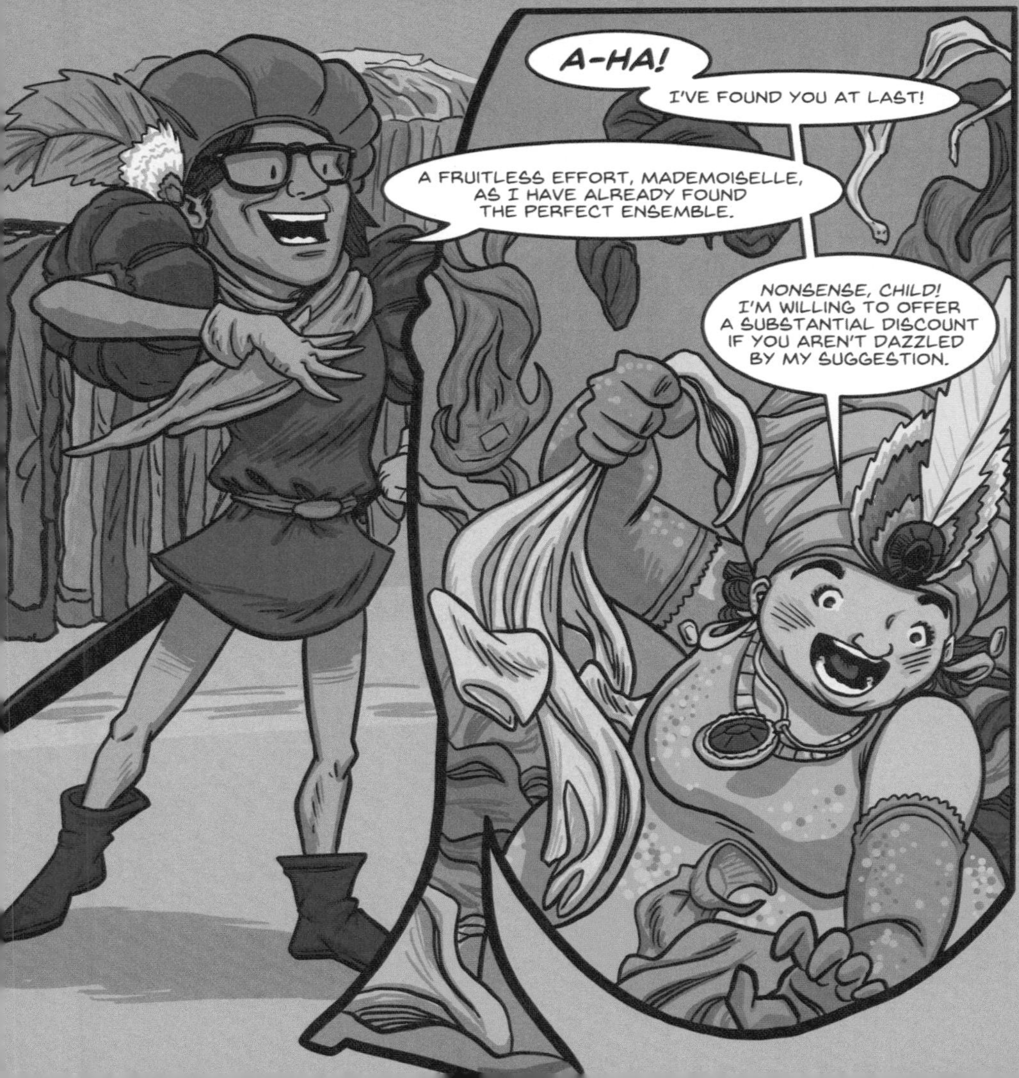
A-HA!
I'VE FOUND YOU AT LAST!
A FRUITLESS EFFORT, MADEMOISELLE, AS I HAVE ALREADY FOUND THE PERFECT ENSEMBLE.
NONSENSE, CHILD! I'M WILLING TO OFFER A SUBSTANTIAL DISCOUNT IF YOU AREN'T DAZZLED BY MY SUGGESTION.

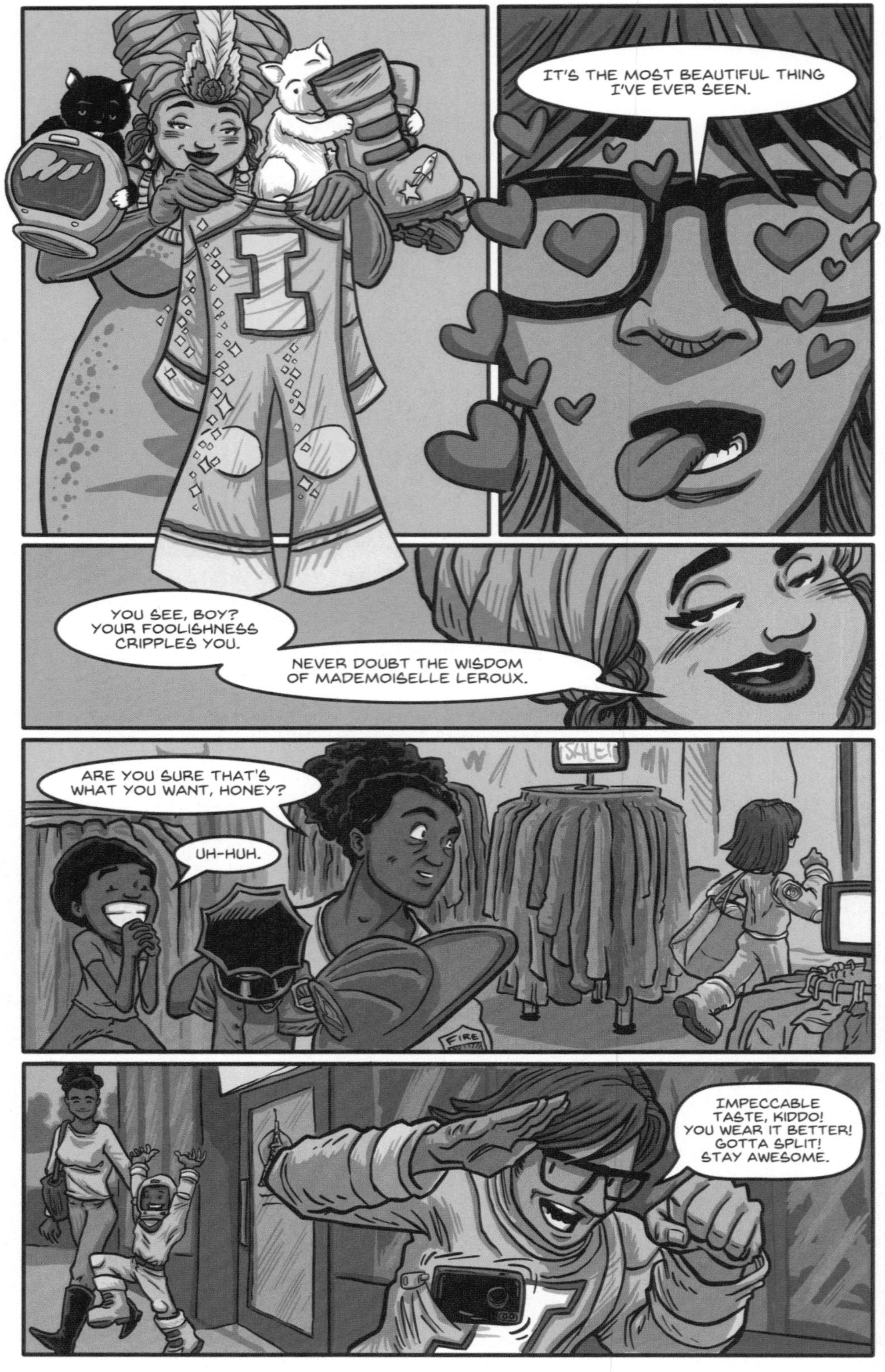
IT'S THE MOST BEAUTIFUL THING I'VE EVER SEEN.
YOU SEE, BOY? YOUR FOOLISHNESS CRIPPLES YOU.
NEVER DOUBT THE WISDOM OF MADEMOISELLE LEROUX.
SALE!
ARE YOU SURE THAT'S WHAT YOU WANT, HONEY?
UH-HUH.
FIRE
IMPECCABLE TASTE, KIDDO! YOU WEAR IT BETTER! GOTTA SPLIT! STAY AWESOME.

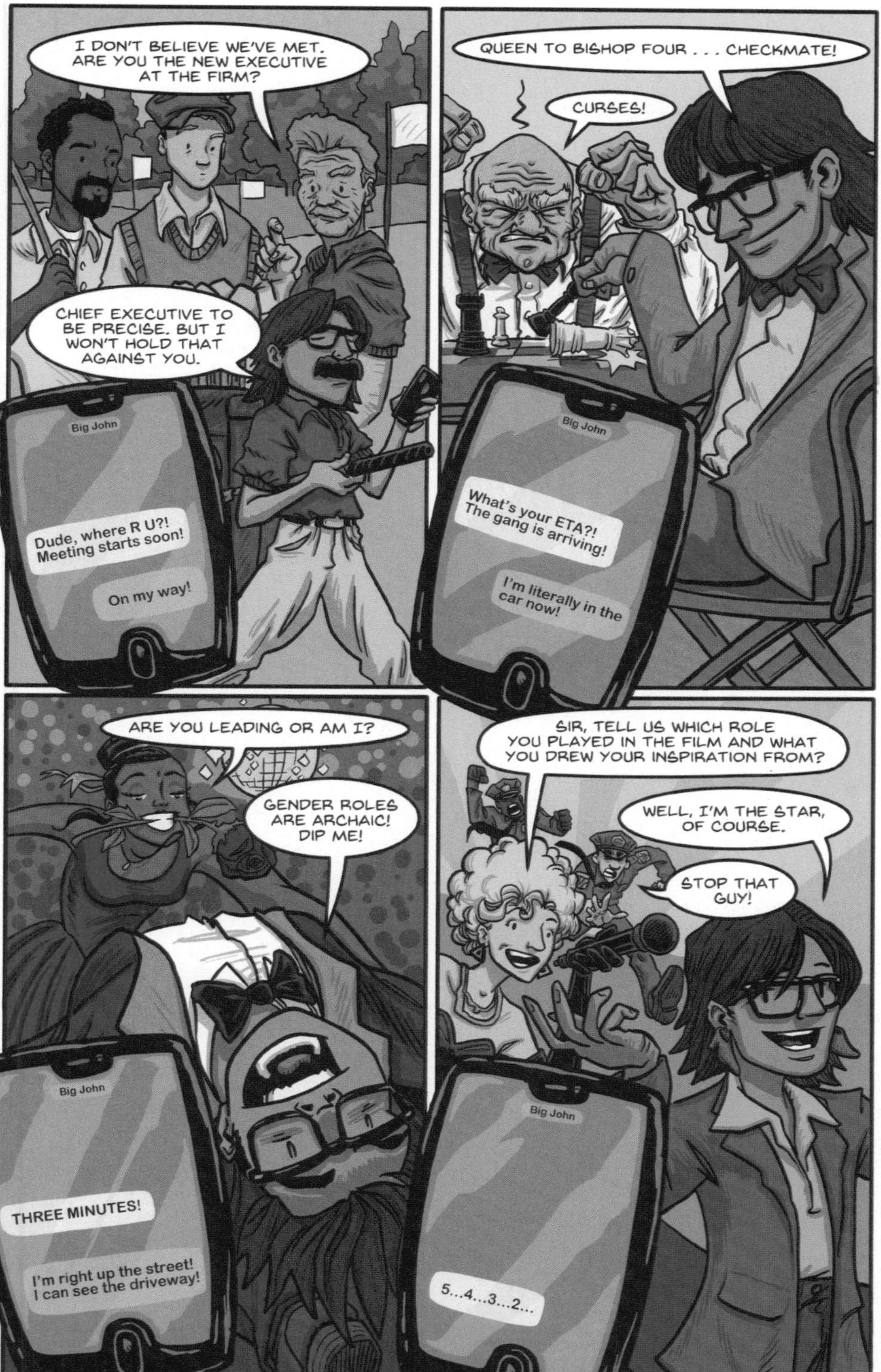

I DON'T BELIEVE WE'VE MET. ARE YOU THE NEW EXECUTIVE AT THE FIRM?
CHIEF EXECUTIVE TO BE PRECISE. BUT I WON'T HOLD THAT AGAINST YOU.
Big John
Dude, where R U?! Meeting starts soon!
On my way!
QUEEN TO BISHOP FOUR . . . CHECKMATE!
CURSES!
Big John
What's your ETA?! The gang is arriving!
I'm literally in the car now!
ARE YOU LEADING OR AM I?
GENDER ROLES ARE ARCHAIC! DIP ME!
Big John
THREE MINUTES!
I'm right up the street! I can see the driveway!
SIR, TELL US WHICH ROLE YOU PLAYED IN THE FILM AND WHAT YOU DREW YOUR INSPIRATION FROM?
WELL, I'M THE STAR, OF COURSE.
STOP THAT GUY!
Big John
5...4...3...2...

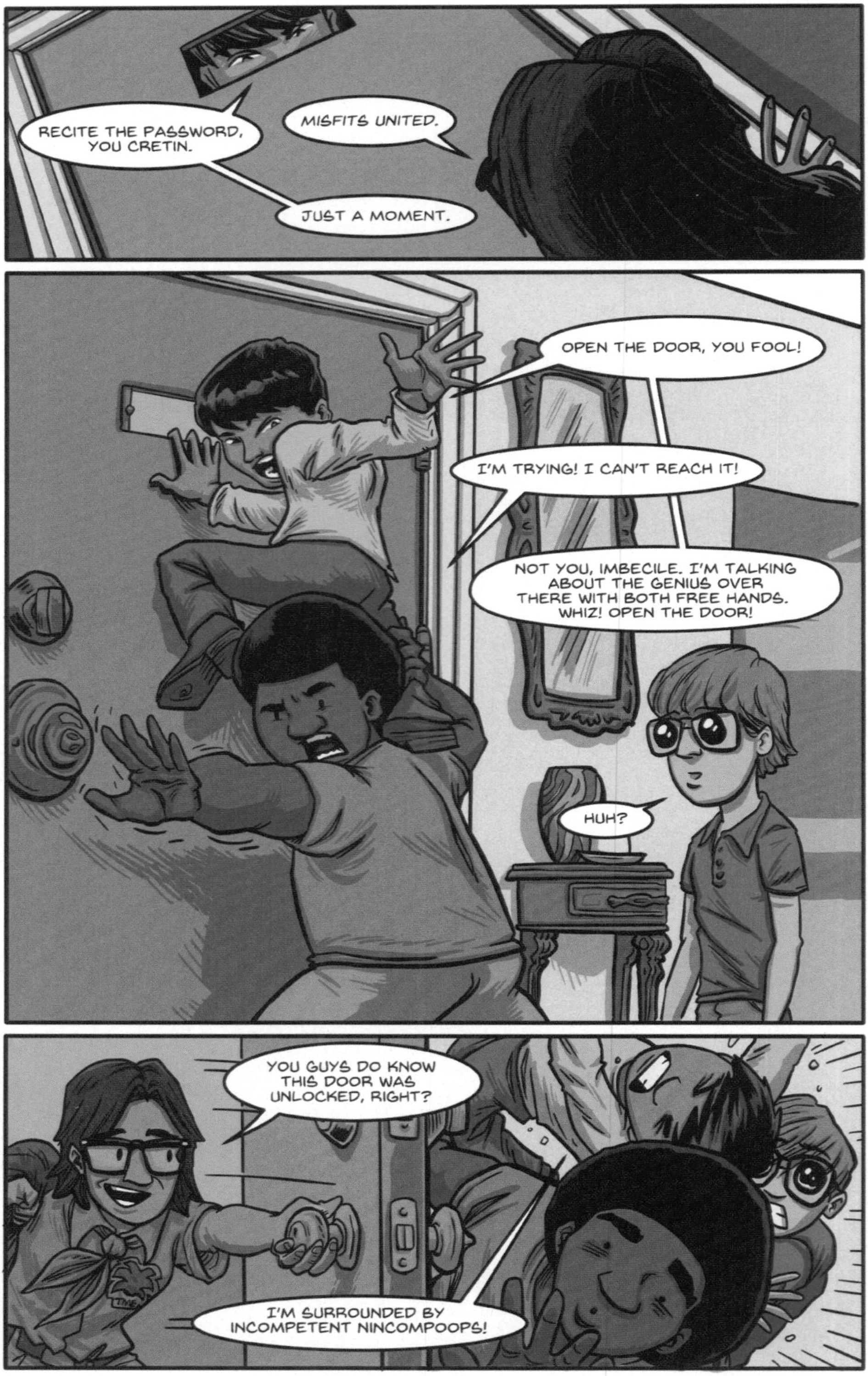
RECITE THE PASSWORD, YOU CRETIN.
MISFITS UNITED.
JUST A MOMENT.
OPEN THE DOOR, YOU FOOL!
I'M TRYING! I CAN'T REACH IT!
NOT YOU, IMBECILE. I'M TALKING ABOUT THE GENIUS OVER THERE WITH BOTH FREE HANDS. WHIZ! OPEN THE DOOR!
HUH?
YOU GUYS DO KNOW THIS DOOR WAS UNLOCKED, RIGHT?
I'M SURROUNDED BY INCOMPETENT NINCOMPOOPS!

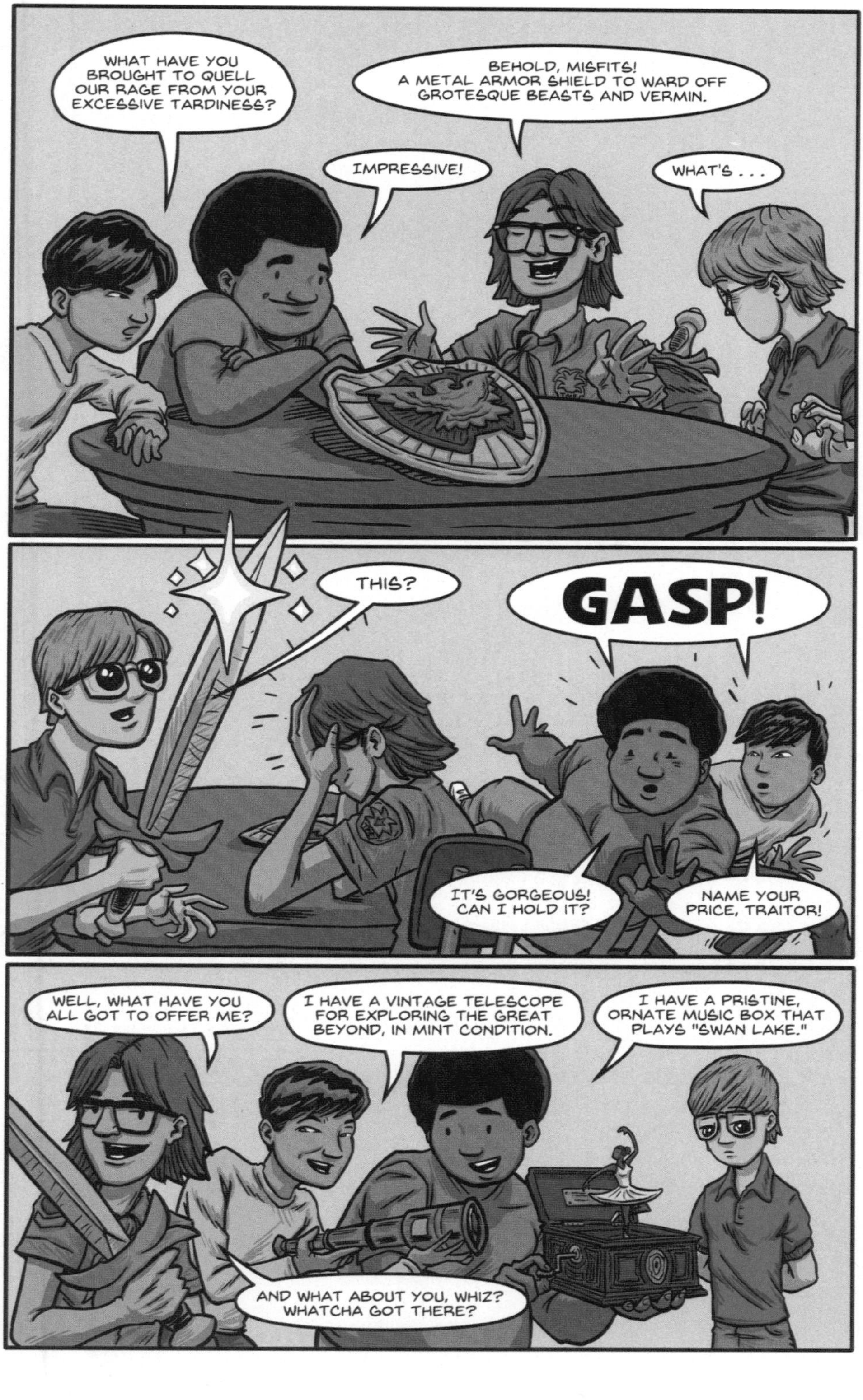
WHAT HAVE YOU BROUGHT TO QUELL OUR RAGE FROM YOUR EXCESSIVE TARDINESS?
BEHOLD, MISFITS! A METAL ARMOR SHIELD TO WARD OFF GROTESQUE BEASTS AND VERMIN.
IMPRESSIVE!
WHAT'S . . .
THIS?
GASP!
IT'S GORGEOUS! CAN I HOLD IT?
NAME YOUR PRICE, TRAITOR!
WELL, WHAT HAVE YOU ALL GOT TO OFFER ME?
I HAVE A VINTAGE TELESCOPE FOR EXPLORING THE GREAT BEYOND, IN MINT CONDITION.
I HAVE A PRISTINE, ORNATE MUSIC BOX THAT PLAYS "SWAN LAKE."
AND WHAT ABOUT YOU, WHIZ? WHATCHA GOT THERE?

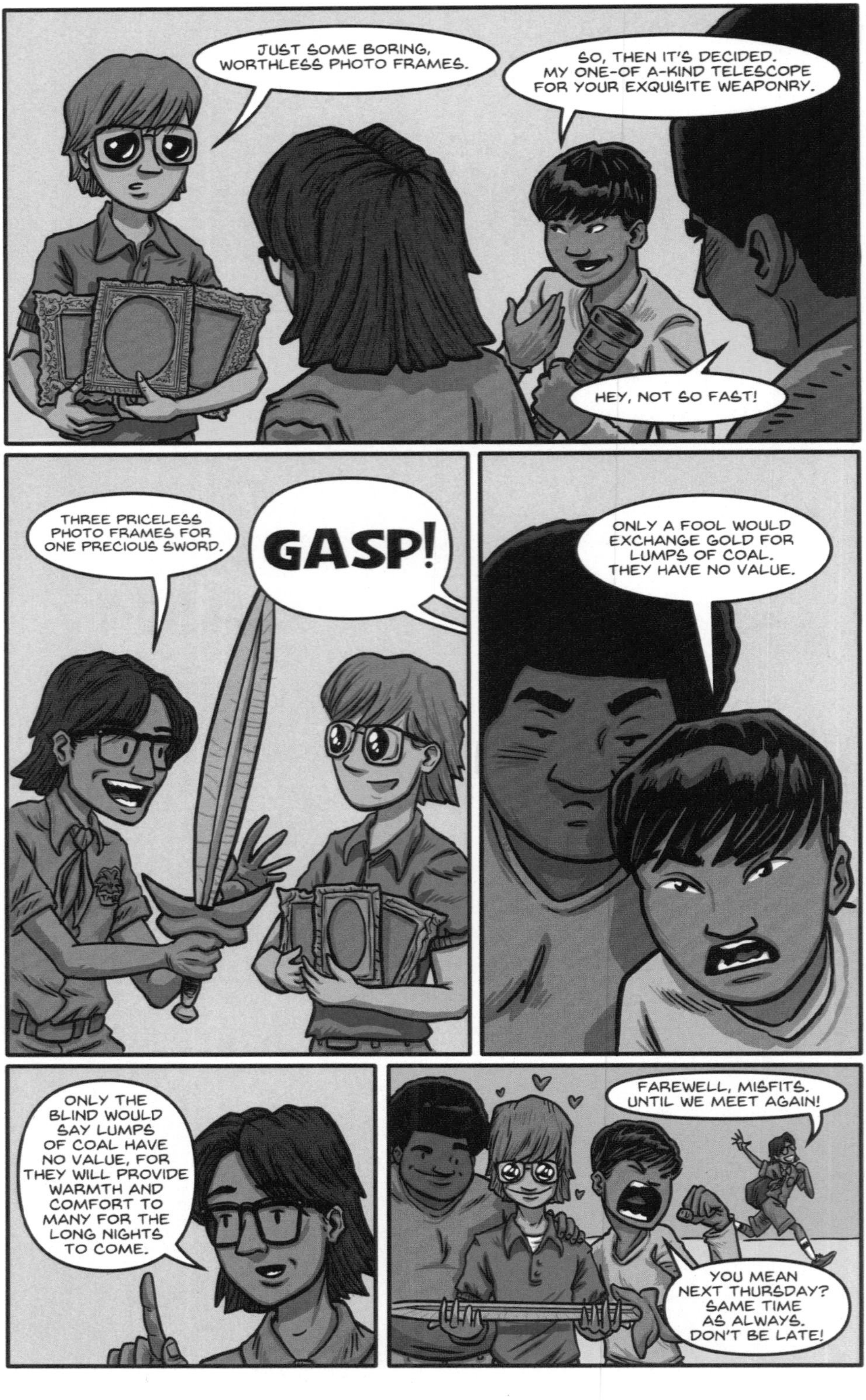
JUST SOME BORING, WORTHLESS PHOTO FRAMES.
SO, THEN IT'S DECIDED. MY ONE-OF A-KIND TELESCOPE FOR YOUR EXQUISITE WEAPONRY.
HEY, NOT SO FAST!
THREE PRICELESS PHOTO FRAMES FOR ONE PRECIOUS SWORD.
GASP!
ONLY A FOOL WOULD EXCHANGE GOLD FOR LUMPS OF COAL. THEY HAVE NO VALUE.
ONLY THE BLIND WOULD SAY LUMPS OF COAL HAVE NO VALUE, FOR THEY WILL PROVIDE WARMTH AND COMFORT TO MANY FOR THE LONG NIGHTS TO COME.
FAREWELL, MISFITS. UNTIL WE MEET AGAIN!
YOU MEAN NEXT THURSDAY? SAME TIME AS ALWAYS. DON'T BE LATE!

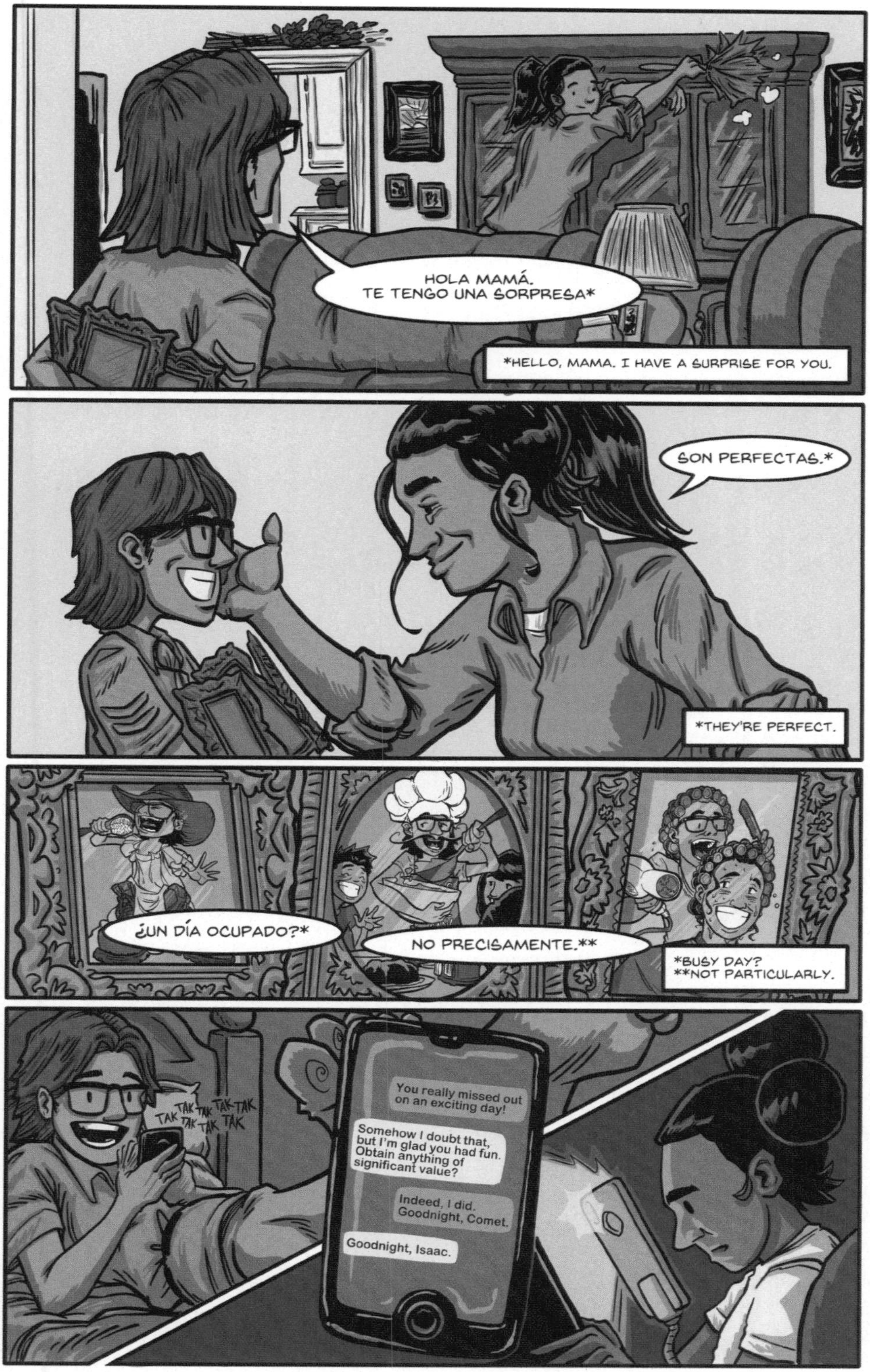
HOLA MAMÁ.
TE TENGO UNA SORPRESA*
*HELLO, MAMA. I HAVE A SURPRISE FOR YOU.
SON PERFECTAS.*
*THEY'RE PERFECT.
¿UN DÍA OCUPADO?*
NO PRECISAMENTE.**
*BUSY DAY?
**NOT PARTICULARLY.
TAK TAK TAK TAK TAK TAK TAK TAK
You really missed out on an exciting day!
Somehow I doubt that, but I'm glad you had fun. Obtain anything of significant value?
Indeed, I did. Goodnight, Comet.
Goodnight, Isaac.

Glamorella's daughter CONCEPT ART!

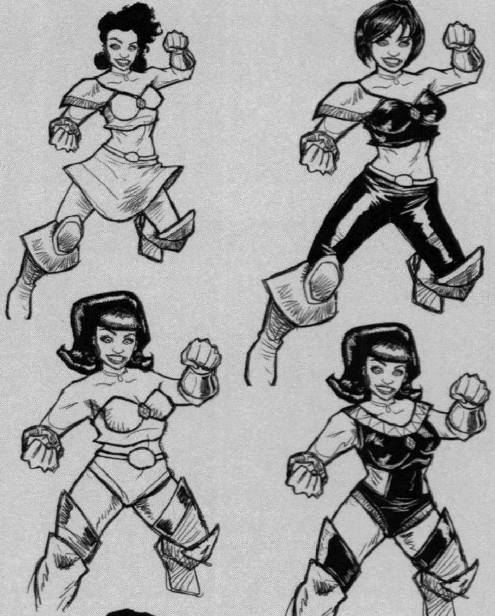

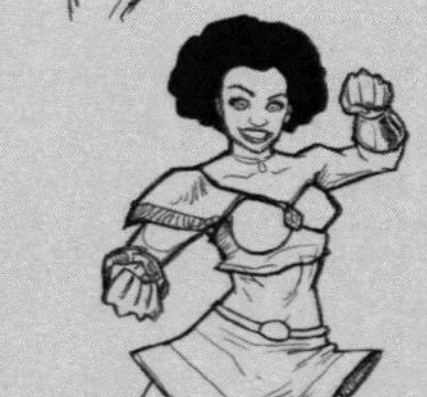

GLAMORELLA WAS A TOUGH ONE TO DESIGN, BECAUSE THERE SEEMED TO BE A MILLION WAYS TO GO WITH HER LOOK THAT WOULD MATCH HER PERSONALITY. WHEN I BEGAN TO THINK ABOUT HER ROLE AS A PARENT, I FINALLY HAD A BETTER SENSE OF HOW TO DESIGN HER UNIFORM.

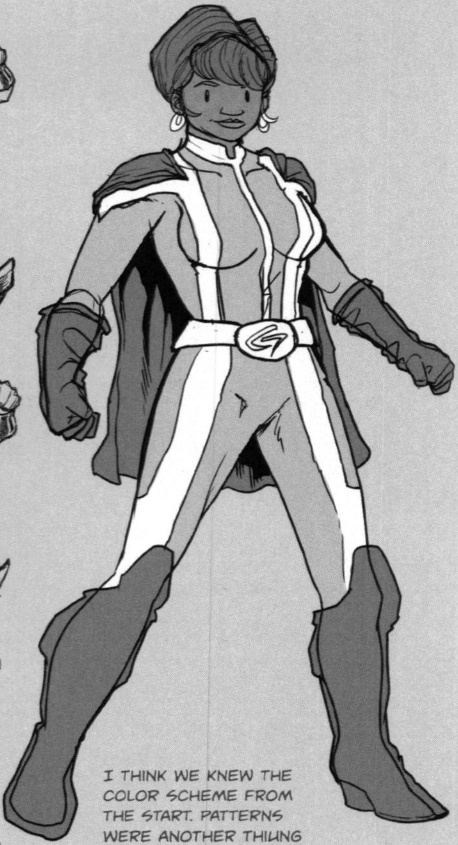

I THINK WE KNEW THE COLOR SCHEME FROM THE START. PATTERNS WERE ANOTHER THIUNG ENTIRELY, BUT WE HAD A BLAST MAKING THEM UP!

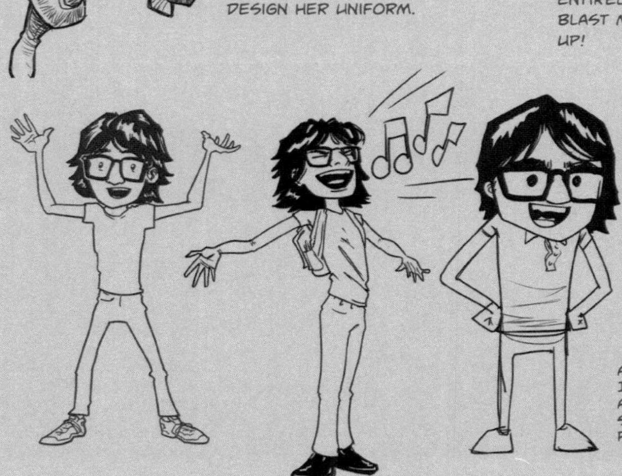

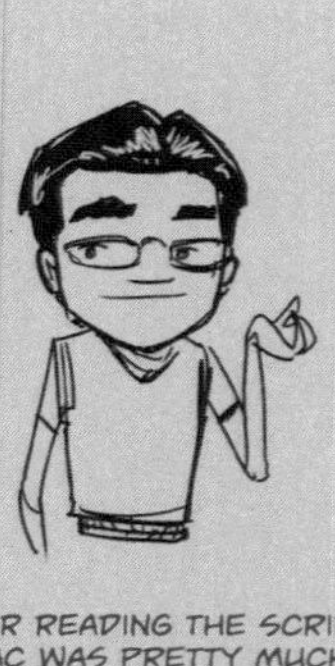

AFTER READING THE SCRIPTS, ISAAC WAS PRETTY MUCH DESIGNED AS AN HOMAGE TO A FRIEND WITH A SIMILAR PERSONALITY WHO PASSED AWAY FAR TOO YOUNG.

CAPTURING GLAMORELLA'S PERSONALITY IN THE ART STYLE CAME PRETTY EASY ONCE I COULD CONSISTENTLY DRAW HER, BUT IT TOOK A LONG TIME TO DECIDE WHAT KIND OF EYES TO GO WITH AND WHAT HAIRSTYLE TO USE. (GLAM DOES INCORPORATE MANY STYLES, WHICH CAN BE SEEN IN PHOTOS THROUGHOUT HER HOME.)

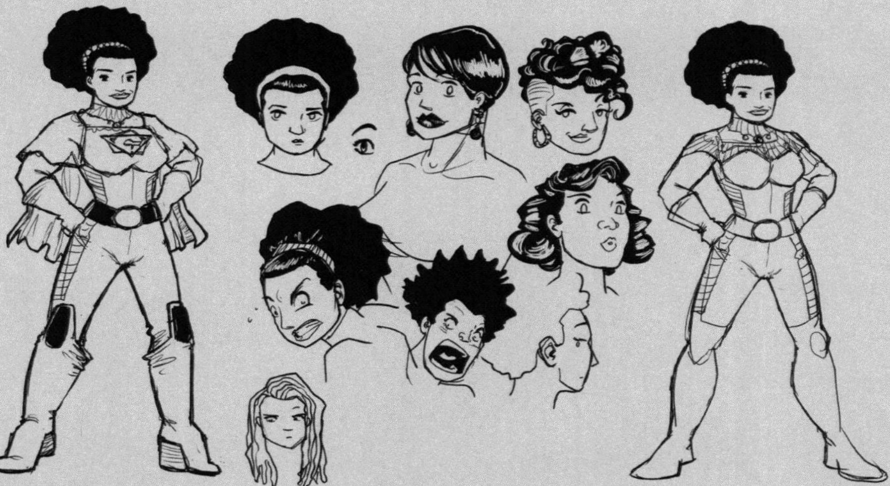

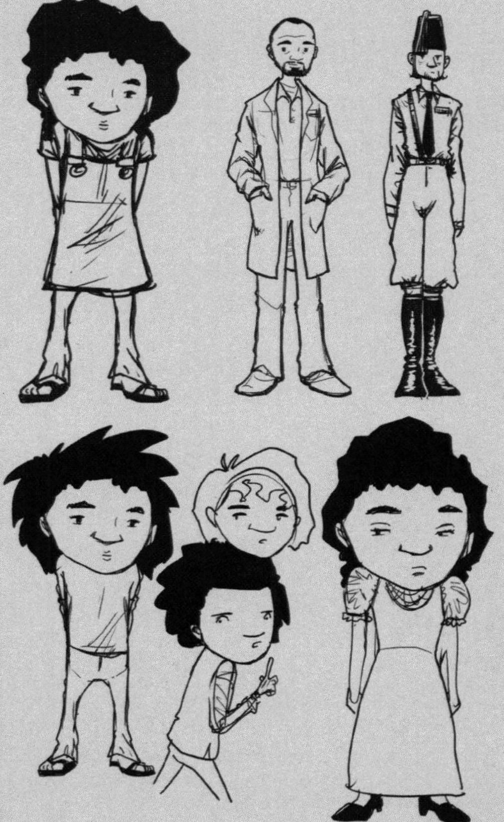

COMET MAY HAVE BEEN THE MOST COMPLEX OF ALL THE CHARACTERS TO DESIGN. WE WANTED TO CAPTURE THE COMPLEXITY OF HER PERSONALITY AND HELP THE READER UNDERSTAND HER THROUGH HER WARDROBE AS WELL AS HER SUBTLE POSING. CHARACTER DESIGN IS CHALLENGING, BUT WHEN DONE RIGHT, CAN BE SO REWARDING FOR NOT ONLY THE CREATORS, BUT FOR THE READERS' EXPERIENCE.

(EARLY PAGE ONE LAYOUT.)

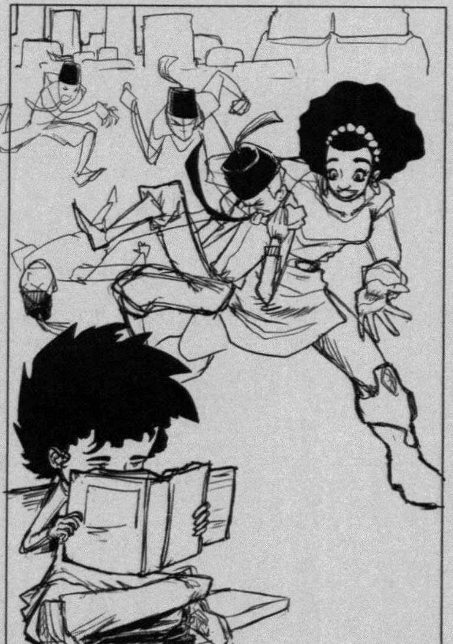

Issue 2 Variant Cover by Jerry Bennett

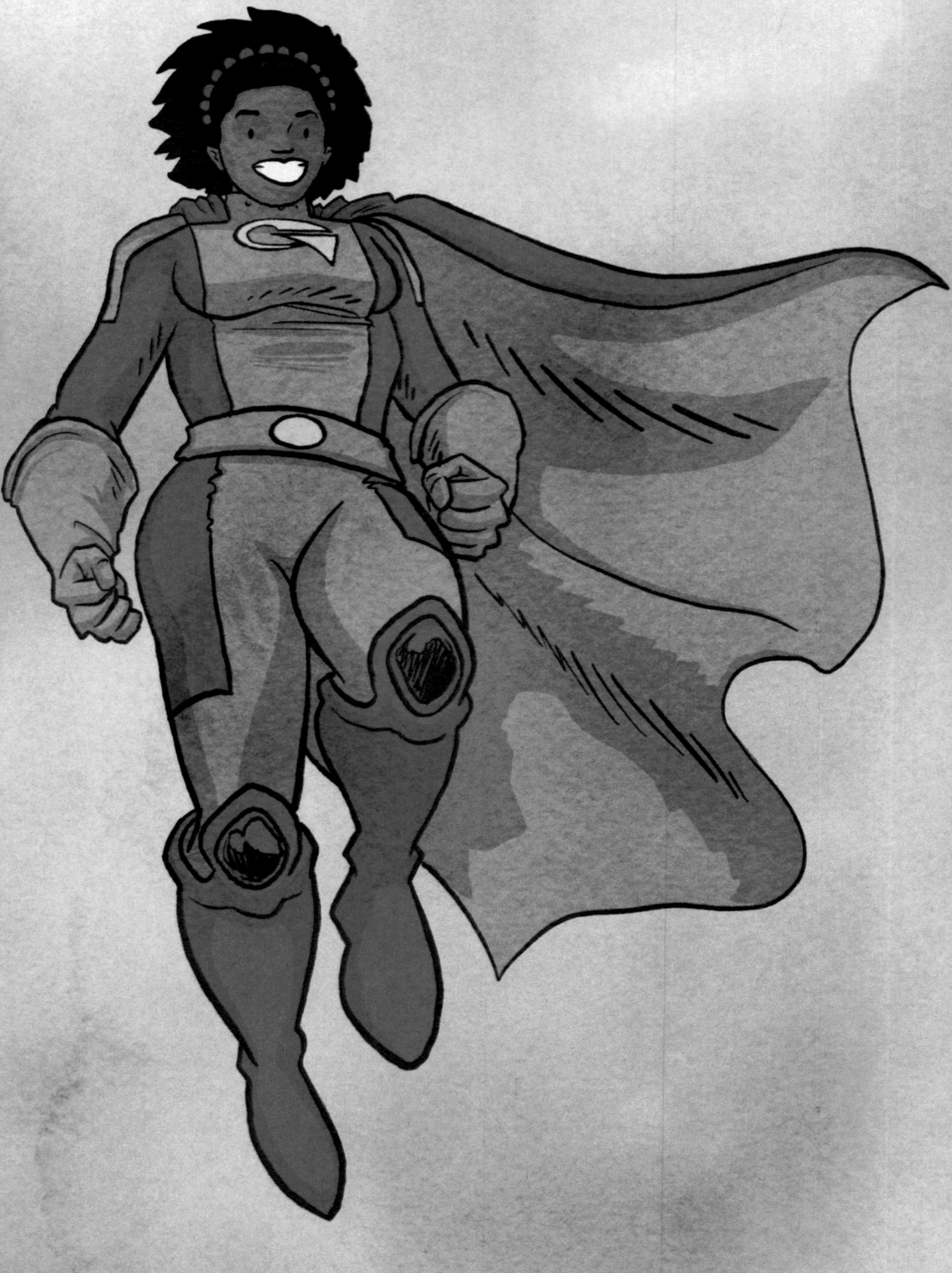

Issue 3 Variant Cover by Jerry Bennett

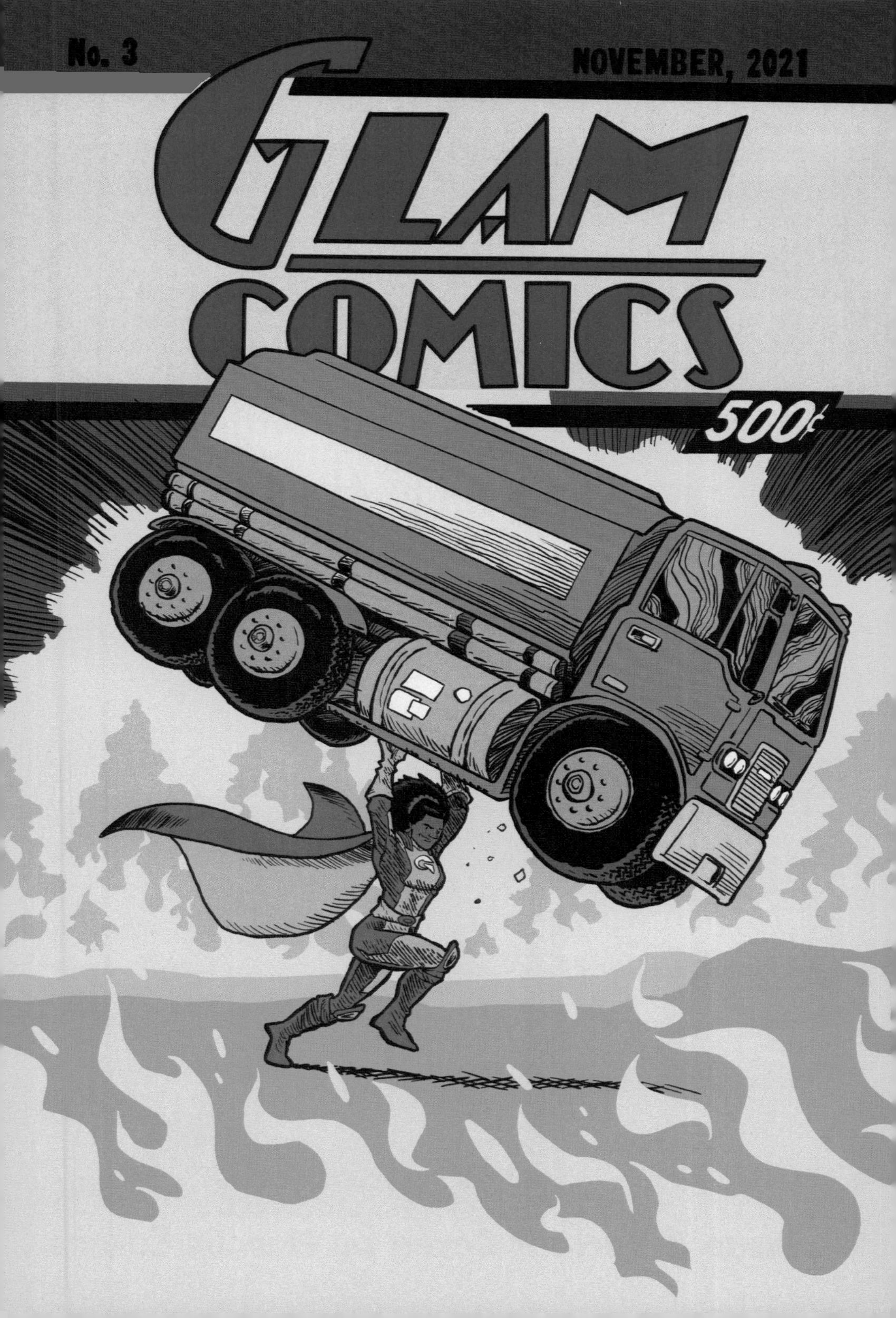
No. 3
NOVEMBER, 2021
GLAM
COMICS
500¢

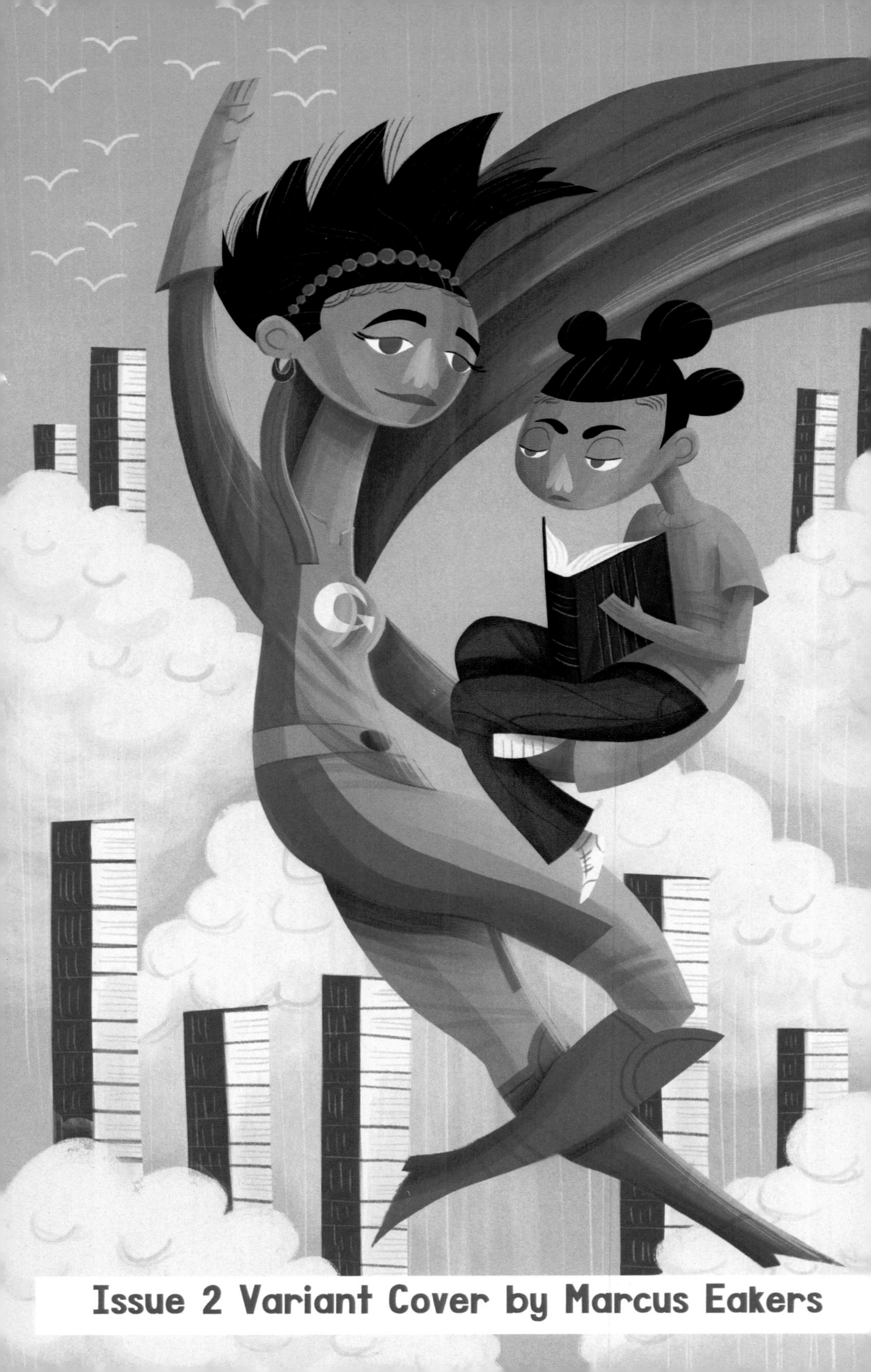

Issue 2 Variant Cover by Marcus Eakers

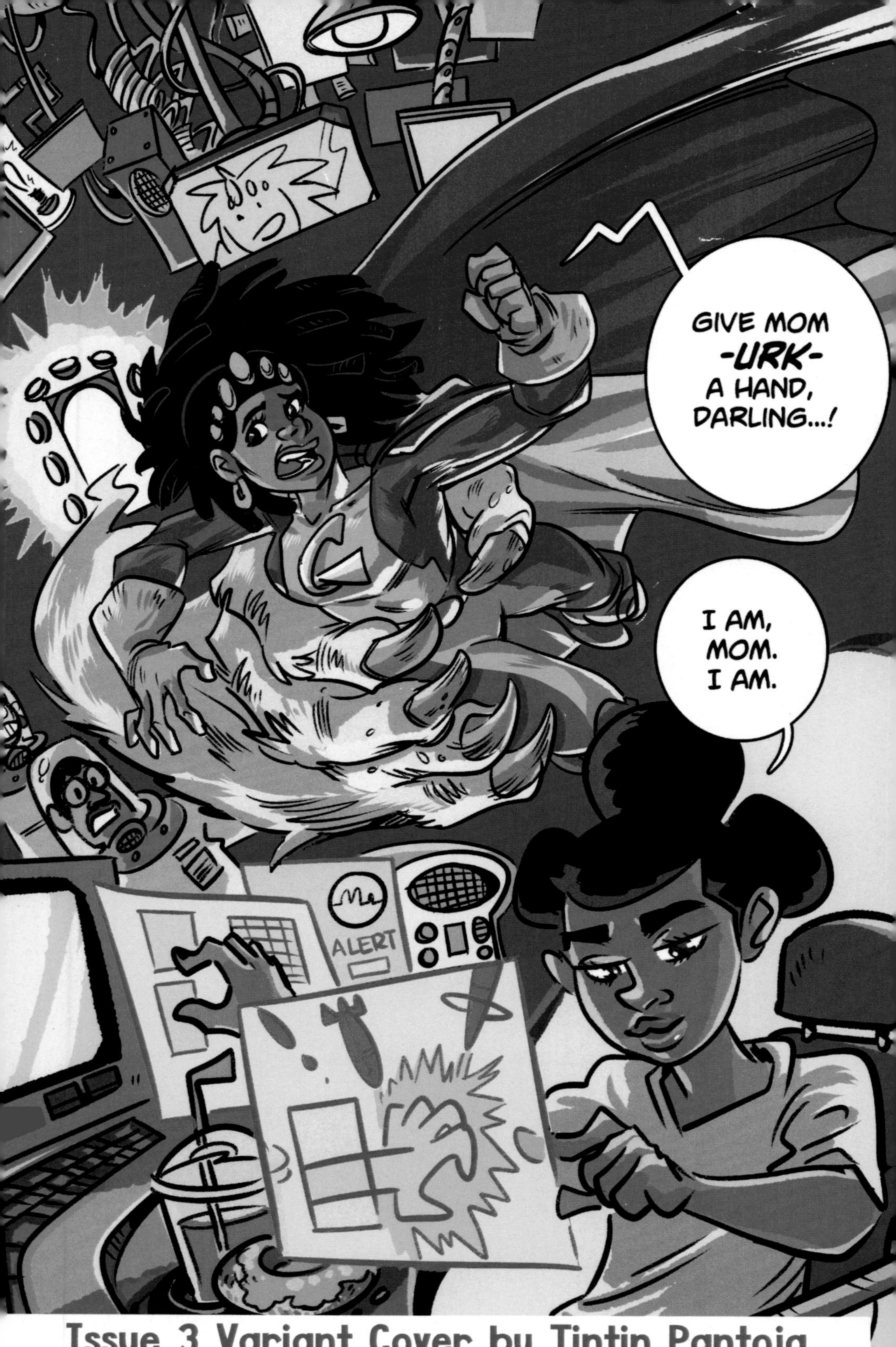
GIVE MOM -URK- A HAND, DARLING...!
I AM, MOM. I AM.

Issue 3 Variant Cover by Tintin Pantoja

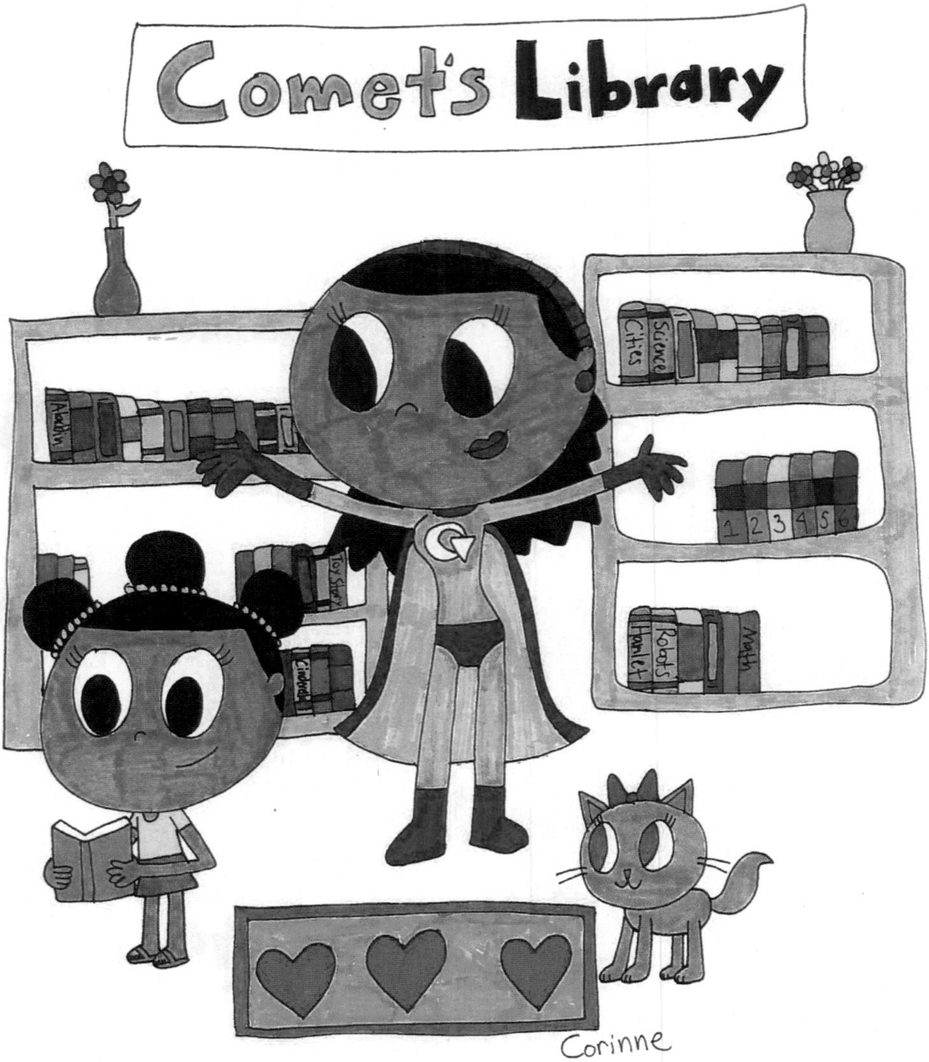
Comet's Library
Aladdin
Cities
Science
Toy Story
1 2 3 4 5
Hamlet
Robots
Math
Corinne

Planet Comicon Variant Cover by Corinne Smith